D1497978

OF MEN AND MUSIC

By Deems Taylor

SIMON AND SCHUSTER
New York · 1937

Published by Simon and Schuster, Inc.
386 Fourth Avenue, New York

Manufactured in the United States of America
By the Stratford Press, Inc., New York

Table of Contents

YESTERDAY

TODAY

CONTENTS

TOMORROW

Introduction

THIS BOOK *began as a series of radio talks that I delivered as part of the Columbia Broadcasting System's broadcasts of the Sunday afternoon concerts of the New York Philharmonic-Symphony Orchestra during the season of 1936–1937. These have been supplemented by material drawn from articles and reviews of mine that appeared originally in the now unhappily extinct New York* World *and New York* American. *Certain chapters were first printed in* The Ladies' Home Journal, The Saturday Evening Post, *and* The New Yorker. *What order and form the volume possesses it owes to the ingenuity of Miss Elisabeth Ingersoll, who accomplished the difficult feat of giving logical sequence to a rather heterogeneous mass of raw material.*

What to call it? I hate to label it a book of essays on music and musicians; first, because so much of it started life as radio scripts, and second, because I fear that "essays" is too flattering a term to apply to many of its chapters. "Observations" might be a better word.

While I can hardly claim for it anything so ambitious as a message, I do find, upon reading it as a whole, that it represents a point of view, one that I have held as long as I can remember. If this book tries to say a few definite things, they are these: that behind every musician lurks a man, who is fully as interesting as the trade he follows; that music is written for our enjoyment, and only incidentally for our edification; and that many a potential music lover is frightened away by the solemnity of music's devotees. They would make more converts if they would rise from their knees.

Hollow Hill,
Stamford, Conn.
October, 1937.

DEEMS TAYLOR.

PART ONE

Yesterday

I

The Monster

HE WAS an undersized little man, with a head too big for his body—a sickly little man. His nerves were bad. He had skin trouble. It was agony for him to wear anything next to his skin coarser than silk. And he had delusions of grandeur.

He was a monster of conceit. Never for one minute did he look at the world or at people, except in relation to himself. He was not only the most important person in the world, to himself; in his own eyes he was the only person who existed. He believed himself to be one of the greatest dramatists in the world, one of the greatest thinkers, and one of the greatest composers. To hear him talk, he was Shakespeare, and Beethoven, and Plato, rolled into one. And you would have had no difficulty in hearing him talk. He was one of the most exhausting conversationalists that ever lived. An evening with him was an evening spent in listening to a monologue. Sometimes he was brilliant; sometimes he was maddeningly tiresome. But whether he was being brilliant or dull, he had one sole topic of conversation: himself. What *he* thought and what *he* did.

He had a mania for being in the right. The slightest hint of disagreement, from anyone, on the most trivial point, was enough to set him off on a harangue that might last for hours, in which he proved himself right in so many ways, and with such exhausting volubility, that in the end his hearer, stunned and deafened, would agree with him, for the sake of peace.

It never occurred to him that he and his doing were not of the most intense and fascinating interest to anyone with whom he came in contact. He had theories about almost any subject under the sun, including vegetarianism, the drama, politics, and music; and in support of these theories he wrote pamphlets, letters, books . . . thousands upon thousands of words, hundreds and hundreds of pages. He not only wrote these things, and published them—usually at somebody else's expense—but he would sit and read them aloud, for hours, to his friends and his family.

He wrote operas; and no sooner did he have the synopsis of a story, but he would invite—or rather summon—a crowd of his friends to his house and read it aloud to them. Not for criticism. For applause. When the complete poem was written, the friends had to come again, and hear *that* read aloud. Then he would publish the poem, sometimes years before the music that went with it was written. He played the piano like a composer, in the worst sense of what that implies, and he would sit down at the piano before parties that included some of the finest pianists of his time, and play for them, by the hour, his own music, needless to say. He had a composer's voice. And he would invite eminent vocalists to his house, and sing them his operas, taking all the parts.

He had the emotional stability of a six-year-old child. When he felt out of sorts, he would rave and stamp, or sink into suicidal gloom and talk darkly of going to the

East to end his days as a Buddhist monk. Ten minutes later, when something pleased him, he would rush out of doors and run around the garden, or jump up and down on the sofa, or stand on his head. He could be grief-stricken over the death of a pet dog, and he could be callous and heartless to a degree that would have made a Roman emperor shudder.

He was almost innocent of any sense of responsibility. Not only did he seem incapable of supporting himself, but it never occurred to him that he was under any obligation to do so. He was convinced that the world owed him a living. In support of this belief, he borrowed money from everybody who was good for a loan—men, women, friends, or strangers. He wrote begging letters by the score, sometimes groveling without shame, at others loftily offering his intended benefactor the privilege of contributing to his support, and being mortally offended if the recipient declined the honor. I have found no record of his ever paying or repaying money to anyone who did not have a legal claim upon it.

What money he could lay his hands on he spent like an Indian rajah. The mere prospect of a performance of one of his operas was enough to set him to running up bills amounting to ten times the amount of his prospective royalties. On an income that would reduce a more scrupulous man to doing his own laundry, he would keep two servants. Without enough money in his pocket to pay his rent, he would have the walls and ceiling of his study lined with pink silk. No one will ever know—certainly he never knew—how much money he owed. We do know that his greatest benefactor gave him $6,000 to pay the most pressing of his debts in one city, and a year later had to give him $16,000 to enable him to live in another city without being thrown into jail for debt.

He was equally unscrupulous in other ways. An endless procession of women marches through his life. His first wife spent twenty years enduring and forgiving his infidelities. His second wife had been the wife of his most devoted friend and admirer, from whom he stole her. And even while he was trying to persuade her to leave her first husband he was writing to a friend to inquire whether he could suggest some wealthy woman—*any* wealthy woman—whom he could marry for her money.

He was completely selfish in his other personal relationships. His liking for his friends was measured solely by the completeness of their devotion to him, or by their usefulness to him, whether financial or artistic. The minute they failed him—even by so much as refusing a dinner invitation—or began to lessen in usefulness, he cast them off without a second thought. At the end of his life he had exactly one friend left whom he had known even in middle age.

He had a genius for making enemies. He would insult a man who disagreed with him about the weather. He would pull endless wires in order to meet some man who admired his work, and was able and anxious to be of use to him—and would proceed to make a mortal enemy of him with some idiotic and wholly uncalled-for exhibition of arrogance and bad manners. A character in one of his operas was a caricature of one of the most powerful music critics of his day. Not content with burlesquing him, he invited the critic to his house and read him the libretto aloud in front of his friends.

The name of this monster was Richard Wagner. Everything that I have said about him you can find on record —in newspapers, in police reports, in the testimony of people who knew him, in his own letters, between the lines of his autobiography. And the curious thing about this record is that it doesn't matter in the least.

Because this undersized, sickly, disagreeable, fascinating little man was right all the time. The joke was on us. He *was* one of the world's great dramatists; he *was* a great thinker; he *was* one of the most stupendous musical geniuses that, up to now, the world has ever seen. The world did owe him a living. People couldn't know those things at the time, I suppose; and yet to us, who know his music, it does seem as though they should have known. What if he did talk about himself all the time? If he had talked about himself for twenty-four hours every day for the span of his life he would not have uttered half the number of words that other men have spoken and written about him since his death.

When you consider what he wrote—thirteen operas and music dramas, eleven of them still holding the stage, eight of them unquestionably worth ranking among the world's great musico-dramatic masterpieces—when you listen to what he wrote, the debts and heartaches that people had to endure from him don't seem much of a price. Eduard Hanslick, the critic whom he caricatured in *Die Meistersinger* and who hated him ever after, now lives only because he was caricatured in *Die Meistersinger*. The women whose hearts he broke are long since dead; and the man who could never love anyone but himself has made them deathless atonement, I think, with *Tristan und Isolde*. Think of the luxury with which for a time, at least, fate rewarded Napoleon, the man who ruined

France and looted Europe; and then perhaps you will agree that a few thousand dollars' worth of debts were not too heavy a price to pay for the *Ring* trilogy.

What if he was faithless to his friends and to his wives? He had one mistress to whom he was faithful to the day of his death: Music. Not for a single moment did he ever compromise with what he believed, with what he dreamed. There is not a line of his music that could have been conceived by a little mind. Even when he is dull, or downright bad, he is dull in the grand manner. There is greatness about his worst mistakes. Listening to his music, one does not forgive him for what he may or may not have been. It is not a matter of forgiveness. It is a matter of being dumb with wonder that his poor brain and body didn't burst under the torment of the demon of creative energy that lived inside him, struggling, clawing, scratching to be released; tearing, shrieking at him to write the music that was in him. The miracle is that what he did in the little space of seventy years could have been done at all, even by a great genius. Is it any wonder that he had no time to be a man?

2

Guide, Philosopher

I NEVER hear the prelude to *Lohengrin* without thinking of Oscar Coon. If any reader happens to come from Oswego, New York, there is a faint possibility that the name might be vaguely familiar. The rest of you, I'm sure, never heard of him. I shall not forget him, because he was my music teacher—about the only one I ever had. He came, as I say, from Oswego, New York. Where he learned music I don't know. I do know that he was a bandsman. He had played second trumpet in the famous band conducted by Patrick Gilmore in the seventies and eighties, and later with Cappa's Seventh Regiment Band, an almost equally famous organization of the nineties. At the time I knew him he was working as a copyist and arranger for a music library. Unlike most good musicians of his time, he was not a German. He spelled his name C, double-O N, and spoke with an uncompromising Yankee accent that scorned any such alien affectations as pronouncing European names in any but the American fashion. He didn't go so far as to call Bach "Batch"; he called him Bok. But Beethoven was "Bee-thowe-ven" and Wagner was "Wag-nurr," and no foreign nonsense about it.

He lived on West Twelfth Street, New York, in a ramshackle old building just off Fifth Avenue. The ground floor was given over to piano warerooms, and the upper stories served as offices, studios, and living quarters, according to the needs and habits of the tenants. He lived in one room whose principal articles of furniture were a cot and a bookkeeper's desk, at which he stood to write music. He subsisted, so far as I was ever able to discover, on Scotch whiskey and bananas exclusively. How long this diet had been going on, I don't know. He was born in 1833, and should have died of dyspepsia about 1870. On the contrary, when I first knew him he was seventy-five and grumbling over the fact that he might have to go back to Oswego and take care of his two older sisters, who seemed to think that they ought to have a man in the house. He wore his white hair rather long, and wore a flowing white beard and mustaches, which gave him the appearance of Shakespeare's King Lear. If King Lear told the stories that my music teacher did, and swore the way he did, he was a far more fascinating character than Shakespeare has allowed us to discover.

Don't get the impression that he was a drunken eccentric. On the contrary, he was a tough-fibered, intellectually honest, fiercely independent upstate Yankee. He was also a profound and devoted musical scholar, and a charming and gallant person. As a teacher he had the knack of imparting knowledge, not with the air of Jehovah handing down the Decalogue, but in terms of casual conversation. By nature he was a liberal. He had a horror of extravagant terms either of censure or approbation. I studied harmony and counterpoint with him, and I remember several occasions on which I brought in what I was sure were perfect exercises in harmony, and perfect workings out of problems in counterpoint, and stood, wrapped in the most completely false assumption of modesty, waiting for his words of praise. And once or twice, when I was right, when the harmony exercise *was* entirely correct, when even he could find nothing to rewrite in the working out of the counterpoint, he would pay me the highest compliment of which he was capable: "Say, you know, that's pretty good." And nothing that any person—or continent—could say to me could puff me up as did that grudging accolade. I studied with him all of one summer and part of a winter, and as I look back now I realize that the hours I spent with Oscar Coon were among the happiest and most profitable of my life.

Lohengrin makes me think of him because it evokes a passage from a treatise on orchestration that Coon once wrote and published. It runs as follows:

"Richard Wagner, without doubt the greatest living master of instrumentation, has taxed every instrument to its utmost. He has sounded them from their lowest note to the top of their compass, made them breathe a zephyr or blow a hurricane, caused them to give 'sweet sounds long drawn out' [*sic*] or rush with the speed of lightning—in short, everything which human endurance and mechanical skill has [*sic*] made possible on musical instruments he has succeeded in drawing from them. In consequence of this his enemies accuse him of creating many difficulties and much noise. However that may be, he has written much music which can hardly be surpassed. What can excel the ethereal beauty of the introduction to his *Lohengrin*, or the massive grandeur of his *Tannhäuser* Overture? Although he may be regarded as a mere charlatan—a musical maniac—by those who have not the ability to appreciate his music; still, the time is not far distant when his genius will be universally admitted."

This was in 1883, the year of Wagner's death. The passage has always stuck in my mind because while I know, as we all do, in principle, that there was a time when Wagner's right to rank among the world's greatest composers was disputed by a great many people, Oscar Coon was one of the few I had ever met who had actually lived through that period, who had ventured to consider Wagner a genius in an era when it took courage and independence to do so. I remember his telling me how, as a very young man, in New York, doing Lord knows what to make a living, he used to save up and go to the concerts given by a co-operative orchestra called the Philharmonic Society. This was about 1852, and on two of the programs of the Philharmonic Society appeared the introductions, respectively, to Wagner's *Lohengrin* and *Tannhäuser*. They were not placed along with the other music, however, but were played at the very end of the concert, with a five-minute intermission separating them from the other works performed. A note on the printed program called attention to this intermission and requested that those of the audience who did not wish to listen to this new music avail themselves of the opportunity to leave the hall. (Behind that polite and rather plaintive request I sense a grim scene—the directors of the Philharmonic Society taking their courage in their hands and putting on the music of this wild man, hoping to goodness that the subscribers who didn't like it would go peaceably, instead of staying around to boo and throw things.)

Coon had three gods: Wagner, Shakespeare, and Bach. There was no musical instrument of any sort in his room, except an aged but respectable cello, which had no strings, and which he couldn't have played if it had had any. But that didn't matter. I have walked into his studio and found him reading a Wagner score, or one of Bach's preludes and fugues, with the absorption that you or I might give to Sherlock Holmes. He had no need to play, or hear played, the music that he loved best. Something inside him played and sang as he read along to himself.

He has been gone some time now. He died, at an incredible age, several years ago. I can only hope that his tolerant spirit will forgive my waiting so long before laying this small verbal wreath upon his grave. I wish it were a bigger one.

3

Two Masters

WAGNER fares pretty well with almost any good orchestra, even under conductors of modest rank. He is such a master of orchestral balance, his knowledge of instrumental color is so profound, his structure is so clearly defined, that if he be conducted in time, and played in tune, much of what he has to say will come through almost automatically. He is a musical dramatist who is a master, not only of construction, but of brilliant dialogue as well.

Brahms is different. If Wagner is Shakespeare, he is Ibsen. The course of his thought is equally rigorous in its logic, equally inevitable in its conclusion; but his speech is more abrupt, less prepossessing in detail, less clearly marked in its trend. It is hard to make Wagner sound scrappy; it is not easy, sometimes, to make Brahms sound anything else. It is not always possible to see the connection between his ideas until he has had his say completely.

Wagner is enthusiastic, voluble, never at a loss for a brilliant phrase, an arresting idea. Brahms is slower, less articulate. His speech is more elliptic; he is more deliberate, and kindles less readily. He picks his phrases with care, with long, ruminative intervals wherein he gropes for the right, the perfect word. To conduct Brahms you must be able to conceive, not one movement, but a whole symphony as a unit; to search out the one climactic point and build everything toward that point—and away from it. And, this granted, you must have an orchestra capable of following Brahms's long, unhurried breathing; an orchestra that, when bidden, can follow a single line through half a hundred bars, that is capable of the crystalline purity and beauty of instrumental tone that, alone, can do justice to the eloquent simplicity of Brahms's musical speech.

4

The Perfect Wagnerite

No one who has never seen *Pelléas et Mélisande* as a play can quite realize what Claude Debussy did for it when he turned it into a music drama. Maeterlinck's *Pelléas et Mélisande* is not quite a good play. Its supply of incident is small, and what incidents it has are so deliberate in their unfolding, and, with the exception of the murder, so slight and underemphasized, that they are not impressive on the spoken stage. Maeterlinck's characters, too, are hazily sketched in, somewhat given to wordiness, and so vague in behavior and motive that they seem at times exasperatingly foolish.

Yet Debussy took this rather tenuous—or, more honestly, uninteresting—stage action and turned it, by his own peculiar alchemy, into a musical and dramatic masterpiece. The faults of the play are the virtues of the lyric drama. The progress of every incident and situation is just deliberate enough to give the music time in which to establish and communicate its mood; and the vagueness of the characters and action becomes simply the inevitable impalpability of that lost land of dreams that emerges dimly through the web of shimmering, pale sound that is Debussy's wonderful music.

There is only one *Pelléas,* and I doubt if there will ever be another. Granted that there ever lives again a composer who has Debussy's uncanny power to suggest the unspoken and the half-seen, I doubt if he would be able to find another such ideal libretto as Maeterlinck's play, so right in its mood, so perfectly imperfect in its realization.

Nor will there ever again be quite another Wagner. For it was Wagner who wrote *Pelléas,* in a way. Had there been no Wagner, Debussy might not have reacted quite so completely from the Bayreuth master's overwhelming articulateness. There would have been no need of a reaction, and the French composer might not have plumbed the furthest depths of his own genius for suggestion. Moreover, *Pelléas* might not have been written at all, had not Wagner formulated the principles upon which it rests. For, ironically enough, Debussy, who disagreed violently with most of Wagner's artistic tenets, has taken Wagner at his literal word in writing this music drama.

"The music must be subordinate to the drama," said Wagner; and with sublime inconsistency proceeded to make the music itself the drama, leaving the actors and scenery to cope with its magnificent explicitness as best they might. Does Wotan surround Brünnhilde with a ring of magic fire? There is, forthwith, such a miracle of seething flame in the orchestra as no stage device could ever hope to approximate. Do Isolde and Tristan confess their love? Up wells music of such torrential passion, such ineffable tenderness, that its poor human protagonists seem dwarfed and foolish.

But *Pelléas* is Wagnerian drama written exactly as Wagner said it should be written. Here the drama comes first, with the music content to hint, to beckon, to clarify with a nod, a faint gesture; above all, to drown the hearer in a soft, audible mist in which shadows are the only realities, and the lovely timid truth steps shyly out of her ugly, clinging garments of fact.

Here, too, is Wagner's leitmotif system—used, however, not with Wagner's eager, explanatory volubility, but only as a hint, a reminding glance to stir the memory and the imagination. Sometimes the music seems meant more for the player than for us. "One never sees the sky here," says Mélisande plaintively to Golaud. "Mélisande, Mélisande," whispers the orchestra, "have you so soon forgotten the well in the wood, and him who stood beside it?" So that Mélisande must add, half against her will, "I saw it for the first time only this morning."

I think there has never been music that combined such apparent fragility with such effortless power. There are whole scenes during which it is scarcely noticeable, even to the attuned and sympathetic ear, and throughout the drama it is, for the most part, felt, rather than heard. Yet there is nothing quite like it, for potency and suggestiveness, in all dramatico-musical literature. It rises from the pit like some drugged perfume, capturing the senses, touching the imagination with soft, relentless fingers, opening doors that we had forgotten were there, and revealing vistas that we never thought to see.

"Hush," it whispers, finger on lip, "tread softly, lest you break the spell. Take my hand and come with me, and we will go down together, into the hidden chambers that lie at the back of the mind, and into the secret places of the heart." And, watching rather than listening, we are suddenly aware of the truth: we see the blind forces back of what men and women call their desires, we know the wordless thoughts that smile derisively at the mind's illusion of freedom. And all the while that marvelous music nods, and murmurs, laughs soundlessly, or stands aside, yearning helplessly over the plight of earth's poor children, struggling mutely in the trap that life has set for them.

5

"Dear Diary"

Two symphonies on the same program: Mozart's Thirty-third, in B flat, and Tchaikovsky's Fifth. As I listened to them, it occurred to me how aptly these two men—the Austrian, who died nearly a century and a half ago, at thirty-five, and the Russian, who died a hundred and two years later, at fifty-three—illustrate, and refute, a highly popular fallacy. That fallacy is the assumption that a composer's work is a direct reflection of his own life.

No one pretends that by looking at a painting you can tell whether or not the artist had the money to pay his rent; and very few people would undertake to tell you, from reading a poem, whether or not the poet was hungry at the time. But people who talk about music, including a good many critics and commentators who ought to know better, insist on confusing the emotions they feel on *hearing* music, with the mental processes of the composer. Most of Mozart's music is simple and cheerful in character; therefore Mozart was a cheerful little man, whose sunny disposition made him impervious to worry. As for Tchaikovsky—I don't have to repeat all the things they say about Tchaikovsky. The general idea is that he led a life of unrelieved tragedy, and that most of his music is a direct expression of his own gloom and despair.

Instead of discussing what we think these two composers thought about, suppose, in the words of a former statesman, we take a look at the record. Let us run over, briefly, the actual, material life that the two men led, and then consider, not only how they reacted to that life, but how far their collected works do constitute a musical autobiography.

Take Mozart first. He was born in domestic service. His father, Leopold Mozart, was a musician attached to the household of the Archbishop of Salzburg. As such, although he was a violinist and composer, he had the standing of a servant. Actually, that isn't as bad as it sounds. Such was the social standing of nearly all composers in his day. Things have improved since then, of course. Formerly, we paid them to compose, and made them eat with the help. Now, we let them eat with the family, and don't pay them anything. At least, Mozart's father had a living. On the other hand, we do know that his brilliant son resented the life he led.

Between his sixth and twenty-first years, Mozart made nine tours of Europe as a pianist and composer. It is customary to assume that his father was a mercenary and heartless tyrant, who exploited his son's talents for his own advantage, and so wore him out with incessant traveling and public appearances that the strain eventually killed him. This isn't strictly true. What Mozart's father was trying to do was to find some European ruler or church dignitary who would engage his talented son as a staff musician—in other words, give him the only opportunity a composer had, in those days, of supporting himself. Incidentally, he never found one. The actual money returns from these trips barely paid expenses. He did make about $3,500 on one tour, but for the most part the elder Mozart would return with his son to Salzburg with a collection of snuffboxes, watches, rings, and fine words —and no money. Nevertheless, I believe that those first twenty years were the happiest in Mozart's life.

In 1772, when he was sixteen, he did get a position as concertmaster to the new Archbishop of Salzburg, at a salary of about $75 a year. Even Mozart couldn't live on that, so in the intervals of turning out musical masterpieces he gave piano lessons. In his twenty-third year the Archbishop raised his salary and made him full *Kapellmeister*. But the two didn't get along. The Archbishop felt that since Mozart was in his employ, he ought to do what he was told, and go *where* he was told. Mozart had different ideas. He felt that his talents entitled him to some freedom of action, and he didn't like being placed above the cook and below the footmen at the dinner table. He and his employer finally had a serious quarrel, and parted forever.

In 1782, when he was twenty-six, Mozart married. And by some grim coincidence, from that time on he never had any permanent source of income. He lived by giving piano lessons—including some that he gave to an eighteen-year-old boy named Beethoven—and by what money he could get from his compositions. It may seem strange that he didn't make a comfortable living out of his operas, many of which, notably *Figaro, Don Giovanni,* and *The Magic Flute,* were extremely popular. But popularity was no source of income in those times. A composer was paid a flat sum for an opera, which then became the property of whichever theatre took it first. It could be resold in turn to dozens of other opera houses, but the money went to the original owner, not to the composer. Even to make a living just above the starvation line, Mozart had to compose continuously, selling outright everything he wrote.

In '87 he did get a $400-a-year job as chamber musician to the court of Vienna. But he lost even that position two years later. His last commission came in the summer of 1791, from a Count von Walsegg, who had a habit of buying works from composers and having them played as his own. The Count wanted a requiem mass, and Mozart set to work on it, although he was on what proved to be his deathbed. Incidentally, to the credit of the Count, be it said that when he did have the mass performed, two years later, it was under the composer's name. Mozart died before the mass was finished, on December 5, just before his thirty-sixth year. Everybody was very much upset by the news. One of his former patrons, the Baron von Swieten, actually called upon his widow, the next day, to advise her not to spend too much money on the funeral. She didn't. She didn't have it to spend. Mozart was buried in the paupers' field in Vienna—just where, no one knows.

What was Tchaikovsky's life? He was born of a family in moderate circumstances, had a conventional schooling, graduated from law school at nineteen, and took a civil service position. Feeling that music was his real life's work, he quit his job and entered the St. Petersburg Conservatory, where he graduated with high honors. He then took a position as professor of harmony in the new Moscow Conservatory. The pay was small, but he had a chance to meet and talk to other musicians, as well as considerable leisure for composition.

His life thereafter, up to his thirty-sixth year, was one of ceaseless composing and genteel, but not abject poverty. He did, however, get heavily in debt. In 1877 a wealthy widow, Natejda von Meck, who was a fervid admirer of his music, offered him a yearly allowance amounting to $3,000—it would be worth about twice that now—so that he could devote all his time to composition. The offer was made on condition that they never meet. Tchaikovsky accepted, and drew the money for thirteen years. At the end of that period Madame von Meck lost a large part of her fortune—or said she did—and discontinued the allowance. Although Tchaikovsky was rather bitter about this, it was really no tremendous hardship, for by this time he was deriving a considerable income from sheet-music royalties and performance fees. In the spring of 1891 he came to the United States and conducted a series of highly successful concerts of his own works. He was a bachelor, except for a brief, extremely unhappy marriage which lasted only three months. He died of cholera in 1893.

Now compare those two lives. I'm not trying to intimate that Tchaikovsky was not an unhappy man. To say that suffering is mental does not make it any the less suffering. But what I am trying to say is that Mozart had his troubles, too. Tchaikovsky knew poverty and worry, true enough, but his real sufferings came from within. He didn't know the ugly, grinding poverty, the ceaseless worry and bewilderment and humiliation that must have dogged Mozart's footsteps during most of his creative life. We know what Tchaikovsky suffered, because he left letters, many of them, that tell us. Mozart suffered, too, but he didn't say much about it. I have great pity for Tchaikovsky, the mental and spiritual invalid, but I must admit that my admiration, as a man, goes to the little Austrian, a great martyr and a great sportsman.

How much actual reflection of Mozart's unhappy life do you find in his music? Almost none at all. Most of his greatest works were written during his worst years, financially, but you will find little in them of gloom or despair. He did write a requiem mass virtually for his own death, but just before that he had written a successful musical comedy, *The Magic Flute,* the champagne of whose score still sparkles.

And what of Tchaikovsky? A great critic once wrote of his work: "Tchaikovsky's music awakens in the breast the haunting, unanswerable questions of life and death that concern us directly and personally." That is quite true. It is also quite true of any great music, whether it be Beethoven's Ninth Symphony, Mozart's G major, Brahms's First, the *Liebestod,* or *The Afternoon of a Faun.*

If you knew nothing of Tchaikovsky's personal life, would you say that the *Nutcracker* suite was the work of a desperately unhappy man? Or the *Sleeping Beauty* ballet? What is there morbid and pessimistic about the B flat piano concerto, or the violin concerto? The *Romeo and Juliet* fantasy is romantic, dramatic, lyric, tragic, if you like. But its tragedy is only the elevated, cleansing, almost stimulating tragedy of the original story. For that matter, what of the Fifth Symphony? You can hardly call a symphony morbid that contains a waltz in both its first and third movements. The second movement, with its wonderful horn melody, is song-like, melancholy, sad, if you will. But doesn't most of the music that affects us most deeply come under the general category of "sad" music? The slow movements of most symphonies are likely to be something other than cheerful and exciting. If Tchaikovsky was at his best—as I think he was—in music that inclines us to melancholy, it is probably only because he had the long line that is the mark of a master, the ability to write powerful, sustained melodic passages that do not depend upon harmonic or rhythmic assistance for their effectiveness. The *"Pathétique"* Symphony *was* Tchaikovsky's avowed personal grief expressed in music, true enough—although even in that work the second and third movements could hardly be called tragic. But it is foolish to let what we know about the writing of the *"Pathétique"* color our view of Tchaikovsky's entire output.

Beethoven is another favorite victim of the "case history" experts. His earlier commentators, from Schindler on, seem to have had a genius for misinterpreting his musical intentions. Virtually everything that they had to say about him was worthless, either as character analysis or musical criticism—which does not in the least prevent their absurdities being embalmed in print for our delectation.

Most of his later biographers have been no better. The most mischievous, probably, is Romain Rolland, whose attitude toward the great Fleming is suspiciously like the attitude of a sentimental housewife toward a motion-picture hero, and who has devoted a six-decker novel and several other detached volumes to trying to make us believe that Beethoven was as sentimental a fellow as himself, and that a Beethoven symphony or overture or quartet is a page, so to speak, out of the composer's diary.

The fact that Beethoven apparently was in the habit of growling and singing and whistling and shaking his fist during the throes of composition seems to have convinced Rolland—and plenty of others—that his music must, therefore, have been a direct expression of his immediate personal feelings; that, if he flew into a rage over the loss of a penny, he forthwith sat down and wrote a rondo about it. He once did just that, of course; and the only thing about the rondo that is in the least expressive of rage over the loss of a penny is its title.

Beethoven, naturally, like any very great artist, devoted his creative hours to solving artistic, not domestic, problems. If he swore and shook his fist while he was composing, it was because some damned modulation wasn't coming out right, not because the Countess Guicciardi had gone to tea with somebody else.

It may be fascinating to read expressions of critical amazement over the fact that such and such a cheerful work was written while the composer was feeling very low; but it is no help toward appreciating the music. Composers do not devote their careers to translating their private feelings into terms of sound, any more than painters spend their entire lives painting portraits of themselves. The very thing that distinguishes a great artist from a small one is his faculty of complete detachment, his ability to stand over his small, weak, everyday self and force that self to the artistic task at hand, whatever it may be. As a man, he may laugh, rage, and despair, starve and freeze, love and hate. Meanwhile his creative self, his oversoul, goes ahead in its own good time, at its own rhythm, watching, weighing, assorting his emotions and experiences, patiently distilling them into the stuff of which art is made. That soul is concerned, not with the griefs and joys of a day, or a year, but with eternal and universal things.

This objectivity, this merciless impersonality, seems so monstrous and inhuman to most of us that even the artists hate to admit that it exists within them. Usually they pretend, even to themselves, that they are normal, uncomplicated creatures of joy and sorrow; that *"aus meinen grossen Schmerzen mach ich die kleine Lieder."* So they do. But the great sorrow may have occurred ten years before the emergence of the little song that is its expression.

If you want to know what a bad time Wagner had during the fifties and sixties, go to his letters, not to his music. In the former you will find the outpourings of a tormented and discouraged man. In the latter you will find only the triumphant achievements of a musical djinn, a creative demon whose sole concern was with turning out masterpieces of art without the slightest regard for the miseries of the highly uncomfortable human being that it happened to be inhabiting.

The intensely satisfactory thing about listening to the Second, Fourth, and Fifth Symphonies of Beethoven—and all the rest of the nine—is the realization that they don't mean a blessed thing. "Mean," that is, in the literary sense of the word. Words have nothing to do with a Beethoven symphony, any more than does Beethoven's private state of mind when he wrote it.

The truth of the matter is that no composer has the time or the energy to spare, when he sits down to write music, to think about his private troubles. When he is writing music he is practicing his profession, and any preoccupation with his own affairs is a hindrance, not a help, in practicing it. If his life is a troubled one, his music is all the more likely to be a refuge, a denial, of that life. I cannot say, with any authority, exactly what went through the minds of Mozart, Beethoven, and Tchaikovsky when they wrote their symphonies. Of one thing I *am* sure: that as they wrote, they were thinking, not about Mozart, Beethoven, and Tchaikovsky, but about music.

6

Reverence for What?

IF SOMEONE should ask me to give a complete course in musical appreciation in one sentence (and it sounds highly improbable), I think I could give it. It would be this: listen to the music, and never by any chance pay any attention to what anyone writes in explanation of it—least of all, the composer. Certainly I would give that advice with the utmost confidence in regard to the works of Richard Wagner. There never lived a composer who was more ready with copious and articulate explanations of what he intended to do in his music—or more certain to do something quite different.

He fulminated against the absurdity of the operatic aria, and wrote Siegmund's Love Song; he excommunicated the operatic duet, and wrote the second act of *Tristan und Isolde;* he cursed the operatic ensemble number, root, stock, and branch, and wrote the quintet from *Die Meistersinger.* He invented the leitmotif system in order to be able to develop his action in accordance with strictly dramatic principles; and proceeded to compose a series of three-act symphonic poems of such eloquence and magnificence that his dazed auditors, to this day, do not realize that the amount of actual dramatic action in any one of them would, by itself, scarcely fill an hour. Most of his theories of music drama were based on the subconscious assumption that their exponent was, incidentally, one of the greatest composers that ever lived; and the failure to realize that assumption, with all its implications, has been the ruin of most of his disciples.

The gap between his theories and his practice looms wide in *Parsifal.* Wagner called his last work a "stage festival play," and succeeded so in impressing the Wagnerites—including the Wagner family—with its essentially religious character that they in turn very nearly succeeded in killing it as a drama. The average *Parsifal* performance has always been approached in the spirit of Oberammergau—be solemn, be reverent, and above all, do not try to be interesting.

I have seen *Die Walküre* acted by singers whose physical grossness was an offense to the eye, whose histrionic gifts were those of the humble semaphore; I have heard it sung by soloists and choruses to whom correct pitch was a sealed book, and played by orchestras whose only ambition, apparently, was to keep awake. No matter. All must be forgiven, because they were all so earnest, so imbued with the solemnity of the master's intentions. If the result was a bore, it must be because I was lacking in reverence.

Unfortunately, in art, reverence alone won't do the trick. Haydn may have put on his best clothes and said a prayer before he sat down to compose; and if the ceremony put him in a better frame of mind for composing, well and good. Nevertheless, it is significant that he did these things *before* he began to compose. The G minor Symphony is fairly conclusive evidence that, once he set to work, his thoughts were, not on God, but on music. And—the G minor Symphony being what it is, God must have been the first to forgive him.

The role of Brünnhilde is as nearly impossible of complete realization as any that even Wagner ever wrote. It demands a singer who must be in turn a dramatic soprano (Acts II and III, first and second scenes), a lyric soprano (Act III, third scene), and a contralto (Act II, fourth scene).

The part is therefore necessarily a compromise. Granted a woman who can sing every note of it right (as I remember, Edyth Walker once did; but I was young, then, and credulous), the odds are a hundred to one against her being able to act the part, and a thousand to one against her looking it. No performance that I have ever seen has justified the lowering of those odds.

The Brünnhilde of *Die Walküre* is not the stately, monumental figure that strides through *Götterdämmerung,* although she is almost invariably so impersonated. Genealogically speaking, she may be the aunt of the hero who awakens her, but that is no excuse for rubbing in the fact. To play her, in *Die Walküre,* as a sort of walking Empire State Building—and they generally do—is to miss the point and throw the drama out of focus.

If Brünnhilde is not young, and hot-blooded, and reckless, she does not make sense. There is no explaining her sudden championing of the two lovers against Wotan. That being so, I would rather have the excitement of seeing a beautiful and vital dramatic performance of the role, and hearing only an adequate vocal one, than insult my eyes and dramatic intelligence for the sake of one perfect vocal moment. That is heresy, and what of it?

7

The Miracle

Coming away from a concert of chamber music, I thought again of the element of mystery that is inseparable from any manifestation of creative genius—the mystery of why one man's way of saying a simple thing is magic, and another man's way is banality.

Brahms sits him down and weaves a few themes together, works them out, takes them apart and puts them together again, with that seemingly plodding, methodical mind of his—and the result is a fabric of extraordinary, quite irrational beauty. Beethoven, searching for a theme for the finale of the cello sonata, hits upon—of all things hackneyed—a major scale. And somehow—something in the way he heard it, probably—it ceases to be a scale and becomes a theme, something that no one had ever quite heard before, a vibrant, shining thing that lives a life of its own, and whispers its own particular message to the mind, and haunts and teases the memory when it is gone.

And Bach. What a man that was. Of all music, his is, I think, at once the most personal and the least contrived. Hearing it, one is conscious of being in the presence of something warm, generous, and friendly, a personality of infinite sympathy and understanding. And yet it is hard to think of anyone's sitting down to make music like this. I never think of Bach as scratching inkily, scowling and erasing, trying out this and that upon a handy and well-tempered clavichord. I see him, rather, out under the morning sun, pruning, raking, watering; tending things—fresh, green, growing things, quivering with life, that put forth tendrils and leaves, that bud and blossom and bear fruit before one's very eyes. And Bach, pleased and beaming, remarking, "I raised that."

8

Orange Grower

HALF a century ago, in the summer of 1884, to be exact, the only music store in Jacksonville, Florida—in fact, the only large music store in that part of the state—was Meredy & Payne's, which sold and rented musical instruments as well as sheet music. One August afternoon a young man came into the store and said that he would like to rent a piano. He was a tall, very diffident young man, who wore thick glasses and spoke with a decided British accent. The clerk showed him several pianos to choose from, and suggested that he try them out. So he sat down and began to play.

He had been playing for about fifteen minutes when the door of the store opened again. And the man who came in went over to the young Englishman and introduced himself. His name, he said, was Thomas F. Ward, and he was organist of the Jesuit church of Sts. Peter and Paul in Brooklyn, New York. His health had begun to give way —in fact, he showed symptoms of tuberculosis—and the fathers of his church had raised the money to send him South for a rest.

"I hope you'll forgive the intrusion," he said, "but as I was coming up the street I heard someone playing in here; and I don't hear many good pianists in this part of the country. I had to come in and find out who it was. Besides, I'm very curious about that music. I'm pretty familiar with organ and piano music, but that piece you were just playing is absolutely new to me. What is it?"

The young man seemed a little embarrassed. "Why . . . er," he stammered, "it's . . . it's really nothing at all. I was just improvising."

Ward, whose interest by this time was beginning to border on excitement, began to ask questions. Yes, the young man was an Englishman, born in Yorkshire. His ancestry, however, could hardly be called extravagantly Anglo-Saxon, inasmuch as he was the son of a naturalized Dutch father and a German mother. His name was Frederick Delius. His father was a wool merchant, and the boy had been traveling, as a salesman, in Germany, Sweden, and France. He had been given some violin and piano lessons, and had developed symptoms of being much more interested in music than in the woolen business. His father, on the other hand, was determined that no son of his should follow a musical career. Finally, as a compromise, his parents had consented to let him try his luck in America. His father had leased him a hundred-acre orange grove near Fernandina, Florida, and he had been there since the spring of the year. The orange grove wasn't doing badly, but after three months of solitude he had decided definitely to devote his life, somehow, to music. He had come up to Jacksonville, he said, because he couldn't stand being without a piano any longer; if he had to stay on the orange grove, he could at least take a piano back there with him.

The two talked for several hours; and the upshot of the matter was that when the boy—he was only twenty-one—went back to the orange grove, Ward went with him. For the next six months the oranges took care of themselves while Ward and the boy played Bach together, and Ward taught his pupil everything he knew about musical theory.

The boy worked as though he were possessed, and finally decided that he must live some place where he could be among musicians and hear more music. He wrote to his father, begging him to let him go to Leipzig, in Germany, where he could attend the conservatory. His father flatly refused. So the son decided to make enough money, somehow, to go over on his own. In the summer of 1885 he and Ward left the plantation and went back to Jacksonville, where, with Ward's help, he set up as a music teacher.

Besides giving music lessons in Jacksonville, Delius sang in the choir of the local synagogue, and occasionally played the organ there. After about six months of this he read in the newspaper that a man named Ruckert, in Danville, Virginia, wanted a music teacher for his two daughters. He offered free board and lodging, a chance to get other pupils in the neighborhood—and no salary.

Delius applied for the job, got it, and thanks to a preliminary story in the local newspaper, which referred to him as "Professor Delius, the eminent violinist and composer, who is prepared to give lessons in violin, piano, harmony, counterpoint, and form," succeeded in getting enough pupils to enable him to live and even save a little money.

Meanwhile his family, who had had no news of him for nearly a year, began to worry. They inquired at Fernandina, and learned that he had gone to Jacksonville. They wrote to Jacksonville, and were told that he had disappeared. His frantic mother finally located him, and wrote to tell him that his father had at last consented to let him go to Leipzig. He went there, and studied under Reinecke, Jadassohn, and Edvard Grieg. But he always said that what he learned at Leipzig did little but add to what he already knew, and that his real training in the technique of music he owed to the Brooklyn organist, Tom Ward.

Delius spent several years abroad, in Germany and France, trying unsuccessfully to get his music played. Not until 1897, in his thirty-fifth year, did he get a performance of any important work. In that year, Doctor Hans Haym conducted his fantasy-overture, *Over the Hills and Far Away,* at a concert in Elberfeld . . . where, it may be said, the members of the town council threatened to dismiss Doctor Haym if he conducted any such music again.

He finally decided to return to London and show his family that at least he hadn't been wasting his time on their money. Accordingly, on May 30, 1899, he gave an orchestral concert of his own works, under the baton of Alfred Hertz—the Hertz who was afterwards, for so many years, a conductor at the Metropolitan and later of the San Francisco Orchestra.

The program lasted from 8:30 to midnight, but the audience stayed. The London critics took him seriously. Some were bewildered, none was contemptuous, and a few even said that he was a genius.

His private life, from then on, was uneventful. He bought a house in Grez-sur-Loing, not far from Paris, where he spent the rest of his life. In his later years he became blind and paralyzed, but thanks to the efforts of his devoted wife, and a young musician named Eric

Fenby, who acted as his amanuensis, continued to compose. He died on the tenth of June, 1934.

Delius occupies a peculiar position in British music. He is generally conceded to be one of England's great composers, and yet his music is surprisingly little known, not only here, but in England. One of his most enthusiastic champions is Sir Thomas Beecham, who conducted the first performances of many of his more important scores. Some of Delius' neglect is probably due to the fact that he always kept very much to himself, was extremely critical of his own work, and never made the slightest effort to have any of his music performed. Even so, it is hard to understand why the man has remained, up to now, so little known.

Perhaps one reason he is not more widely recognized is that his music is difficult to catalogue as to nationality. A man who was born in England, sold woolen goods in Scandinavia, raised oranges in Florida, studied music in Germany, and lived in France, could hardly be expected to show any strongly nationalistic traits. And Delius doesn't. His music has a quality of German solidity about it, but in its impressionism and objectivity is much more French than German. On the other hand, while he has been compared to Debussy in his harmonic scheme, he speaks with more clarity, with much less reticence, than the French master. And while there is a certain British austerity about his style that occasionally reminds one of Vaughan Williams, the warmth of his orchestral coloring is much more suggestive of Florida than Yorkshire. In short, he is a cosmopolitan in music. You can't describe him accurately beyond saying that he is Delius.

9

Visiting Muscovite

DELIUS was not the only European composer to visit America in his youth. We had another, even earlier, young visitor. To meet him, we shall have to go back, in time, nearly three-quarters of a century, and travel, in space, to Niagara Falls. There, in the autumn of 1863, we shall find a group of Russian naval officers whose ship, the frigate *Almaz,* is anchored in New York harbor, and who are on a sightseeing trip to see one of the wonders of the Western world. The American Civil War has been going on for three years, but it is not the immediate cause of their visit. An uprising in Poland, with which the English are openly sympathetic, has brought on an international crisis that looks as if it were about to develop into a war between England and Russia. Five vessels of the Russian fleet have been sent to America with secret orders to attack English shipping if hostilities should break out.

Among the officers of the *Almaz* was a midshipman named Nicholas Rimsky-Korsakoff; and in spite of the serious nature of his mission, and the state of war that existed in America, he seems to have had a very good time. He and his fellow officers had come up from New York to Albany by boat, and then by train to Niagara, where they stopped at the Niagara Hotel as guests of some American friends. He spent two days there, in the course of which he hired a rowboat and went as close to the falls as he could get, then made a roundabout journey back to New York by way of Elmira. He spent about seven months, altogether, in America, during five of which he was in and around New York, where he went to the theatre, sampled what the restaurants and wine shops had to offer, and saw two rather bad performances of Meyerbeer's *Robert le Diable* and Gounod's *Faust.*

Young Rimsky-Korsakoff—he was twenty at the time—already had a reputation among his fellow naval officers as a talented amateur musician. He played the piano fairly well, chiefly by ear, and one of his American friends, a pilot named Thompson, played the violin—also by ear; and Thompson and Rimsky-Korsakoff used to give concerts in the wardroom of the *Almaz.* On the whole, he seems to have been a much better musician than naval officer. He himself said, much later, that he had absolutely no talent for a naval career, because he didn't like to give orders, didn't like inflicting punishments, and had no gift at all for swearing at sailors. His voyage to America constituted the bulk of what sea service he ever saw, and on his return to Russia, although he did remain a navy man for many years, it was in the rather pacific position of inspector of navy bands.

His musical education, such as it was, had begun before his American trip, and continued in what was then St. Petersburg, after it. I say "such as it was" because it could hardly be called an education in any strict sense of the word. His master was Balakireff, who was the head of a more or less revolutionary movement among the younger Russian composers. Their avowed mission was to free Russian music from the Italian, French, and German influences that had, in their opinion, corrupted it. Of course, in their enthusiasm for their cause, they did what revolutionaries generally do—attacked everything, bad *or* good, that symbolized the old regime in any way. The great thing in music, they decided, was to have color and rhythm. Harmony must be instinctive, counterpoint was to be avoided as interfering with inspiration, form must be absolutely free, and melody was a sign of weakness. In this last respect Beethoven, especially in his symphonies, was highly objectionable, only less so, in fact, than Chopin, who was looked upon as a drawing-room composer. For some reason they approved of Schumann, but Bach was not a composer at all, and Wagner was an unknown foreign curiosity. In fact, reading their opinions on composing and music in general, it is hard to keep remembering that what they said was being said in the sixties and seventies, and not in the 1920's.

With all these libertarian ideas in the air, you can readily imagine that Rimsky-Korsakoff and his contemporaries, who included César Cui and Mussorgsky, had a grand time studying. Balakireff started to teach Rimsky-Korsakoff to play the piano, but deciding that his pupil would never make a really fine pianist, persuaded him to drop the whole matter. In composition, Balakireff's pupils were not encouraged to bother with harmony, or counterpoint, or other theoretical studies. They just went ahead and composed. Rimsky-Korsakoff, in fact, virtually began his career as a composer, at the age of seventeen, by writing a symphony, under Balakireff's direction. On his return from America he settled down to his combined naval and musical career in earnest, and for the ensuing seven years spent from two to three hours a day filling out reports and writing form letters for the navy, and the rest of the time in talking, playing, and writing music in the company of Balakireff, Cui, Borodine, and Mussorgsky. The five had a wonderful time, criticizing each other's music, hearing it played, and meeting the other musicians, Russian and foreign, of their day. Wagner had conducted some concerts of his music in Russia, and while he exerted amazingly little influence as a composer, he did make a decided impression as a conductor. Among other things, he introduced a new technique of conducting whereby, instead of facing the audience, the conductor turned his back to the audience and faced the orchestra. Apparently this was a great novelty, at least in Russia, and Russian conductors immediately took up the new method, with great success.

There is no particular point in my burdening you here with a detailed biography of Rimsky-Korsakoff. To do so would only be to do, badly, what he himself has done superlatively in his autobiography,* one of the most honest and entertaining personal documents ever written. There is one incident in his life, however, that will bear some discussion. It is an amusing one, but it is likewise not uninstructive.

In 1871, when Rimsky was twenty-seven, the new head of the St. Petersburg Conservatory, Azanchevsky, asked him to accept the position of professor of practical composition and orchestration, and conductor of the student orchestra. Now although Rimsky had already written an opera and several orchestral pieces, including *Sadko,* his theoretical knowledge of music was almost non-existent, and he showed a certain degree of understandable reluc-

* *My Life in Music,* by Nikolai Rimsky-Korsakoff, Alfred A. Knopf, New York, 1923.

tance about taking such a responsibility. But his friends were all for it, particularly Balakireff, who thought it would be a good idea to have one of his revolutionary young men in an academic post. So Rimsky finally did accept.

Writing about this venture, years later, he says: "Had I ever studied at all, had I possessed a fraction more of knowledge than I actually did, it would have been obvious to me that I could not and should not accept the proffered appointment, that it was foolish and dishonest of me to become a professor. . . At the time, I not only could not decently harmonize a chorale, had not written a single counterpoint in my life, but I had hardly any notion of the structure of a fugue. . . As to the conductor's art, having never conducted an orchestra, nor even rehearsed a single orchestral piece, of course I had no conception of it."

He took the job, nevertheless, and made a surprising success of it, helped, as he says, by the fact that his pupils would hardly venture to suspect that he knew no more than they did. "By the time they had learned enough to see through me, I had learned something myself. Thus, having been undeservedly accepted at the conservatory as a professor, I soon became . . . one of its very best pupils!"

There is a moral to that. While I would hardly recommend Rimsky-Korsakoff's methods of acquiring a musical education to the average student, I must say that I think he started composing at the right end. Inspiration doesn't depend on theory, and doesn't wait upon it. I think you will find that in the career of any real creative artist, his ideas have sprouted, so to speak, well in advance of his technical ability to handle them. Moreover, I think Rimsky-Korsakoff is a more severe critic of his own shortcomings than he would be of a stranger's. Technique and form are, in the last analysis, more or less intuitive. Almost any artist is born knowing, or discovers for himself, most of what is between the covers of his text-books. A formal training in the technique of his craft is a valuable tool for an artist to have; for a formal education is a time-saver. It gives him the benefit of other men's discoveries; it teaches him methods of shaping and polishing a work of art with a minimum expenditure of time and a minimum waste of energy. But if a man has the character to be a great artist, he generally has enough application and intelligence to educate himself. At the time he took his position in the conservatory, Rimsky-Korsakoff may not have known the names of things; but hearing the music that he had already composed, much of which still survives, you can't escape the realization that he knew his business; that he must have been studying for years, even if unconsciously, under a professor named Rimsky-Korsakoff.

The history of music has always been, that the theorists of one generation collect examples, and make rules out of them, from the works produced by the preceding generation, which didn't know that it was making rules. I've often thought that if there is any one thing wrong with modern music, it is that it is not unconscious enough; in a sense it is too well schooled. I can't help distrusting artists who are too conscious of being path-breakers. When I see composers issuing statements, and essays, and pamphlets, explaining, not the aesthetic qualities of their work, but its technical virtues, I become uneasy. I begin to wonder whether they haven't spent too much time writing the words and not enough in writing the music. Ernest Newman once said that most of the great technical discoveries and innovations in music have been made by composers without talent; because the geniuses were too busy creating masterpieces out of familiar materials to have time to experiment with new ones.

Yesterday, a musician wrote music; then came the professors to explain how he did it and what he meant by it. Today, too often, the musician first writes a treatise on harmony and then composes music to conform to the rules that he has just made up. He may be right. What sounds to me so pedantic, so colorless and arbitrary about the conscientious bleakness of some contemporary music may sound profound and beautiful to another generation. Just the same, there is something to be said for Rimsky-Korsakoff's method of writing it first and finding out later how it was done. At least, up to now, it has produced some highly attractive results.

10

Pure Reading Matter

IN SPEAKING of the elaborate apologias that so many contemporary composers furnish as a sort of guide-book to their work, I am not referring to the program notes that accompany pieces of a descriptive or narrative character. The symphonic poem, a rendering in terms of music of something that originally existed in terms of literature or drama, has long since become as accepted and respectable a musical form as the symphony. It appeals to our incorrigibly childish desire to have someone tell us a story. Audiences love to read program notes—if you could watch a room full of symphony subscribers during a performance of, say, Strauss's *Ein Heldenleben* without hearing the music, you might be forgiven for wondering whether you were in a concert hall or the reading room of a public library.

Incidentally, there has been considerable finger-pointing at Richard Strauss because he so elaborately tried to conceal the programs of several of his symphonic poems. Many of his commentators seem to feel that it was not quite nice of Strauss to have a program if he was going to pretend he had none. I think, on the contrary, that Strauss was obeying a very sound instinct in trying to keep his programs to himself, and that it would have been far better for him, as a composer, never to have revealed them.

A program is a wonderful springboard for the imagination of a composer whose tendencies, like Strauss's are dramatic. It gives him a ready-made framework for his music, and a prescribed set of emotions and impressions to convey. But a piece of music lives or dies, in the long run, by reason of its success or failure as a piece of music, and not as a sort of aural Baedeker. The composer who writes a tone poem, and publishes his program, runs a great risk of having his critics spend most of their time deciding whether or not he has followed his program, and very little of it in listening to whatever music he may have written. Moreover, the composer himself frequently ends by doing the same thing.

In his earlier works, Strauss was content to convey the general mood and spiritual content of his program, and let things go at that. But as he became increasingly successful in making his music say definite things, he became increasingly indifferent as to whether those things were worth much after they had been said. Of all Strauss's tone poems, those that I still hear with the greatest pleasure and profit are *Don Juan, Till Eulenspiegel,* and *Death and Transfiguration;* and it is precisely those three, I think, that need no libretto to make their structure and utterances intelligible.

The others, *Zarathustra, Don Quixote, Ein Heldenleben,* despite many pages of beauty and eloquence, involve a fearful amount of required reading to make them completely understandable. By the time we get to the *Domestica* and the "Alpine" Symphony we find a Strauss whose entire interest, apparently, is in his literary structure—who assembles a great heap of heterogeneous material—gold, silver, bronze, marble, scrap iron, bits of broken bottles, old bones, and half-bricks—and plasters it into the walls of his edifice with hardly a second glance.

Eventually, all program notes run out of print. The programs are forgotten, and the brilliant descriptive bits lose their salience. Only the music—if any—survives.

11

Music Lives Long

EVERY time I hear the Schumann Piano Concerto, I'm impressed all over again by its extraordinary youthfulness and vitality. It's amazing to see how little it shows its age. I've often wondered whether anyone, someone who had never heard of Schumann, hearing this work for the first time, could guess within fifty years the period in which it was written. I'm inclined to think that this faculty of remaining contemporary is a characteristic of most great music. It ages much less rapidly than some of the other arts.

The Schumann work, for example, is nearly a hundred years old. Now if you saw a painting that was done nearly a hundred years ago, I doubt whether you would have any great difficulty in recognizing its approximate age. Even if the colors hadn't darkened and the varnish cracked, something about the drawing, the way the paint was applied, even the arrangement of the colors, would betray the fact that it wasn't the work of any contemporary artist. Rembrandt, Rubens, Michelangelo, Velasquez, Goya, the great masters of the past, are modern in that they represent a point of view that is timeless, but the *manner* in which they paint is unmistakably that of another day. You wouldn't be likely to mistake a verse by Edgar Allan Poe for the work of a contemporary poet; Dickens, stylistically, certainly has little in common with

H. G. Wells, or Joseph Conrad, or Willa Cather, or Edna Ferber.

But in music, which apparently changes its style from one week to another nowadays, the great composers work astonishingly alike. If Sibelius has been called the modern Beethoven, it is perhaps because there is many a passage in his symphonies that Beethoven would have written in the same manner. Eighteenth-century music *is* dated, I grant you. No one would be likely to mistake Händel or Haydn or Mozart or the early Beethoven for a living composer. But once we're in the nineteenth century, the trouble begins. Not long ago I heard Paul Whiteman conduct a medley of waltzes, and—if you'll forgive the blasphemy—enjoyed it. Among others, it included themes in waltz time from Chopin, Tchaikovsky, Gounod, and Johann Strauss. Here was music by four composers whose combined birth and death dates covered a span of ninety years. Yet it all went together, perfectly. There was no perceptible change in method and feeling in moving from one to another. Schumann and Richard Strauss are certainly different in their individual styles; yet the musical materials of the former—melody, harmony, and rhythm—are not so different from those of the latter that you would inevitably know that Schumann died before Strauss was born.

12

Richard Himself

I NEVER did see Shelley plain, but I once had tea with Richard Strauss at his summer home in Bavaria. Tea and an interview. It was several years ago, when I was music critic of the now unhappily extinct New York *World*. Perhaps, in the interests of honesty, I might qualify that statement about interviewing Strauss. The actual asking of the questions was done by the late Harry O. Osgood, of the *Musical Courier*, who had made the appointment with Dr. Strauss and took me along, introduced me, and conducted the ensuing conversation with a pyrotechnic fluency that made any display of my own rather disheveled command of the German language mercifully unnecessary. However, I would have asked the same questions that Osgood did if I could have had a few days in which to commit them to memory, and I did understand Strauss's answers with practically no outside help; so, for publication purposes at least, I like to think of it as my interview with Strauss.

When you see Garmisch, where Strauss spends his summers, you begin to understand his success. No wonder he can write music there! The only mystery, in fact, is that any of the inhabitants waste time doing anything else. It is a toy village at the extreme southern end of Germany, about four hours by rail from Munich, set down upon a plateau about three miles wide, as flat and green as a pool table and ringed in by the Bavarian Alps. There are no foothills to these mountains. They rise from the flat ground with a smoothness and swiftness that give dramatic emphasis to their towering immensity. Beyond them are other peaks, all snow-capped and gleaming, the farthest ridge of all marking the boundary line between Germany and Austria. One might easily be crushed by the huge impassiveness of these masses of rock and ice, as well as be exhilarated by their beauty; but it seems impossible that anyone could live unmoved in their presence. From his study window Strauss can look out upon a willow-fringed river, two miles of meadowland, vast black stretches of pine forest, seven mountain peaks, and a glacier. The comparative failure of the "Alpine" Symphony becomes understandable. No man living could quite translate that view into terms of music.

We had a little trouble in finding the Strauss villa. We had heard of Garmisch solely because Strauss lived there, yet not all of the inhabitants of Garmisch, apparently, had heard of Strauss. The first three people of whom we asked the way were regretful but vague, and the fourth, a housewife whom we interrupted in the process of chasing a goose out of her garden, was positive but, as our subsequent wanderings proved, highly inaccurate. Most of the Garmisch villagers were aware in a general way that the *Herr Doktor* was a famous composer; but his local fame seemed to rest chiefly upon the fact that he is the best skat and pinochle player for miles around.

The Villa Strauss finally revealed itself as a baroque structure surrounded by rather extensive grounds and almost completely hidden from the road by maple and linden trees. Strauss's horror of unexpected visitors was evidenced by a high stone fence that completely surrounded the property, pierced by an equally high iron gate ornamented with ferocious signs about being ware of dogs. Set into the gate were a push button and an apartment-house telephone. Our companion pushed one and applied his ear to the other, with prompt results. "She says he's out," he remarked to us and then explained to the gatepost that it was two *Herrn* from New York, who had an appointment with the *Herr Doktor* for 4 o'clock. The gatepost relented on the spot and asked us to come in and wait. A starched little maidservant emerged from the house, opened the gate for us, and led us down a graveled walk to where some iron chairs and a table clustered sociably under a tree at the edge of a little lawn starred with buttercups and cornflowers. The *Herr Doktor* was writing letters, she thought. She would call him.

To be a good interview, this chronicle should go on from here to relate how I put Dr. Strauss at his ease when he appeared, what he said to me, and with what brilliant sallies I kept the conversational ball rolling. But in such respects this is not going to be much of an interview. As I explained before, my companion did most of the talking, my sole vocal contributions, as I remember them, being to say *"Es freut mich sehr"* upon being introduced (that may be bad German, but that is what I said) and to murmur *"Leider nein"* when Strauss asked me if we were related to Loomis Taylor of the Metropolitan Opera House. Otherwise I listened and tried to look like a German-speaking music critic.

Dr. Strauss hadn't been writing letters, after all. He came round the corner of the house in golf trousers and a beautiful plum velvet smoking jacket, to explain that he had been pruning the fruit trees in the back garden. He looked tanned and healthy, easily a decade younger than his actual years, and was cordial and talkative. He was likewise extremely diplomatic at first. His answers to all questions regarding his recent American trip were deliberate and for the most part carefully noncommittal. Had he enjoyed the trip? Yes, greatly. It was a wonderfully gratifying experience. How about music in America? Did Americans seem more interested in music than when he toured in 1904? A shrug and a smile: possibly; one could hardly say. What about the orchestras? Here he grew more positive. "Excellent. A very high standard of playing."

His remarks about opera in New York, and particularly his views upon the language in which opera should be given, were his most interesting contributions of the afternoon. He admired the gorgeousness of the Metropolitan Opera House productions and the perfection of organization that enabled the Metropolitan to perform eight different works in a week, but he did not think much of the Metropolitan staging. "They have no dramatic instinct there," he remarked. "Everything is the singing—always the voice." Jeritza, he thought, was a great artist—the greatest Salome, perhaps, that he had ever seen. One of us—it hardly matters which—happened to ask him if he had seen the Metropolitan production of Mozart's *Così fan tutte,* and thereby incidentally elicited his views regarding opera in English. No, he had not seen *Così fan tutte* in New York. "It was very fine, I hear, but I should not care to see it. The Metropolitan is too big for such a work. It must have been lost there. Besides"—he grew animated—"I understand they gave it in Italian. That was a mistake, a great mistake. A work like *Così fan tutte,* where the words are so important and where there is so much parlando recitative, should always be given in the language of the country where it is being performed. What interest can there be for the audience to hear those long parlandos in Italian? There is no musical interest in such passages. Unless one understands every word the characters are saying, they are bound to be boresome—*sehr langweilich!*"

Asked to name some other works that should be done in English in New York, he considered a moment. "Well, *The Barber of Seville,* for one. That is full of *recitativo secco.* It should surely be done in English. Any *opera buffa* where the individual words are important should be done in English in New York, or not at all. My own operas? With *Die Rosenkavalier* that is not particularly necessary, perhaps; but *Salome*—yes, the words are very important in *Salome;* that might be sung in English. And if they ever give me *Ariadne auf Naxos,* they should certainly give it in English, for that is modeled in form after Mozart."

At this juncture the starched little maid appeared to announce that tea was served, and would the *Herrschaft* come in and have some? They would, and did. Unfortunately, my recollection of the rest of the afternoon is a little dim. I do recall that Frau Strauss was there, speaking excellent English that fell soothingly upon the ear of one of the *Herrn* from New York; that I was further comforted to discover that Dr. Strauss's English was about on a par with my brand of German; that the widow of Johann Strauss was also there, very interesting and interested, and apparently immortal; that the tea included whipped cream, an unheard-of delicacy in Germany; and that a pleasant time was had by all.

We did see the dogs of which the signs on the gate had spoken so threateningly. They were rather small and brown, and they slept, prodigiously chained, in two small kennels beside the front door. At that same front door occurred one of those small incident that are remembered for years afterward. As Dr. Richard Strauss, Director of the Vienna Opera, composer of *Till Eulenspiegel, Don Quixote,* and other works too numerous to mention, approached the threshold of his own home, he paused and wiped his feet carefully upon a small square of dampened doormat that lay before the door. Advancing a step, he wiped his feet once more, this time upon a small dry doormat. Stepping across the doorsill he stopped and wiped his feet for a third and final time upon a small rubber doormat that lay just inside the door. A weight fell from my shoulders that will never again rest upon them. Strauss may be a good conductor and a great composer, and I shall always respect him, but I could never again be afraid of him. For in that moment I saw, for a flash, the truth. Here was no Titan or demigod; before me stood only a married man.

13

Bandmaster

I READ an editorial on band music recently, in which one sentence began, "While it can hardly be said that John Philip Sousa was a great musician—" I am not so sure of that. So much depends upon your definition of greatness. For me, a great musician, like any other great artist, is one whose name identifies his work.

There is another type of artist who survives: the one whose work identifies his name. Scattered through the pages of aesthetic history you will find a host of men who had the luck to turn out one work of genius. Thomas Gray was—who? The man who wrote Gray's *Elegy.* The *Rubáiyát of Omar Khayyám* does not survive because its translation is one of the works of Edward FitzGerald. On the contrary, FitzGerald survives because he wrote the translation. Mention the name of Henry Bishop to the average person, and that which you have mentioned will probably kindle no light of recognition in his eye. To identify Bishop, you must explain that he wrote "Home, Sweet Home."

In these cases, and a good many others, the work is more famous than the man. The light in which he stands is a reflected one. The truly great ones survive without explanatory footnotes. We say, "a play by Shakespeare," "a symphony by Beethoven," or "a statue by Michelangelo." We do not ask, "What play?" or, "What symphony?" or, "What statue?" We take it for granted, hearing the name of the artist, that any work of his is worth our attention. Even his failures, whose actual merits warrant them no such distinction, usually survive because they bear his name. That name is, if you like, a trade-mark; and, like any good trade-mark, is a guarantee of worth.

Sousa was no Beethoven. Nevertheless he was Sousa. When you said "a Sousa march," the phrase meant something pretty definite to almost anyone who heard you. He did not ask, "What Sousa march?" It did not matter. Any one of them bore the impress of a vigorous, clear-cut, and decidedly original musical personality. They were not —they are not, for that matter—"festival" marches, or any other concert variant of the original form. They were intensely practical. Sousa started as a navy bandmaster (that is, after he had left off being a boy violinist), and did most of his work in the open air, and in motion. The marches he wrote, first for the Marine Band and later for his own, were intended to set the pace for marching men. They were for the feet, not for the head.

They have a deceptive simplicity, those Sousa marches. Their tunes are so uncomplicated, so easy to catch, so essentially spontaneous and diatonic, that one can easily underrate them. Simple as they may be, they are Sousa's tunes, and no one's else. It took only a minor grade of inspiration to write them, perhaps. It is none the less genuine inspiration.

His career is not unlike that of Johann Strauss, Jr. Like the Viennese, he wrote operettas (you may still remember *El Capitan*) whose scores always contained at least one number couched in the composer's characteristic rhythmic idiom. In Strauss's case, it was a waltz; in Sousa's, a march. Gradually each man became famous for that particular sort of instrumental number, and grew to specialize in it. Strauss became the Waltz King; Sousa became the March King.

A composer whose music is in the permanent repertoire of virtually every brass band in the world may not be a great musician, but he is none the less someone to take into account. I have heard *The Washington Post* March played in Munich, and the *High School Cadets* played in Paris. *The Stars and Stripes Forever,* it is safe to say, is better liked in many lands than the actual Stars and Stripes themselves. Wherever men march, they march, sooner or later, to the music of John Philip Sousa.

We do rightly, of course, to judge a man by his reach as well as his grasp. It is only fitting to admire Beethoven and Wagner for their pretensions as well as for their achievement. They dared more than other men. If they won greater glory, they also risked a more disastrous failure. Yet I think it is not always necessary to be technically "great" in order to be immortal. The giants of art stir our hearts and souls and imaginations. Sousa stirs only our feet. Nevertheless, he does stir them.

Wherever he has gone, I am sure he has found a welcome. There is a dining hall in the Elysian Fields, marked Grade A Composers Only. If you could look in at the door tonight, you would probably see him there; perhaps not at the speakers' table, with Wagner and Beethoven and Mozart and Bach and Debussy and the rest, but somewhere in the room—at a small table, possibly, with Herbert and Strauss and Delibes.

"However did *he* get in here?" asks some disapproving

shade—a small-town *Kapellmeister,* probably. "He was a good craftsman, and did an honest job, no doubt. But so am I, and so did I. Yet when I applied, they black-balled me. Who got him in?"

The guide smiles. "The marching men. The men who have had to go long miles, on an empty belly, under a hot sun, or through a driving rain. They made us take him in. They said he made things easier for them."

14

The Brave Days of Old

I HAD a letter a short time ago that raises a question that I don't remember ever having heard discussed at any particular length. In writing of the relation between the composer and his public, my correspondent said: "Isn't it possible that one reason why the greatness of certain works by the earlier composers failed to be recognized at once was the fact that they were badly played?"

That question opens up a wide field of speculation. One of the striking characteristics of this musical generation, particularly, I might say, in America, is the fact that in the performance of music we take the mechanical perfection of the instruments, and the technical perfection of the performer, entirely for granted. When a famous violinist or pianist plays a new concerto, we assume, as a matter of course, that the instrument upon which he plays is capable of producing the required sounds, and that he himself is capable of playing any sequence of notes that the composer may choose to write. The day of the old-fashioned virtuoso, who dazzled his hearers with acrobatic musical feats, is entirely over. We're no longer interested in the fact that a musician can play or sing very loudly and very fast. What we say now is, "Granted all that, how *expressively* does he sing or play?"

That was not always so. We can only guess, of course, at what the earlier performances of some of the familiar masterworks must have sounded like; but the history books do occasionally let slip certain isolated facts that justify us in the suspicion that, up to the very third quarter of the nineteenth century, a composer not only had to struggle to get his ideas down on paper, but then had to worry about getting a decent performance.

Nobody claims that certain musical instruments, as they exist today—the harp, for instance—have reached their final pitch of mechanical perfection. But it is hard for us to realize how enormously improved they are over what our forefathers had to cope with. Consider the pipe organ, for instance, for which Bach wrote his contrapuntal masterpieces. The wind for it was provided by a huge pair of bellows, the handles of which had to be yanked up and down by one, sometimes two or three men. The player was more or less at the mercy of these organ pumpers. If they worked the bellows in a regular rhythm, supplied the organ with a continuous supply of the right amount of air, a long, sustained passage might sound reasonably like what the composer had written. But if they pulled the handles irregularly, or waited too long between pulls, that same passage would emerge as a series of gasps and grunts and moans that would drive a modern organist to murder or suicide.

The action of the organ was entirely mechanical, and the weight of the action was determined by the number of pipes that were playing at any one time. If one stop—that is, one set of pipes—necessitated a pressure of four or five ounces in order to depress the keys, the minute the organist coupled in another stop, the key pressure increased. If he threw in all the stops at once, he might have to exert a force of one or two pounds in order to depress one key; or, granted that he had the strength to do that, if he had forgotten to notify the organ pumper that he was coming to a full organ passage, there might not be enough air in the wind chest to make the pipes sound at all. Not only that, but the action was noisy, as it involved a whole machine shop of arms and levers, and the pipes were slow in responding to the keys, so that very rapid passages were likely to have notes missing.

Compare that primitive mechanism with the modern organ, wholly electrical in its action, with motored blowers automatically supplying just the right amount of air, with three, four, sometimes five banks of keys, and with pipes running into the thousands, supplying a range of power and tone color of which Bach never dreamed. And don't blame the modern organ for the fact that it is usually housed in a motion-picture theatre, and is used more for jazz than for Bach. The fact that the movie-house organist spends most of his time playing "Mother Machree" with chime effects doesn't alter the other fact that the instrument upon which he commits this outrage is a mechanical miracle that Bach would never have hoped to see this side of heaven.

The piano upon which we now play Bach and Mozart is not the clavichord or so-called pianoforte for which those composers had to write. That was an evolutionary instrument, halfway between the harpsichord, with its jacks and quills, and the modern piano. It did possess a rudimentary dynamic range—its very name, pianoforte, is the perpetuated boast of its inventor that it could play both soft *and* loud; but its tone was a pale, characterless tinkle, compared with the singing thunders of a modern grand piano. Whenever I hear a good pianist play Mozart's G major Concerto, I can't help wishing that Mozart might be in the audience to hear it as it sounds, not on the instrument for which he was forced to write, but the instrument of which he must, wistfully, have dreamed.

Orchestral composers had their troubles, too. Their stringed instruments, of course, were perfection, the finest ever made; but wind instruments were anything but perfect. The ancestor of the tuba, in the brass choir, for instance, was a thing called, appropriately enough, the serpent. It was built of wood, covered with leather, was pierced with finger-holes, and in general appearance resembled the death agonies of a boa constrictor. The sounds it emitted, indescribably horrible in themselves, were not even in tune; for the finger-holes were placed, not where they would produce notes of the correct pitch, but where the player's fingers could reach them. This same habit of favoring the player's comfort over the laws of acoustics made the flutes and clarinets of the eighteenth and early nineteenth centuries instruments whose intonation would make a modern symphony subscriber squirm.

In Weber's overture to *Der Freischütz* there is a passage for bassoons in octaves. It takes the second bassoon player down to his lowest possible note, the low B flat. But on the way up, while the first bassoon plays the octave B natural, the second bassoon plays nothing at all; not because Weber didn't want it, but because the bassoon of the 1820's had no low B natural. Neither the trumpets nor the horns, almost up to Wagner's time, had valves. They were so-called "natural" instruments—which is to say that they could play only bugle calls. They couldn't play an ordinary diatonic scale, let alone a chromatic one. In other words, when a composer of those days wrote for brass instruments, he couldn't write scales, except for the highest and loudest notes of the instruments, and he couldn't change key without changing the instrument. If Richard Strauss had been born in 1764 instead of 1864, he never would have written the horn and trumpet parts of *Ein Heldenleben,* for the simple reason that there existed no instruments that could have played them. Even as late as 1845, Wagner, in writing *Tannhäuser,* does not dare take it for granted that any particular opera house will have more than two valve horns. His score calls for two valve horns, to play the sharps and flats, and two natural horns to play the open notes.

But imperfect instruments were not the chief affliction of the classic composers. The quality of the average performance must have been something that we wouldn't tolerate in a high school orchestra. Consider the simple fact, for instance, that the vibrato, in violin playing, is a comparatively modern invention. You've noticed that when a violinist draws his bow across the string, the finger of his left hand that is resting on the string doesn't remain motionless. It vibrates. It is that vibration of the left hand that gives the tone the undulatory, singing quality that makes the violin such an eloquent instrument. Now players of the elder days of orchestral music didn't bother with any such nonsense. The violinist clamped the fingers of his left hand on the strings, and held them there, and sawed wood with his right. And only if you've ever heard the sound produced by a class of beginners in a conservatory, playing violins in unison, without vibrato, can you realize what a dead, depressing sound that is.

A second violinist or viola player in a modern symphony orchestra is an artist in his own right. He plays the supporting, rather than the leading roles; but there is no question of his technical mastery. In the orchestras of the good old days, a second violinist was somebody who wasn't good enough to be a first violinist, and a viola player was a disappointed second violinist. The great English composer, Henry Purcell, confines the violin parts of his works largely to the limits of the first position; because, as he himself said, he didn't dare take them out of the first position for fear they wouldn't play in tune.

In orchestral works written before Beethoven's time, the cellos almost invariably play in unison with the basses, partly because that was the custom, but also because no composer thought of trusting the cellos to play melodic passages. I've often wondered what the fugal passage in Beethoven's C minor Symphony, and the double-bass recitatives in the Ninth sounded like at the first rehearsal. Musicians who had spent their lives playing an endless succession of "vump, vump" bass parts must have swooned in terror at being asked to play eighth- and sixteenth-note scale passages in quick time. Rehearsals for Schubert's C major Symphony (the 1828 one) had to be abandoned temporarily because the string section announced that the music couldn't be played.

There is an amusing example of orchestral incompetence in the score of Liszt's E flat Piano Concerto. In the original version he has a short section in which the triangle is supposed to play a little rhythmic pattern all by himself. But even after several rehearsals, at the first performance the triangle player was so terrified by his sudden emergence into prominence that he missed his cue and never came in at all. So, in the revised edition of the score, the original triangle passage has been handed over to the flutes and oboes. Another one of those is in the overture to Wagner's *Flying Dutchman.* In one place the theme of Senta's ballad is given to a solo oboe. The passage ends on a high C and a high D, both of which notes ought, logically, to be played by the oboe, and which any modern oboist would play as a matter of course. But if you'll look at the score you'll find that Wagner suddenly brings in the flute to play the last three notes of the phrase. He did this because, at the first rehearsals, the oboe player wasn't able to play those notes without breaking. It's a familiar matter of history, of course, that as late as 1862, another of Wagner's works, *Tristan und Isolde,* had to be abandoned as unplayable after fifty-four rehearsals.

It was not only the orchestral musicians who hampered so many great composers. The soloists and the singers were just as bad, sometimes. The *Tristan* rehearsals were given up, not only on account of the orchestra, but because the tenor Ander, who was supposed to sing Tristan, couldn't learn the role. He spent a winter at it, and finally announced that as fast as he learned one act he forgot another, and threw up the part in despair. In 1881 Tchaikovsky dedicated his violin concerto to Leopold Auer, the great Hungarian virtuoso and teacher. Auer refused to play the first performance and turned down the dedication, on the ground that it wasn't violin music, and couldn't be played anyhow. Incidentally, he spent the later years of his life teaching that same concerto to such pupils as Hubermann, Zimbalist, and Heifetz.

The general level of performance, in the past, must

have been far below what we now take for granted. Thirteen or fourteen years ago I heard a performance of Bach's B minor Mass in Carnegie Hall, by the Schola Cantorum, numbering about two hundred and fifty voices, with an orchestra of nearly one hundred musicians. The soloists were, of course, skilled and highly paid artists—many members of the chorus, as a matter of fact, ranked as professionals. And I couldn't help comparing that performance with an account I once read of the *first* performance of the B minor Mass, in St. Thomas' Church at Leipzig. I may not be strictly accurate as to details, as I haven't the description handy; but in general, it related how no pains had been spared to make the performance a brilliant and sumptuous one. The orchestra had been augmented to more than thirty players, the chorus numbered nearly forty, and two of the soloists were professionals. I'm pretty sure that what Bach had heard was not as good as what I heard.

There were other factors about those early performances that must have been disturbing. Apparently the public of those days was satisfied more or less by the sheer *sound* of the music. Expressiveness doesn't seem to have counted for much, and such a thing as "interpretation," as we understand the term, must hardly have existed. Notice the simple, but rather significant fact, that music, from Purcell to Bach, was printed, as a rule, without any marks of expression whatsoever, beyond a simple indication of the speed at which it was to be played—and not always that. The *fortes* and *pianos* and *crescendos* and *rallentandos* that we expect to find in a modern piece of printed music were simply not there. Of course, that lack has been a golden harvest for the editors of the classic masterworks; but it also makes one wonder what the average performance of a Bach suite must have sounded like in those days.

Nor would the conductor, in a case like that, be much help. Strictly speaking, there were no conductors in those days, as we understand the word conductor. Mendelssohn was about the first musician really to conduct an orchestra, to play upon it as one plays on an instrument. The conductor was a time-beater, sometimes using a violin bow as a baton, or a roll of paper, or leading the orchestra from his place at the harpsichord. Sometimes, when merely waving something wasn't enough to keep the orchestra together, the leader would pound on the floor with a cane. The great French operatic master, Lully, used to conduct performances of his operas in this manner; and at one performance pounded his foot by mistake. The foot developed gangrene, and he died of it.

You remember the passage in Thayer's biography of Beethoven that describes the first performance of his Ninth Symphony? The orchestra numbered about seventy-five players, and Beethoven himself conducted. That is, he stood in the orchestra pit, turned the leaves of his score, and beat time. But since Beethoven was by that time stone-deaf, the official leader of the orchestra, Umlauf, instructed the orchestra to pay no attention to Beethoven, but watch *him.* At the end of his scherzo, the audience burst into thunders of applause, but Beethoven, whose back was to the house, stood, still turning the pages of his score, until his friend, Fraülein Unger, plucked him by the sleeve and turned him around, to bow.

That is a pathetic, a tragic incident. But part of the tragedy is what the performance must have been like, despite the applause of the audience. To grasp the musical standards of Beethoven's time, try to imagine a first performance, in Carnegie Hall, of a new symphony by a great modern composer, at which a deaf man is placed on the conductor's stand, with the orchestra under orders to take its *cues* (no time for shading or details, of course) from the concertmaster.

I think there is no doubt that the average concert played today, by a first-rate symphony orchestra under a first-rate conductor, offers a performance that, in technical smoothness, beauty of tone, and variety of light and shade, is something of which an eighteenth-century listener could have had no possible conception; that the great masters of the past, whatever they may have heard in imagination, as they wrote their scores, never in real life heard the perfect performances of their works that we now take so for granted.

PART TWO

Today

I

The End of a Chapter

THIS may not, in the long run, turn out to have been a very productive period, musically speaking, but it is an interesting one, none the less. For we are living through a period that occurs only about once in a century; the period when one "school" of music gives way to another—in other words, when composers, obeying some obscure and uncodified psychic law, stop writing one kind of music and begin writing some other kind. That is what is happening just now. We have about come to the end of one epoch and are entering another.

The one out of which we are passing is what we might call the Jazz Epoch, using "jazz" in the broadest sense of the word. It began during the war, and very abruptly. Jazz is amusing and exciting. It stimulates the nervous system and the motor centres. At the same time, most jazz is fundamentally regular and unvarying in rhythm, so that its montonous, reiterated underlying beat has a curiously hypnotic, anaesthetizing effect. But jazz, as a class of music, is not moving. In the rare moments when it does attempt to stir the emotions it usually becomes merely sentimental and hollow. At its best and worthiest, it is bright, vigorous, and hard as nails.

That, of course, was just what we wanted—"we" meaning most of the so-called civilized world—during the years of the war, and just after it. We were not, generally speaking, cold and hungry. There was money to spend, and things to buy with it. We ate, drank, and slept in comfort. Some were away, fighting or getting ready to fight; but music did not figure much in their lives, one way or the other. When they came back on leave, here and abroad, they did as we did. It was not our bodies that were particularly uncomfortable. Two things troubled us, haunted us night and day: fear and grief. The fear of death, if we were soldiers; if we were not, the fear of death for those that we might lose, or grief over those we had lost. Even in Germany, which was starving, it was not hunger that was hardest to bear. What haunted her were the same twin spectres that haunted the rest of us.

Naturally, what we needed most was to get away from our emotions. We wanted—exactly—to forget; and jazz helped us to do just that. "Don't think," it said. "Don't feel. Listen to me. I will stir your feet, and keep you in a world where you won't have to think about anything. Above all, I promise never to make you feel, or remind you of what you would rather not hear mentioned." For more than a decade after the war we were in much the same state. Many of us who had stayed at home had cause—all too real cause—for grief. Those who came back had had all they wanted of violent emotions. All of us were disappointed and disillusioned. We had put our faith and our ideals into a war that had turned out to be, not a crusade, but just another war. We were going to make a new, and a better world; and aside from the blood and the mess, it was just the same world. So, the hell with it. We were through with feelings.

So jazz was still what we wanted. When the serious composers got to work again, the spiritual equivalent of jazz was what they turned out. Stravinsky wrote an *Octuor* that was, he said, "to be listened to as one looks at a piece of sculpture," whatever that meant. Any emotional element in music was sentimentalism, to be avoided like the black plague. We were handed intellectual concepts set to music, arrangements of notes which, their composers assured us, were to be played without expression, and heard as studies in abstract form, and listened to as studies in sonority, and appreciated as arrangements of sound-planes—as anything, in short, that could be described without employing the words "beauty" or "emotion."

Well, the war is over—spiritually, at least. The old griefs have stopped aching, the old fears and memories are not so sharp, even the old disillusionment is less keen. We are still troubled, but our trouble is almost exactly the opposite of the old one. Where it was death and separation that tormented us before, it is hunger and cold and discomfort that worry us now. The world is paying for the war, and the bill is a large one. The times are uncertain; jobs are uncertain. Taxes are heavy. Even so, things are not as bad as they were. The fear of unemployment and want is a very real one, but it is something that gnaws the mind rather than a torment to the soul. Our souls, as a matter of fact, are not involved. We are worried; but worry at its worst is mental.

We are beginning to look, not for something to keep us from feeling, but something to keep us from thinking; something, in fact, that will reassure us, remind us that the material world, which is so precarious just now, is not the only one, or even the most important one; something, in short, that the hard-boiled music of the last decade cannot do for us.

It seems to be a law of art that when men are troubled in their souls they turn to such aesthetic diversions as will allow them to forget everything but their bodies. When their troubles are material and physical, they search for an art that will help them to escape from the body. We have passed through the first sort of trouble, and are into the second, which means that the days of Weber and Schumann and Wagner are about to dawn again. Another romantic age of music is not far off.

2

On Kicking up a Row

IT SEEMS incredible, now, that music such as the prelude to *Lohengrin* should ever have seemed strange, discordant, and revolutionary. Yet we have the record of history that, to certain people at least, it did. For that matter, even so harmless a work as the Beethoven violin concerto drew a considerable amount of critical disapproval after its first performance. They thought it was pretty radical and eccentric, and one critic even said that if Beethoven kept on in this way, he and the public were going to have a very bad time together.

Of course, ever since Wagner's overwhelming refutation of his critics, people have stopped condemning new music as much as they used to do. There never was a composer so abused as Wagner was, and never in the lifetime of any composer did so many critics live to eat their words. I sometimes wish his victory had been a little less complete; for since his day there has been a most unfortunate decline in intolerance in musical circles. I think a few sturdy, bitter, whole-hearted haters of his work are a good thing for any artist, particularly a composer. It's very hard for a man's champions to answer dispassionate criticism or courteous disapproval; but let a composer's audience tear up a few benches, and his critics call him a few wholly unwarranted names—then his friends get mad, and go to work for him in earnest.

Stravinsky's *Le Sacre du Printemps* is one of the few modern works to draw a really riotous audience at its *première;* and the riot was the making of it. Everybody, naturally, wanted to hear the music that could drive its hearers to such a frenzy of disapproval.

Of course, the trouble is that we're all so frightened to death of being wrong about some genius that we thought was a fool, of being laughed at as one of those who were too dull-witted to recognize a masterpiece when we heard it, that we tend to cultivate a great pose of tolerance. We hear a new piece of music. We don't like it. Then some enthusiast rushes up and says, "How did you like it? Wasn't it wonderful?" And instead of being honest, and saying, "I'm not sure, but I *think* it was terrible," we scowl judicially and finally say, "Well, of course, it's an idiom that's rather new to me, and I wouldn't want to give a snap verdict. But even on a first hearing I can see that it has some very interesting things in it."

Now part of that attitude is sheer social cowardice. And the rest is, I suppose, a dread of being less than fair. But a love of art has nothing to do with justice. Being tolerant of a work of art that you dislike is like inviting a man to dinner because you think that he can't be as unpleasant as you think he is. Critical disapproval never killed a genuine work of art of any kind. It has killed the artist, on occasion, but it never shortened the life of his work. Any masterpiece outlives its audience and its critics. If a piece of music can't survive your dislike, or mine, it hasn't got the breath of life in it.

In my lifetime, in New York, I remember only one

really good, exciting musical row. And that was the rumpus that attended the first production here of Strauss's *Salome.* Oscar Hammerstein, having built the Manhattan Opera House on West Thirty-fourth Street, had installed a company there, in 1907, with the avowed intention of rendering the Metropolitan Opera Company obsolete. He didn't quite do that, but he did introduce a number of operatic works, including *Louise* and *Pelléas et Mélisande,* that we had never heard before, and a roster of singers that included Maurice Renaud, Mario Sammarco, and, above all, Mary Garden—and bluffed the Metropolitan into giving him a million dollars to get out of New York, in 1909, just as he was about to go bankrupt.

Among the forthcoming productions that he announced was *Salome,* with Mary Garden in the title role. Whereupon the Metropolitan announced *its* production of *Salome,* with Olive Fremstad as the prophet-sharing princess. It lasted one performance. On that occasion the critics went up into the attic and dusted off adjectives that hadn't been in use since Ibsen was first produced in London. I remember that "bestial," "fetid," "slimy," and "nauseous" were among the more complimentary terms that they applied to the score. Furthermore, one of the feminine members of the Metropolitan's board of directors took one look at Madame Fremstad's version of the Dance of the Seven Veils, called a hasty meeting of the board, and announced that curfew would not ring that night—or, more accurately, that *Salome* would not again be performed at the Metropolitan. And it was not. (For a long time, that is. Years later, when

Salome was revived at the Metropolitan, the critics found fault with Maria Jeritza's performance of the title role on the score that it was too schoolgirlish!)

But even the *Salome* episode was a matter of critical malediction and private censorship, rather than of audience misbehavior. As a matter of fact, I've never seen a really first-class musical riot in New York. American audiences are, of course, notoriously indulgent toward those who appear before them. They order things differently in many part of Europe, where listeners shout, hiss, whistle, and even resort to physical violence when they hear a performance of which they happen to disapprove. The American, however, seldom gives vent to any audible manifestations of annoyance; he will even applaud, politely, what he actively dislikes. I have heard hissing in Carnegie Hall, upon occasion; but it was not very earnest hissing, and seemed to be emitted more to annoy those who were applauding than to rebuke the entertainment.

This excess of exuberance is supposed to show that the European takes his music much more seriously, and feels it much more profoundly, and resents bad work much more bitterly, than the American, who does not know good work from bad and would not care if he did know. That, I submit, is a theory invented and supported largely by Europeans. Why on earth should a public display of bad manners be a sign of superior culture? If you go to a party, and meet a man who insults all the other guests and breaks the furniture, you do not instantly assume that he is the most cultured person present. You do not even think of culture in connection with him.

They say we are timid and uncertain in our judgements, and that the European auditor has the courage of his convictions. Bosh! It is simply that we have other ways. We're a more polite audience. We don't whistle and stamp and boo when we don't like something. On the contrary, whistling, with us, is often a sign of supreme approval. When Ernestine Schumann-Heink made her debut at the Metropolitan Opera House, she went off the stage heartbroken, because the gallery began to whistle when she left. She thought they hated her, when they were really trying to induce her to give an encore.

But if our means of showing our dislikes are less obstreperous than those in vogue in Europe, they are none the less effectual, and, I'm inclined to think, sometimes a little more cruel. I've never heard a New York audience hiss new music with any particular energy, but I have seen a concert of modern music open to a full house and resume, after the intermission, to seventy-five people. I have seen a New York audience applaud one ultra-modern piece so thunderously and insistently that it had to be played over again three times, to the joy of the deluded composer, who failed to notice that his hearers were howling with laughter as they applauded and stamped. And I once heard George Antheil's *Ballet Méchanique* produced in Carnegie Hall. I forget the entire instrumentation of this work, but I do recall that the score, among other things, called for ten grand pianos, one player-piano, six xylophones, four bass drums, a couple of automobile klaxons, a fire-alarm siren, and an airplane propeller—from which you can form a rough idea of how it sounded. The piece began before a silent and attentive audience. After five minutes of it, a few began to fidget; after six minutes a few more began to cough; after seven, a few more began to giggle. At the eighth minute precisely, a man in the third row raised his cane, to which he had tied his handkerchief. And at the sight of that white flag the entire house, simultaneously, gave up trying not to laugh. I don't know how the *Ballet Méchanique* ends. I am not even prepared to discuss its possible musical value: but I do know that as a comedy hit it was one of the biggest successes that ever played Carnegie Hall.

3

The Scorned Ingredient

NOT long ago the Moscow Art Theatre and a Soviet newspaper offered a series of prizes for an opera and a ballet to celebrate some anniversary of the Bolshevist revolution in Russia. According to the terms of the contest, the music "must develop new forms which will not only synthesize the musical culture of the past, but also be a monumental expression of humanity transformed by the proletarian socialist regime." Among the themes suggested for development by the composers and their librettists or scenarists were: socialist industrialization; socialist reconstruction of agriculture; the class war in the villages; the technical revolution; the Union of Socialist Soviet Republics; and the cultural improvements and the question of nationalities along the lines laid down by Lenin. There were others, but these are enough to give you a general idea of the fare upon which the Russian muse was expected to subsist.

I am ashamed to say that I lost interest in the contest and never knew who won the prizes and with what. I mention it only because Russia is not the only place that has produced extraordinary conceptions of the nature and function and limitations of music. Only the other day I read an eminent American critic's review of some new music. In the course of his discussion he remarked: "Like all other modernist music, naturally, this work is not to be approached from the old angles."

Why not? Music—or any other art, for that matter—has always been approached, up to now, from angles that are as old as art itself. Why this sudden demand of the right, not only to change the forms and substances of an art, but to invent a brand-new set of standards by which to judge it? Naturally, I am not arguing that music should never progress, that we should expect it to have an unalterable set of harmonies and melodic progressions, and an unchangeable set of forms and rhythms. But I must say I don't see why we should be asked to judge a contemporary radical composer by standards other than those to which we hold every other composer from Bach to Stravinsky.

I have found it a good plan, whenever I am in doubt concerning some question about music, to translate the discussion into terms of cookery. It is astonishing how much alike food and music are. They are so, of course, because music is decidedly a variety of food. So is all art. We feel the pangs of bodily hunger, and put things into our mouths in order to stay them. Similarly, we feel certain emotional or spiritual cravings that can be satisfied only by religion or art—frequently both. We ask two simple questions regarding any food: Does it taste good? Does it nourish me? Now many modernist composers and their advocates remind me of a cook who should suddenly tire of doing things with the same old flour and salt and pepper and beans and lamb chops, and should forthwith proceed to invent dishes composed of benzine, shavings, quinine, oystershells, and crank-case lubricant.

The cook would have a perfect right to do this, of course. But it would hardly prove him to be a good cook, if when you exclaimed, "This is nasty, and I don't think it agrees with me," he were to reply, simply: "But, you fool, it's supposed to be nasty! The old flavors are outmoded. The old conceptions of sweet and sour and bitter must give way before a newer, freer handling of flavor, more closely akin to the pulsating, unsentimental, clean-cut life of the machine age. As for its not agreeing with you, that is no concern of mine. Food must be purified, purged of its nineteenth-century burden of bourgeois nutritive values."

This is nonsense, of course, coming from a cook. Coming from a musician, it gets a serious hearing from a surprisingly large number of intelligent people. I hear a new piece of music which seems to me to be deficient in most of the qualities that have made music good in the past. I find its essential musical ideas poverty-stricken, and either developed by the simple process of reiteration, or else stated and immediately abandoned in favor of others equally barren. I find its harmony so completely stripped of any vestige of assonance that its monotonous series of dissonances sound merely dull. I find its structure vague and apparently planless, and its emotional content simply zero.

Whereupon the composer announces that I am not approaching it from the right angle. I must expect none of the abstract qualities that I look for in other music, ancient and modern. Just what I am to look for he does not always say, but he is always emphatic about one thing: emotional content is old stuff. It simply is not being done. I am not supposed to be moved by his music, as I am moved by Corelli, or Händel, or Wagner, or Brahms, or Debussy. I must not, in short, look for beauty. No matter how willing I may be to stretch my conception of what beauty might be, I must not call it that.

Which is where the modern misunderstood artist, be he painter, poet, or composer, differs from his forebears. In the days when they were being misunderstood by people who said, "I don't call that beautiful," they replied: "Just the same it is beautiful; and some day you will find it out."

Frequently, after an interval, we did. But we need not expect to do so any longer. Say to a modern artist, "I find your work neither beautiful nor expressive," and he does not mind. He merely remarks, "It isn't supposed to be." It is not a bad idea. At least it wins arguments. The tailors in Hans Christian Andersen's tale of "The Emperor's New Clothes" were unfortunate. They were ahead of their time. Were they alive today, and the little girl should say, "But the emperor has no clothes on!" they would need only to say, triumphantly, "Who said he had?" Whereupon the little girl would have been properly spanked and sent to bed supperless.

4

Sound—and a Little Fury

STRAVINSKY'S *Symphonies d'instruments à vent* is a perfect example of the sort of thing I have just been discussing—the contemporary composer's practice of asking his audience to make over all their previous conceptions of the nature of music before listening to his work. When he wrote *Le Sacre du Printemps* the gifted Russian demanded that we listen to it as absolute music, even though it had been written as a ballet-pantomime. We did our dutiful best, and so far succeeded that *Le Sacre* is now fairly well established in the repertoire of symphonic music. The *Symphonies* is the work of a Stravinsky who is seven years older than the composer of *Le Sacre,* and seven years further advanced in his journey across the no-man's land of aesthetic experimentation. In presenting the score to the public he accompanied it with a set of fairly specific directions for listening to it, which, simple as they may appear, ask of the hearer a frame of mind rarefied beyond anything that has been hitherto demanded of a concert-goer.

Stravinsky presents the *Symphonies* as a study in sound, a purely abstract "arrangement," as a modernist painter would call it, of contrasted, juxtaposed tone-sensations. He looks upon this music as something analogous to a piece of sculpture, and insists that "the tonal masses are to be regarded objectively by the ear." Now these are hard words, and I am not at all sure that I know precisely what they mean. On the surface they sound as if Stravinsky were again asking that his work be regarded as absolute music; but if that were all, he would not have to go to such elaborate pains to elucidate his request. He must want something more, and that something more is, I believe, that the listener approach the *Symphonies* with complete detachment, with purely intellectual curiosity, deriving satisfaction, not from the emotional effect of the music (he is specifically enjoined from looking for any such thing) but from the pleasure he takes in observing the clash and concord of rhythms and sounds. In other words, the hearer is requested to appreciate, rather than feel.

Leaving aside for a moment the actual effect of this music in performance, what about the theory upon which it is based? It seems to me to have two defects: first, the difficulty of putting it into effect, and second, its dubious value if it could be realized. Stravinsky speaks of his music as being "sculptured in marble." Now music is a great many things, but it is not sculpture or painting or architecture (though it is closer to architecture than the first two). It bears a relation to time that sculpture and painting do not recognize. It is quite possible to look at a painting or a statue dispassionately, admiring certain qualities that distinguish it as a whole, to get away from it, so to speak, observing it merely as an arrangement of colors or masses. There is no time limit upon such scrutiny. You may glance at *The Winged Victory* for three seconds, or you may gaze at her for a full hour. If your grasp of design is immediate, a minute's time may suffice for you to absorb the essentials of a Rembrandt; or, if your apprehensive power works more slowly, you may spend a morning upon it. You may consider details in any order you wish, spending as much or as little time upon any one of them as you please. You can walk around the statue, studying it from any angle or elevation, and you can scrutinize the painting from left to right, or from top to bottom, even turning it upside down if you like. In brief, the method or the amount of time you employ in studying a work of plastic or graphic art is determined wholly by yourself.

Time enters into the reading of a book or the hearing of a play, but only insofar as it determines the order in which you receive your first impressions. You can turn back the pages of the book in order better to assimilate a passage that has eluded you, or you can buy a copy of the play and read the scenes in any order whatsoever. You can, in fact, even read the play without seeing it at all.

None of these things is completely possible with music. For the moment a single note of musical composition has been heard it has begun to die: another note succeeds it, and it has vanished utterly. The order of these successions is vitally important, for the effect of music is almost entirely contextual; the major seventh chord that opens the second act of *Tristan* never sounds quite the same again, when it recurs between other chords. Nor can you stop the music, or turn it back, the better to grasp it; for not only the order but the speed of the sound successions is one of its essential elements. The moment you hasten or retard this speed, the music becomes different music. The effect of music, in other words, is not immediate, as in the case of painting or sculpture, but cumulative. People speak of "reading" printed music as if the process were analogous to that of reading printed words. Words, either spoken or written, are a medium, a medium for ideas and images. A printed word does double duty. It is, first of all, a set of directions to the reader, directing him to utter certain sounds. If he obeys these directions he utters words, which in turn convey ideas to himself and others. But printed words are also the direct symbols of ideas. You may read a play without ever once imagining the sound of its speeches. You may have a perfect reading knowledge of the French language without being able to pronounce one word of it. You may be born stone-deaf and still learn to write and read words without associating them with any aural concept whatsoever.

That is not true of printed music. It is a set of directions pure and simple, ordering the violinist to draw the bow across a certain string, or the trumpeter to press certain valves and blow into a metal tube, or the singer to produce certain sounds with his vocal cords. If you derive any satisfaction from reading a printed score it is only because you have acquired the ability to imagine the sounds resulting from these actions. What you receive is a series of mental images, so to speak, of the sounds. But they are not the sounds themselves, or any complete equivalent of them, any more than a photograph of Stravinsky is actually the composer. You form some idea of what the music is going to sound like, just as you gain some idea of a projected building from looking at the architect's blueprints. The musical symbols mean nothing in themselves, in the sense that printed words do. I know of nothing in music that really and completely corresponds with an abstract idea. What you get from music is what you get, not through your mind, primarily, but through your emotions. You may thrill at a printed page of *Le Sacre du Printemps,* just as you may thrill at a set of plans of Notre Dame de Paris; but it is your own imagination, in both cases, that thrills you, not the music or the cathedral.

And so how can "the tonal masses" be "regarded objectively by the ear," as Mr. Stravinsky insists that they must? How can you use your mind to receive an art that, of all others, enters the consciousness not through the mind at all—an art that can move an idiot to tears, that can put a two-weeks-old child to sleep, that can arouse to frenzy a savage whose vocabulary contains only forty words and to whom a painting is nothing but a flat mass of paint? How can you intellectualize about the one purely emotional art?

In actual performance, Stravinsky's *Symphonies* does little to prove his case. To begin with, after writing this—to his view—purely abstract arrangement of tonal masses, he subtitles it "In Memory of Claude Debussy" —and if those words do not convey an emotional connotation, what do they convey? Parts of the music are very beautiful; in other words—which Mr. Stravinsky will not like—they arouse emotion in the listener. Other parts are decidedly uninteresting. Still others do, perhaps, carry out their composer's program: one admires their workmanship, without experiencing any emotion at all. A few passages arouse a definite feeling of repulsion. Here are four kinds of music; and the second and third kinds evoke not the slightest desire ever to hear them again. The interesting part of the *Symphonies* is the emotional part, in short. As a whole, the work sounds curiously frustrated and invertebrate, as if the composer, in his anxiety to avoid emotional effects, had tried to impose his will upon, not the form but the substance of his work, suppressing where, normally, he would have been moved to create—fashioning robot-music that, having no feeling, would do his bidding even at the cost of destroying itself.

The *Symphonies* is, I think, reactionary music—in the literal sense of the word. Mr. Stravinsky, being a genius, is alert, impatient, and sensitive. He has a far keener mind than most geniuses, and is something of a scientist at heart, as well as an artist. He has seen program music carried to the lengths of Strauss's *Don Quixote* (which requires five pages of program notes); he has seen the emotional power of music degraded to sentimentality at the hands of little men. Having mastered the art of complex orchestration as nearly completely as any man ever has in all probability, he is now experimenting with simplification. He is revolted by over-literalness, and angered by sentimentality. He lives on a continent that is busy destroying itself through using its emotions as a substitute for thought. And so he is sick of imaginings, sick of dreams, sick of feelings. He would purify his art, and the only way he sees to do so is by leading it out of the realm of emotion entirely, into the domain of pure reason. I think he is wrong. Bad art may be beneath thought, but great art is beyond it; and an art that asks men only to think is doing badly what science does supremely well.

5

Playing with Paint

A FEW seasons' exposure to ultra-modern music leads one to the conclusion that, regardless of their tenets and theoretical pronunciamentos, the majority of present-day composers have one preoccupation in common. Almost without exception their work can be classified as a series of experiments in dissonant harmony. Atonality, polytonality, liberated counterpoint, and all the other ities and isms are, when you boil them down, efforts to arrange combinations of tones such as have never been heard before. The polytonal experts hold that you can listen to music in two or three simultaneous keys without discomfort; the atonalists want you to listen to notes combined into chords that have no relation to any key whatsoever.

Where Richter would tolerate a chord of the ninth only through the rather sneaking subterfuge of calling it a suspension to a seventh, the modern harmonist faces chords of the thirteenth-and-a-half without a quiver, tosses minor ninths over his shoulder with the greatest ease, and toys carelessly with anomalous horrors the mere thought of which would have sent Richter to a sanitarium.

It is not always safe to pursue analogies between the arts too closely, but one is, I think, fairly safe in assuming that harmony in music corresponds with color in painting, in that the kinds of emotional response they arouse are approximately the same. We shrink from an unexpected combination of notes very much as we shrink from an unexpected combination of colors.

In other words, then, the modern composer is under the spell of what, in a young painter, would be an intense preoccupation with color. But if the history of painting teaches anything it surely teaches that no painter achieves immortality through his actual colors. There have been, and are, great colorists, but their fame rests not on the fact that they evolved new and unheard-of pigments but that they managed to combine their new pigments—or even the old ones—in an individual way. No single color remains interesting very long; it is the relation between colors, their balance and contrast, that counts in the end.

It is not even necessary to use different pigments to obtain color effects. We speak of an etching by Pennell or Whistler or Rembrandt as being "full of color." Why? Because these men can so manipulate various shades of one color—brown—as to produce a brilliance and vibrancy that a less skilled craftsman could not produce with the whole spectrum. If the color effect is in the picture, it is there almost regardless of the pigments. A half-tone reproduction of a great painting will probably render its essential values as well as the original. But if it happens to be a poor half-tone of a different subject, and so loses the values, you may print it in crimson or purple or emerald green, if you like, without restoring those values one particle or altering its essentially monochromatic nature.

It is in this matter of values that so many modern

composers seem entirely astray. They devise a startling chord and think it means something by itself, or they arrange sixteen bars of extreme dissonances in a certain order without leaving any convincing impression that they could not have been arranged in some other order just as well. I don't mind the so-called discords in their music; one gets used to anything. But I do mind the absence of any discernible inevitability of relationship between those discords.

Besides, the more familiar I become with much of it, the less its dissonances come as a shock to the ear, the less impressive it becomes. The polytonal and atonal excursions of a good many contemporary composers, once they cease to frighten me, seem monotonous and lacking in—shall we say eloquence? The colors are loud enough, heaven knows, but their final effect is monochromatic. There is a string quartet by Mozart—the sixth, in C major—with an adagio opening whose first sixteen bars are as startling and impressive an example of exotic harmony as I know. There is not a chord in them that Mendelssohn would have shuddered at; but the cunning with which they are juxtaposed, the fundamental rightness of their values is such that they are unforgettable.

So many of the moderns seem to forget that a new chord, or a combination of them, is valuable for its shock effect only so long as it is new. It is easy enough to jolt an audience into paying attention to you. One could doubtless attract the attention of a roomful of the most sophisticated people in the world by flinging open the door and shouting, "Boo!" But, their attention duly attracted, what then?

6

The Tolerant Ear—I

IF RALPH WALDO EMERSON is not the patron saint of all those who write on controversial subjects, including music, he ought to be. For it was Emerson who invented that God-given line about consistency being "the hobgoblin of little minds." My other favorite author is Walt Whitman, with his "I contradict myself? Very well, I contradict myself"—or words to that effect. All of which is a more—or less—graceful way of leading up to the fact that, having just pleaded for a revival of intolerance in listening to new music, I am about to plead, with equal eloquence, on the other side. In short, while I do feel that a good many of us could afford to be a bit more honest in expressing our musical dislikes, we might, on the other hand, be a little slower in forming them; we ought to be quite sure that we know what it is that we do not like about music that repels us.

Let me get to my text. It is a letter from a radio listener to the Philharmonic-Symphony concerts, and reads, in part, as follows:

"I have been listening for many years to the works of the great masters as rendered by the best orchestras on two continents, and think I know a little about good music. But I am unable to appreciate the modern composers. Such music seems to me to be without melody, harmony, or form, and literally gives me a pain. And yet there must be something in it, or the great orchestras would not play this kind of music. What must I listen for? How should I listen? There must be something I have missed, and I am sincere in my desire to know what it is. I am sure there are thousands like myself, asking the same questions. Could you say a few words on this subject some time? I feel that many of your listeners would be grateful for some advice on this point."

Naturally, I cannot undertake to write an exhaustive and authoritative treatise on How to Listen to Modern Music, for the three excellent reasons that I haven't space enough, you haven't patience enough, and I don't know enough. But I might be able to make a few suggestions that would possibly be useful to anyone hearing ultra-modern music for the first time.

First and foremost, when you sit down to a piece of ultra-modern music, try to rid yourself of . . . fear. I make that suggestion in all seriousness. Don't be afraid. It may seem silly to imply that people are frightened by modern music. Just the same, I think they are. A good deal of the fury with which people denounce the new and unfamiliar in art is the result of a very real terror. Let me illustrate.

When I was a good deal younger than I am now—in fact, when I was four years old—my most precious possession was an iron fire engine drawn by two galloping iron horses. That engine and its horses never left me. It stayed with me through the day and went to bed with me at night. One day, when I was supposedly playing with it, contentedly, my mother came into the room and found me dissolved in tears. After a good deal of questioning she found out what the trouble was. I forget how I worded my explanation, but the gist of it was that I had just realized that when I grew up I wouldn't be able to play with my fire engine any more. She tried to comfort me by assuring me that I could have my engine as long as I liked; that I could play with it even when I was grown up. "But," I said, miserably, "I'm afraid I won't *want* to."

I think that particular fear lies at the root of a great deal of people's unwillingness to give even a first hearing to modern music. It's a sort of "I'm-glad-I-don't-like-lemonade-because-if-I-did-I'd-drink-it-and-I-hate-it" attitude. How many times I've heard people say, "Well, if *this* is music, what's going to become of Bach and Beethoven and Mozart and Wagner?" We're really afraid of getting to like this new stuff, for fear that it might destroy our taste for the older music that we've known and loved all our lives.

Or, if our reactions are a little less naïve, we have a subconscious—or perhaps conscious—fear that if too many people grow to like this new music the old will lose its popularity, orchestras will stop playing it, singers and instrumentalists will stop putting it on their programs, and we shan't be able to hear the classics any more.

Now granted that you may be haunted by that fear, look about you—or rather, use your ears. Is Bach extinct because Strauss wrote *Ein Heldenleben?* Is Beethoven on the ash-heap because Stravinsky wrote *The Rites of Spring?* Is Wagner no longer heard because Debussy wrote *Pelléas et Mélisande?* Has Brahms been scrapped to make room for Shostakóvich? If the history of the race tells us anything, it tells us that art is not a branch of the automobile industry or the millinery trade. This year's model does not render last year's model obsolete. The music you have always liked will continue to be played. There is no limit to the library of the world's music. There's plenty of room on its shelves for new scores, without throwing out any old ones.

Another thing of which not to be frightened. Don't be too much impressed by what people have to say about how this ultra-modern music marks a complete smashup of all our previous conceptions of what music ought to be, the destruction of all pre-existing laws of melody, harmony, and whatnot. Some of the most repellent characteristics of much modern music have been in existence for centuries. In the Confucian temples of China, for instance, the priests sing certain prescribed hymns in unison; but every priest is at liberty to choose whatever key is best suited to his voice. That's polytonality. The so-called harmony of the Middle Ages would sound unbearably awkward and ugly to us. There is much talk of twelve-note scales and quarter-tones today. In Hindu music today, as there always has been, there are sixty-three well-defined different scales. So don't get to thinking of this break-up of existing musical theories in terms of the fall of the Roman Empire or the destruction of civilization. It's only the breakup of a lot of rules made up by people who weren't composers. The so-called laws of musical theory are rules of procedure, codified from what composers of the past did more or less instinctively, in order to allow composers of the present to write music that will at least be inoffensive.

Great music can be written that conforms to the strictest rules ever laid down. But the fact that music conforms to the rules is no guarantee that it will be great. Bach and Mozart and Beethoven broke as many rules in their day as Schönberg is breaking in his. Most great composers are aesthetic anarchists; so don't let people scare you by tales of the Red menace. Particularly, don't let us critics frighten you. The people who stand most stubbornly in the way of progress in any art are generally the very people who know most about it. They *know* what rules are being broken, and are correspondingly horrified. The general public likes the new work or doesn't like it, and so keeps it alive or kills it.

Furthermore, if you honestly want to understand this new music, don't pay much attention to what its composers have to say about it. Every artist desires ardently to be understood, and his natural impulse is to burst into words in order to help you see what he is driving at. But music happens to be a language—a very definite language—for the expression of just those ideas and moods and emotions that cannot be expressed in words. So don't trust words. If a piece of music can be completely expressed in words, and the intellectual ideas of which words are the supreme medium, there never was any need to compose it.

And don't wonder what Beethoven or Wagner would have said of it. If what their fellow composers had to say of their music is any criterion, Beethoven and Wagner would loathe it. Don't take the word of the past, no matter how great a past. Ancestor worship does not make for a healthy nation or a healthy art. God help us if the younger generation ever stops being the despair of its grandparents, or turns out no music of which its spiritual ancestors would have thoroughly approved.

Another thing. If music means anything to you, if it is a source of pleasure, inspiration, or spiritual nourishment to you, you owe something to music. It is your duty to help to keep it a living, growing art. You must not be selfishly content merely to sit in the shade of the tree. Water it occasionally. The least you can do, as a lover of music, is to be willing to listen to what a new composer has to say, whether you like it or not. People write me despairing letters, pointing out our dearth of great composers, our lack of a Beethoven, a Wagner, or a Brahms. I don't say that that is true or not true. I don't know. But if it is true, at least let us make it possible for the great man to get a hearing when he does arrive. And make no mistake. When he does arrive, many of you will not like him. To some of us at least, Debussy's *Afternoon of a Faun* is one of the loveliest pieces of music ever written. Even those who may not care for it hardly find it ugly or incoherent. Yet at the first performance of the *Faun* there was a riot in the hall. The audience laughed and yelled and hissed and whistled so loudly that the piece went virtually unheard. That was in 1894, less than half a century ago. The human ear is a very adaptable instrument.

"All right," you say, "I'll listen. Now what do I listen for?" That question is not so easy to answer. Or perhaps it is. I think I would say, listen for the same things that you expect to find in any piece of music; but don't make your definitions too rigid. There are four elements that are present in any piece of good music: melody, which is design; harmony, which is color;

rhythm, which is proportion; and form, which is the ground plan. Listen for them. Ask yourself, does this music contain themes that possess a definite contour and outline, regardless of whether they happen to please me or not? Do they exist? Granted that its harmonies may offend my ear, is there any element of contrast among them? Is there any discernible difference between one ugly chord and another, or is the general impression of all this cacophony one of monotony? Does the music possess some underlying rhythmic pattern that keeps it going, or does it give the effect of moving in a circle? Does it possess any plan that I can discern, no matter how unfamiliar or unlike the traditional forms? Does it seem to possess a beginning, and middle, and an end, or does it just start and stop?

Now a word of warning about the harmony. Bear in mind that in recent years composers have taken to using strongly dissonant chords very often not as harmony is conventionally used, but to give an effect of color. It is a device that is hard to explain in words. One simple example is the silver-rose theme in Strauss's *Der Rosenkavalier*, where the celeste plays a series of chords that has nothing in common with the harmony of the strings that underlie it. If you're familiar with that theme, you can't deny that the dissonant harmonies give it a silvery, metallic quality that has nothing to do with the tone quality of the instruments that are playing it. Look for a similar intention in a piece of new music before you decide that the composer was just trying to annoy you with a series of discords.

One thing about form. Music has always been inspired by the mediums through which it is transmitted—in other words, has always been written for whichever medium would give it the most performances. If Haydn and Mozart and Beethoven wrote a great many symphonies and string quartets, one reason is that almost every wealthy man of their times maintained a private orchestra or a private quartet. He would order a new symphony or a new piece of chamber music much as you would order a new overcoat. Today there are no more private orchestras and very few patrons. But one medium that is becoming increasingly hospitable to composers is the theatre. Of fifteen works by modern composers played by the Philharmonic-Symphony Orchestra during the season of 1936–37, only two of them were absolute—that is, abstract—music. Five were program music—told a definite story—and eight had been written for the stage, and particularly for ballets and pantomimes.

Now stage music must base its form, not on a musical structure, but on a dramatic one, which is frequently quite foreign to musical logic. To develop a musical idea clearly and coherently takes a certain amount of time; but when music accompanies a dramatic story, or the gestures of a pantomimist, it must frequently turn in its own length, so to speak, long before it would naturally do so. The consequence is, that when such music is played on a concert stage, without the pantomime or the ballet as a clue to what it is trying to express, it is often likely to sound formless and incoherent. Parts of Stravinsky's *Petrushka* and *The Rites of Spring,* for instance, are almost meaningless without the accompanying stage action. This is no fault of the music; it is the fault of playing the music out of its proper place—exhibiting the costume, so to speak, without bothering to bring on the actor. Bear that handicap in mind when you listen to a new ballet or pantomime in concert form.

And now, having dutifully listened, suppose you still don't like this new music? Hear it again. Give it several hearings, if you possibly can, no matter how much they may hurt. And then, if you are absolutely sure that you really don't like it, or that you really do, don't be afraid to say so. Don't be afraid to be wrong. Don't pretend, either way, out of deference to your friends, or a fear of being thought old-fashioned. Furthermore, if you dislike one ultra-modern work, don't take it for granted that no ultra-modern music is for you. On the other hand, don't assume that every new piece, however outrageous, is the voice of the future. The proportion of rubbish to great music that is being written today is what it always has been: about ninety per cent.

When we hear two men speaking in a foreign language, if we don't happen to know that language, everything they say sounds like gibberish. Only after we have begun to grasp their language can we decide whether they are talking wisdom or nonsense. Composers today are experimenting with a new musical language. There is as yet no dictionary for it, and no way of studying it except to listen to it without panic and without mental reservations. And the more we listen, the better able shall we be to weigh and estimate the value of what present-day composers are saying. Some of them are just talking pig-Latin; but others may be saying something that we may all, some day, be grateful to hear.

7

The Tolerant Ear—II

PERHAPS it would be well, in pursuing this discussion further, not to use the term, "modern music." It is vague at best, and no two people necessarily agree as to what they mean by it. One man's conception of a modern composer is Shostakóvich, while another's may be Strauss or Debussy—or even Bach. It is safer and more precise, I think, to be simple; to group all unfamiliar works under the general head of "new" music.

It is important and only fair, as I said before, to give this new music a hearing. Let us assume that you have done so; and the next time we meet you say, "All right, I listened, as you suggested, and I still say it's nothing but ugliness and noise."

That is exactly why I suggested that you make it a point to hear a piece of new music at least twice before you make up your mind about it. Your first impression is only a reaction; and a reaction is not an opinion. While first impressions of *people* you meet may be the ones you come back to as you get to know them better, your first impression of *music* that you meet for the first time is not necessarily a safe guide. Theodore Thomas, when he was doing missionary work for Wagner's music in this country, placing Wagnerian excerpts on his programs over the protests of his subscribers, once said, "Popular music is familiar music." You know yourself that certain songs or dance tunes that you heard as a child have an emotional effect on you that may be all out of proportion to the actual merit of the music. You like that music because it's been with you a long time. Its tunes have worn little tracks in your brain, and once they start, they glide through your head easily, gently, without friction. Now along comes a new tune, by a new man, who has a new musical vocabulary. There's no mental track for it to run. It has to plow its own track. And that, almost literally, hurts your mind. You resent it, and you say, "I don't like that music. I don't want to hear it." And I ask you, "Why?" And you say, "It's ugly and noisy."

That sort of reaction means very little. The great handicap under which the new music and the new composers labor today is the lack of intelligent criticism. Opinion about it is roughly divided into two camps: the people who rave about it simply because it *is* new, and swallow anything, so long as it isn't like anything else ever written; and the people who simply refuse to have anything to do with it. Both groups are doing nothing for music. As I said before, I believe, of the music being written today, exactly as of the music that was being written a hundred years ago, that ten per cent is good, and ninety per cent is rubbish. But it's that ten per cent of good that it is important to unearth, if only to get rid of the rubbish.

The way to do that is to make some effort to understand what the composer is trying to say—if he is trying to say anything at all. In the previous chapter I compared hearing new music to overhearing a conversation between two men speaking in a foreign tongue. Let me carry that analogy a little further. We assume that they are speaking in Russian. You don't know a word of Russian, and the sound of it grates on your ears. You say, "That's a hideous language. Nothing anybody could say in a language like that could possibly be worth listening to." Then, suppose you take the trouble to learn a little Russian. As you study it, its sounds grate less and less on your ear. Finally you know enough Russian to understand the conversation of these two men, and you discover that one of them, as you suspected all along, is talking complete nonsense. The other man, however, is saying some tremendously important and interesting things; things that you might have missed; things that may mean a great deal to you.

And so I repeat: before you dismiss a piece of new music, be sure that you understand it. The mere fact that you like it or don't like it is of no importance to me or anybody else. But if you can tell me exactly *why* you do or don't like it, that is extremely important, not only to me, but to the composer and to music in general. Because the final verdict on every work of art is delivered, not by the critics, not by the experts, but by the public. If Beethoven has survived a hundred years it is because successive generations of ordinary listeners have heard something in his music that meant something to them.

Ah, but that was Beethoven! Nobody could fail to recognize *his* greatness, at once. Oh, yes, they could. The history of music is a chronicle of the human animal's incredible capacity for being wrong about it. That is why a criticism such as this one must not be taken too seriously:

"The old masters allowed themselves a certain license, to be sure, but always made the ear the judge. But now that barbarians have begun to write music, we get passages that make us shudder. From two fragments of this new quartet we can decide that the composer (whom I do not know and do not want to know) is only a piano player with a depraved ear."

That is not a letter from an outraged radio fan, nor is it taken from a contemporary newspaper. It is an excerpt from some observations by an eighteenth-century Italian music critic, named Sarti, concerning Mozart's D minor Quartet. Even professional musicians are not always sound in their judgment. Listen to this:

"Yesterday we studied the new symphony of Brahms —a composer who is praised to heaven in Germany. I don't understand his attraction. In my opinion he is dark, cold, and full of pretense, of obscurity without true depth. I think Germany is on the decline musically, and that the French are now due on the scene."

That is Tchaikovsky, writing about an eminent contemporary. And here is what one of Tchaikovsky's fellow composers, Taneieff, had to say about Tchaikovsky's own Fourth Symphony:

"The first movement is too long in proportion to the others; it gives the effect of a symphonic poem to which the composer has slapped on three more movements and called it a symphony. The rhythm is repeated too often, and is tedious. There is one defect in this symphony to which I shall never become reconciled; every movement contains places that remind one of ballet music."

I don't want to labor my point, but let me give you one more excerpt:

"Some assert that it is just this symphony which is his masterpiece, that this is the true style for high-class music, and that if it does not please now, it is because the public is not cultured enough, artistically, to grasp all these lofty beauties. Another faction denies that the work has any artistic value, and profess to see in it an untamed striving for singularity. . . . By means of strange modulations and violent transitions, by combining the most heterogeneous elements, a certain undesirable originality may be achieved without much trouble; but genius proclaims itself not in the unusual and fantastic, but in the beautiful and sublime. A third party, a very small one . . . admits that the symphony contains many beauties, but concedes that the connection is often disrupted entirely, and that the inordinate length of this, the longest and perhaps most difficult of all symphonies, wearies even the cognoscenti, and is unendurable to the mere music-lover. It fears that if Beethoven continues on his present path both he and the public will be the sufferers."

That is an early nineteenth-century critic discussing the first performance of the "Eroica" Symphony. There is no need to remind you of the sort of comment that Wagner's music aroused when it was first played, or of Gounod's famous characterization of the Franck D minor Symphony: "The affirmation of incompetence pushed to dogmatic lengths."

Please do not assume that I am trying to imply that because good music has been abused, abused music is good; that a new symphony is a masterpiece simply because people say hard things about it. All that I say is, when you hear a new work, don't assume that it's worthless merely because it comes into more or less violent collision with some of your preconceived ideas as to how good music ought to sound. The great English critic, Ernest Newman, in his enchanting book, *A Music Critic's Holiday,* remarks: "It is a curious thing, the cynic may reflect, that the music of every period lacks melody as compared with the music of the past. Yet there is any amount of melody in music. The explanation of this strange circumstance seems to be that melody is always in the music of the generation before, never in the present generation. People who reject Stravinsky or Schönberg because they have no melody hark back regretfully to the melodies of Richard Strauss. But it was only a few years ago that we were being assured that Strauss had no melody—that there had been no melody in music, in fact, since Wagner and Brahms and Schumann. Yet one seems to remember that Wagner and Schumann in their day were accused of melodic poverty or melodic ugliness; and no doubt the charge goes back long past St. Cecilia, to the very days of Tubal Cain."

The music of Bach and Beethoven and Mozart will never be written again. They said what they had to say, in the vocabulary of their times, and they said it perfectly. If they were alive today they would not use that same vocabulary. I have often wondered what our verdict would be if some conductor were to discover a Tenth Symphony by Beethoven, and present it to us as the work of a little-known contemporary composer. I have an idea that while we might find in it much that was impressive, we would criticize the composer's form and style as being utterly old-fashioned. Hearing Beethoven's music, and knowing that it *is* Beethoven's, we accept the way in which he expresses himself as appropriate to him and the age in which he lived, just as we accept the language of Shakespeare in his plays. But a modern playwright, such as Maxwell Anderson, writing a play in verse, uses an English vocabulary that is utterly different from Shakespeare's. Beethoven's greatness is in the spirituality and eloquence of his musical ideas, not in the particular set of harmonies or the conventional turns of melody that he employs. The harmonies —or lack of them, if you like—in a piece of new music that sound so grotesque to you are merely the language in which the composer is expressing himself. You must hear deeper than that to discover whatever greatness his music may possess.

Not that it necessarily possesses any greatness at all. I am no devoted admirer of the new music. An enormous proportion of it strikes me as being highly tentative and empirical, and I frequently suspect some of its composers of trying to find a substitute for creative talent. Even so, no one who pretends to a love for music has any right to dismiss a new work without a fair hearing.

Let me quote Newman again: "The greatest geniuses . . . . have always been rather conservative, and, indeed, have always come at the end of a long period of development, never at the beginning of one. It is generally the men of the second or third order who experiment, and in no case do they use their medium with the ease and variety and force with which the geniuses use theirs."

That, I believe, is true. On the other hand, these contemporary experiments in broadening the language of music are not particularly new; they have been going on for some time (*Le Sacre du Printemps,* for example, dates from 1911). And, even granted the synthetic quality of much of the new music that we hear, it is quite possible that the period of development to which Newman refers may be nearing its close.

It is wholly possible that before very long, composers will arrive on the scene to whom these new harmonies and rhythms and melodic twists are not experiments, but their natural musical speech, composers whom even the most stubborn conservative will recognize as men of genius. Which is why I say, keep on listening. You owe it to the future. The great men may be here now, unrecognized. Even if they aren't, see to it that when they do arrive, they don't have to face an audience that has made up its mind beforehand not to give them a hearing.

Suppose, however, that a new piece of music remains stubbornly incomprehensible even after a conscientious hearing; is there any way of arriving at a defensible opinion of it?

There is no sure way, of course; but one or two hints may be useful. When you hear a particular piece by a new composer, does the music annoy you? Does it make you angry? If it does, give it a second hearing. There may be something in it. For nothing is more irritating than a new thought. It strikes a part of your mind that has never been disturbed before . . . and you draw back. Try again. The second time it may not be so bad. If the piece *bores* you, however, if you can honestly yawn at it, without having your temperature rise by a single degree, the chances are that you're safe in letting it go. Another thing: let us assume that you have heard a work by a new composer. You didn't like it. A week or so later, you hear another piece. And without knowing who wrote it, you say, "Oh,

Lord, that must be that frightful Russian, what's-his-name." If it *is* by him, go back and give the first piece another hearing. For if a composer possesses enough individuality to make you recognize his style, he is, however irritating, a personality. And personalities are rare, and precious, in music.

There's one other thing to listen for. It is hard to define. The easiest way of expressing it is by asking the question: does the music seem to run under its own power? In other words, does it give the impression of possessing some spark of life of its own, something that makes it go without your being conscious of the composer constantly trying to push it along? Stravinsky's *Le Sacre du Printemps* is a good example of what I mean. You may like it, or you may hate it. In either case you cannot deny that the music has the breath of life in it. You haven't the feeling that it is about to fall to the ground at any moment. You may wish it would, but you have no hope that it will. It soars, like an airplane, not like a kite.

8

A Masterpiece

In the last chapter I mentioned the possiblity that before long composers would arrive to whom the strange harmonic and rhythmic idiom of so-called ultra-modern music would be their natural musical speech, and whose talents would be patent even to those who happened to dislike their music. The statement was over-cautious. Such a composer has arrived, in my opinion, and has produced at least one musical work of enduring value. He will not produce another, more's the pity. He was Alban Berg, the Austrian composer who died not long ago, at fifty, long before his task was finished. The work that he produced is his opera, *Wozzeck,* which, to one of its hearers at least, towers high above most contemporary music. I am not sure that I like *Wozzeck;* I cannot quite imagine dropping in at a performance of it at the Metropolitan to hear that delicious bit in the third act. Still—I might. And I do consider it an authentic work of genius.

Wozzeck made its initial appearance at the Berlin Staatsoper on the night of December 14, 1925. Savagely attacked from the start, and as savagely defended, it made its way through the opera houses of Germany and Austria, and for a time was a favorite topic of debate in European musical circles. It reached this country six years later, when it had two performances by the Philadelphia

Opera Company, under Leopold Stokowski. I saw them both, and I shall not soon forget them.

Berg arranged his libretto from a play by Georg Büchner, a curious and tragic early nineteenth-century combination of scientist, mathematician, and poet, who died in 1837, in this twenty-fifty year. The manuscript was lost at the time of its author's death, and was not found and published until 1879. Originally in some twenty-odd loosely connected scenes, it was compressed by Berg into fifteen, distributed equally through three acts.

The story of *Wozzeck* is, briefly, the story of a poor devil. Nominally, Wozzeck is a conscript, a captain's orderly, garrisoned in a small German town, but in a broader sense he is the common man of any time and place, the eternal underdog, the little fellow at the bottom of the pile. He is a stupid, trustful fool, bullied by his captain, who loves to jeer at his thick-wittedness, and exploited by the town doctor, who uses him for some idiotic experiments in psychiatry. Dumb brute as he is, he has got himself a mistress, Marie, whom he worships and who has borne him a child. Marie, who was a rather shopworn blossom even when Wozzeck gathered her, wearies of him and falls a willing victim to the wiles of a handsome dog of a drum-major. The captain and the doctor have great sport hinting to Wozzeck that he has been betrayed. He rushes to Marie, bewildered and suspicious. She laughs at his forebodings; furious, he raises his hand against her. "Don't touch me!" she screams. "Rather a knife in my heart than a hand laid upon me!"

Baffled and jealous, he wanders into a summer garden, where he sees Marie and the drum-major dancing. He goes back to the barracks, but he cannot sleep. The drum-major comes in, drunk, taunts Wozzeck with his conquest, and when he refuses a drink, beats him up. The poor, half-mad, abandoned lover takes Marie for a last walk in the country, by a pond. There he stabs her. He goes back to a tavern, but the revellers look at him in horror; there is blood on his hands. The knife! He must find the knife. He goes to the pond once more, but the knife is gone. Wholly mad now, he wades in the pond, and is drowned. The doctor and the captain happen by, and hear his dying gasps; but they hurry away. In the town, the children hear the news of the murder, and rush to tell Marie's little son that his mother is dead. But he is too young to understand. They run off, leaving the little boy riding his hobbyhorse.

Grewsome as this story may sound, outlined thus baldly, it is told with such pity, in language and scenes of such simple pathos, that its horrors are softened, quite dimmed, in fact, by the spectator's profound sense of sympathy and pity for its people in general and Wozzeck in particular. For its expounding, Berg wove a musical integument of enormous complication and great dramatic power. He was, as you have been told many times, a pupil of Arnold Schönberg, and his score is written in the atonal manner of his master—that is, in complete disregard of what are still the orthodox notions of concord and discord. The orchestral voices go their way in what seems like complete independence, in totally unrelated keys, and in rhythms as complex as the harmony.

But, like it or not, the music of *Wozzeck* is not to be dismissed with a word—or with many words. It is music written by a man who has enormous talent for the theatre, who can isolate, as it were, the emotion of a scene, and convey it, who has an unerring sense of timing and an almost unfaltering command of climax. *Wozzeck* is a true music drama, written by a dramatic artist of the first order.

What impresses one first of all about the score of *Wozzeck* is the technical mastery of its composer, his complete control of his medium. Berg himself has written that the composer of opera must be a super stage director, a statement whose truth ought to be—and is not—self-evident to any assiduous opera-goer. For it is the composer who, in the last analysis, not only establishes the mood of the scenes, but dictates the pace at which they are taken, the pauses between speeches, the time allowed for stage business, the emphasis and inflections with which the speeches are delivered, the very speed with which the curtain goes up and down. To be a master-musician avails an operatic composer very little if he be not also a man of the theatre.

And this Berg is. Throughout the three acts and fifteen scenes of his astonishing opera he seldom relaxes, and never loses, his hold upon the hearer. He displays an admirable sense of just how long the tension of a given mood can be sustained without snapping, how long or short an interlude should be, just what sort of music is needed to effect the transition between two disparate scenes, exactly where the music should be lyric, where graphic and dramatic, where reflective.

The score of *Wozzeck* is an extraordinary contrapuntal achievement. It is not, perhaps, the sort of counterpoint that would appeal to a German musical scholar of the old school. Hearing it, Jadassohn would probably go mad, and Fuchs would assuredly hang himself. Bach, however, while he might have made a wry face over it, would have rendered its creator a grudging respect. For the voices in Berg's orchestra are manipulated with great skill. Their progressions have little to do with accepted notions of concord and key-relationship; but they are real progressions. His canons are canons, and his fugues are real fugues.

The least successful element in the work seems to me to be the vocal writing. Berg's idea, presumably, is to get away from the idiom of traditional operatic singing, to make the musical speech of the singers approximate the rise and fall and intonation of the spoken speech of actors. Much of the time he directs them to use a tone that preserves the relations of the written notes to one another, without trying for exact intonation (a procedure that is almost imposed by the impossibility of singing true notes against an atonal orchestra). This is an excellent idea, but in carrying it out he elects to write the vocal parts in a register that is practically impossible for the singers. The Captain, sung by a tenor, spends most of his time in a register that would be comfortable only for a contralto. Wozzeck must be prepared to negotiate a low E natural in the bass clef, yet sings most of his lines in a fairly high tenor register. Berg, who would not dream of asking a French horn to spend half the evening screaming away on its top C, does not hesitate to demand that Marie do just that.

As a result, the actors neither speak nor sing. They just holler. On the rare occasions when they do manage to sing-speak as Berg demands, their vocal loops and nosedives are so abrupt and far-reaching that they sound like bad actors ranting. When it comes to reading lines, Berg could have learned something from almost any good American stage director.

But far more important than Berg the technician is Berg the artist and thinker. He has caught and intensified with amazing power the mood of terror and nameless horror that hangs over the story of Wozzeck. The plot is only a framework for the inner, personal drama that he sets to music. Most of the time his music is not objective at all. It concerns itself, not with the external horrors of lust and murder, but with the secret terrors of the mind, the thoughts that gnaw the brain like maggots, the chucklings and whisperings of the little devils of madness.

Even when his music is descriptive it contrives to be introspective, to be both a picture and a comment. The distorted harmonies of the band in the beer garden, the drunken dissonances of the revelers, contrive to saturate the scene with the nightmare quality of a Goya etching. The rising tide of swirling chromatics that engulfs the orchestra after Wozzeck's death is the voice of the water as it must have sounded in the ears of the dying man. The incredible interlude that follows the murder scene—a stupendous unison *crescendo* on the note B—creates in the brain the same intolerable tension that slow realization must have wrought in the brain of the poor, bewildered murderer.

The music is, of course, almost wholly dissonant. There is hardly a chord that does not bristle with unreconciled sharps and flats, scarcely a progression that does not bite like acid. Yet there is a curiously reassuring quality in Berg's music. You feel that he is writing, not to a formula, but from necessity. The music is so completely appropriate to the dramatic theme that it is easy to believe that it is not the only music its composer can write. His themes have bite and salience; they stand on their own feet and move of their own vitality. Upon occasion he can write simply, almost diatonically. The interlude between the second and third scenes of the first act; Marie's *berceuse* and her recital of the story of Mary Magdalene; the last intermezzo of the third act, and the pitying and rueful finale—all these possess a quality of lifting and eloquent beauty that speaks to the heart direct, needing neither analysis nor explanation.

I have never heard any excerpts from the score of *Wozzeck* played in concert. It is quite possible that, divorced from the stage action of which it so eloquent an interpreter, the music might sound arbitrary and formless. That, however, is only a negative way of saying that it fits its own frame to perfection, that its creator, in setting out to write a musical setting for a drama that would express, not only its action but its emotional overtones, has succeeded, as Debussy did in setting a not dissimilar drama, in producing an unforgettable masterpiece.

9

Music and the Flag

PEOPLE seem to be worrying almost continuously because they can see no sign of an American "school" of music. They seem to feel that it is very slow in getting under way, and keep poking at it in an effort to make it move faster. Opinions differ as to what kind of school it ought to be, and just what should be its characteristics. Some think it ought to convey the spirit of American independence and initiative, the spaciousness of the windswept prairies and the solitude of the Grand Canyon; the uncurbed spirit of the Boston Tea Party, coupled with a slight hint of the Monroe Doctrine.

There are others who think it should convey the roar of the cities, the mechanical perfection of the airplane engine, and the relentless mechanization of a Ford plant. Still others want it to be expressive of our idealism and international goodwill—the Ku Klux Klan and the brotherhood of man.

All, however, are agreed as to two things. First, that there should be a school. Apparently composers, in their opinion, are something like flying fish, and can get nowhere unless they are moving in a body. Second, they are positive that our music should be founded upon our folk-songs. Hardly a week goes by that some newspaper does not print a letter from some onlooker who wants to know, with considerable heat, why American composers do not utilize the mine of native musical lore that lies at their feet.

There are three kinds of folksongs in this country upon which various enthusiasts think our American school of music should be based. The first is made up of the songs and dances of the American Indian. These have strength, and simplicity, and are undeniably primitive; but wherein are they particularly American? That is, wherein do they express anything of *us?* Just what response is going to be stirred in the blood of a New Yorker of mixed Russian, Italian, and Irish extraction, or a Chicagoan whose forebears were Swedish, Czechoslovak, and German, when he hears a Zuñi medicine song, or an Apache war-dance? We have stolen everything else from the Indian that he ever owned; we might at least let him have his own music for himself.

Not that good music cannot be written on Indian themes. MacDowell's "Indian" Suite is proof enough of that. But the "Indian" Suite is Indian, not American.

The same objection holds, I think, against trying to make Negro spirituals the basis of American music. They were undoubtedly created in this country, and they are a mine of magnificent musical material. But they are not American—that is, in the sense of expressing the soul of the average white American. We may be thrilled by their beauty. But beauty is not enough, at least in a folksong. What we are looking for is some common fund of music that awakens ancestral echoes within us; and so far as blood is concerned, the finale of the Ninth Symphony is more likely to do that than "Swing Low, Sweet Chariot."

There remain certain local folksong, such as the songs of the Kentucky mountains that Loraine Wyman and

Howard Brockway collected, and the cowboy songs. The Kentucky songs are beautiful, but they are English, where they are not Scotch. Most of them have easily traceable English archetypes; and the lovely "Nightingale" song from the first Wyman-Brockway book is, if you play it a bit faster, not far removed from "The Campbells Are Coming." This is all very well for the Anglo-Saxon American, but it leaves the Scandinavian, Irish, Italian, Russian, French, Jewish, Greek, Czechoslovak or what-have-you American out in the cold.

Which brings us to the cowboy songs. As folk poems, as verses that convey something characteristically and inescapably American, they are superb. But their music is deplorable. The words of "Jesse James was a man who killed a-many a man" are grand; but the music to which they are set is pretty meagre stuff upon which to base symphonies and tone-poems. To read the words of "Whoopy ty-yi-yi, get along, little dogies," and then to hear the music, is a complete course in anticlimax. The cowboy songs, for the most part, are ballads, sung narratives in which the words (as they are everywhere) are of primary importance. Judging from the tunes, and what little I know about horses, it is not easy to compose good music while riding horseback.

There is much talk in contemporary circles of making jazz the basis of American music. Thus far only one composer, the lamented George Gershwin, has done anything memorable in that idiom. The *Rhapsody in Blue,* the Concerto in F, and *An American in Paris* may be reckoned as genuine, if not monumental, contributions to contemporary music; but I am inclined to credit their achievement to Gershwin rather than to jazz. The trouble with jazz, to this observer at least, is twofold. First, it is, so far, extremely limited in its emotional range. The best jazz appeals, as Gilbert Seldes once put it, exclusively to the feet. It stimulates, it stirs, it cheers—even inebriates; but it opens no doors to the unseen and the inexpressible. It neither inspires nor consoles. When it does essay the tragic mood, as in the much-admired "blues," it is merely mawkish.

Moreover, jazz is not a wellspring of music; it is a method of writing music, a rhythmic idiom, a formula. And formulas are pretty sterile ground upon which to grow the flower of art. Those of us who look to jazz to save American music might glance at Spain, whose music is also based on a formula, and most of whose composers have gone from the cradle to the grave with the accursed "TUM-de-UM-tum, TUM-de-UM-tum" rhythm of the fandango and habanera ringing in their ears and echoing throughout their pages.

But the quest continues, the search for an American musical speech, some characteristic turn of harmony, melody, or rhythm that will stamp its creator's nationality beyond the possibility of doubt, the search that has bedevilled American music and musicians for a century. It is a vain one, I think. There is no American school of music, and I doubt if there will ever be one. As a matter of fact, I have an idea that "schools" of art are about over, everywhere. In their heyday they were largely a product of times when the artist was esteemed as a craftsman first, and as an original creator second. In the great Italian and Flemish schools of painting, for instance, it was considered no disgrace for one painter to imitate the technique, and even the actual composition and arrangement of another. Provided he turned out good work, no one criticized him if it bore a more than superficial resemblance to the work of his master. Even as late as the eighteenth century composers borrowed themes from one another with no self-consciousness whatsoever, and without exciting any particular adverse comment.

But now the emphasis has shifted from the work as a thing in itself to the work as an expression of the individual artist. We do not expect the pupils of a certain painter to paint indefinitely in faithful imitation of his style. Composers no longer borrow or lend themes. The luckless musician who borrows somebody else's tune is regarded, not as a borrower, but as an embezzler. In short, the very people who yearn after definite schools of thought and technique are likewise insistent that the artist be uniquely and recognizably himself. Unless he can create pictures and words and music that are his own and nobody else's they refuse to recognize him as an artist at all.

One other factor made for schools of art: nationalism. A school, in its less obvious aspect, is the result of a common fund of thought and feeling—particularly feeling. Talk to a Paris taxicab driver, and you find the same rigorous sense of logic, the same utter innocence of sentimentality that make Debussy's *Pelléas,* for all its wraith-like fragility and suggestiveness, a solid, firmly built work of art. The reiterated tonic chords at the close of Beethoven's Fifth Symphony are but a sublimated and happier manifestation of the Teutonic habit of laboriously pounding home a point long after the listener has wearily conceded it. English painting, on the average, is one vast betrayal of the sentimentalism for which the average Englishman's monosyllabic matter-of-factness is a cloak.

At that, when it comes to music, I suspect us of being a good deal more confident of detecting national characteristics than we have any right to be. I have often thought what an interesting experiment it would be to find some person who was sensitive to music, but knew neither the name nor nationality of a single composer; to take him to hear operas and concert works, and ask him to guess the countries of their origin.

Some he could undoubtedly guess. I would try him on a Chopin polonaise or mazurka. "Polish," he would say. The "Ritual Dance" from De Falla's *El Amor Brujo*. He would probably guess, "Spanish." A gavotte by Lully he would undoubtedly identify as French (Lully was an Italian who founded French opera), and he might find a waltz by Johann Strauss unmistakably German—or, let us say, Teutonic. If I played him a tarantella he would probably identify it as coming from Italy.

But, just as he was beginning to wax a bit boastful, I would play him the exquisite "Fisherman's Tale" from that same *El Amor Brujo,* and ask him—or, rather dare him—to tell me the nationality of the composer. I would play him the Russian national anthem by Lvoff, and the Austrian national anthem by Haydn, and ask him to tell me which was the Russian and which the Austrian, and why. If I played him the *"Marche des Rois"* from the *Arlésienne* suite, and the "Habanera" from *Carmen,* I would be extremely curious to see whether he would guess that the same Frenchman had written both.

It is perfectly true that we associate certain rhythms,

and certain conventional phrases of musical speech, with definite nationalities. I think it is equally true, however, that nationalism is only for the middling good artist; that when a composer begins to search for some music that will express universal human ideas and emotions, and succeeds, he generally far transcends the bounds of any national idiom. The Wagner of the first scene of the last act of *Parsifal* is no more German to me than the Debussy of the closing scene of *Pelléas et Mélisande* is French.

Just what is the common characteristic that would make you sure of identifying the music of Corelli, Respighi, Verdi, and Pizzetti as unmistakably Italian? What is there French, beyond the composer's name, about Ravel's *Bolero?* The slow movement of the "From the New World" Symphony is accepted as so completely American that, with words by William Arms Fisher and entitled "Goin' Home," it is accepted by thousands of Americans as a genuine Negro spiritual (in other words, American. Anyone who lives in America, particularly an Indian or a Negro, is, musically speaking, an American).

Even if it were true that a common fund of racial experience and emotion invariably produces music whose nationality is unmistakable, we would be no better off. For we Americans are not a race. America is a club, not a motherland. Her people have almost no common thoughts and feelings and instincts. We talk a good deal about the Spirit of '76, and the ideals of the Founding Fathers. They once existed, too; but that was long ago, when we were a race of transplanted Englishmen. By now, our blood is such a conglomeration of diverse racial strains that we have hardly any nationalistic feeling at all, in the European sense. Inland, we are parochial; on our eastern coast we are international-minded; in the extreme west we are anti-Oriental—a purely negative kind of nationalism.

All of which does not make for a national school of music or any sort of art. It is not easy to find in our painting or poetry or music any unmistakably American characteristics, to isolate, as it were, an aesthetic bacillus that flourishes exclusively in our own culture. Edward MacDowell, George Chadwick—German composers, both of them, the former with a deliberate added touch of Amerindian. Sargent was a superb painter of the French school, a brilliant blood relation of Boldini. Our best novelists seem purely American—frequently for no other reason than that their subject-matter is American. But read a poem by Edna Millay or Archibald MacLeish without knowing the poet's name, and (disregarding geographical allusions) tell me the poet's nationality.

I am not prepared to say that there are absolutely no national characteristics in the music of great composers; but I do believe that they are not nearly so clear-cut or important as we have deluded ourselves into thinking they are. In general, a great composer is national only when he is at his second best. At the height of his powers, when he has ceased being decorative or merely exciting, and becomes eloquent and moving, he is likely to sound merely like himself. The great American music of the future will be a music to which America will listen and respond. But it will not be the music of Sitting Bull, or Booker T. Washington—or even George. It will belong to us, because one of us made it; but it will, like all great music, belong to the world. And the world will not be curious regarding the name and address of the composer.

10

Ishmael

NO SCHOOL, no folksongs, no particular stream of racial consciousness. Deprived of these props, how is the American composer faring? He is faring, on the whole, rather well, certainly a thousand times better than he did even so recently as a quarter of a century ago. His fellow countrymen are beginning to realize that he exists, broadcasting companies are beginning to commission works from him, symphony conductors are displaying a reasonable willingness to program his works. Even so, it would be absurd to pretend that he cuts a particularly important figure in the world's music as yet. He has plenty of talent; but he seems to develop it only so far. There is something he lacks, something he needs. What is it?

I have a suspicion. To open the discussion, suppose we consider this passage from a letter that came in after the broadcast of an American work by the Philharmonic-Symphony Society: "I should like to take a shot or two at that old question, why can't the American composer stand on the same step with his European contemporary? The plaintive answer that he doesn't get a chance to be heard in his native country isn't accepted any more. All he has to do is write, and he'll find a chance to get heard. And it is my guess that he doesn't write or compose one quarter of the amount he should. If the output of an American composer could be placed alongside the output of a European, how would it compare? . . . Quantity is lacking in the case of the American composer. If you fire often enough at a target you'll learn to hit the bull's-eye."

On the whole, I agree with that. American composers, as a rule, do *not* write enough. One reason is the economic one, of course. The American must spend a large part of his working time in making a living, before he can sit down to compose. That is largely true of all composers, European as well as Americans. But the European has one advantage. It's no disgrace for an artist to be poor, in Europe; in fact, it's rather expected of him. It *is* a disgrace here. It is taken as a sign of incompetence for anyone to be poor in this country. When I say that a composer who doesn't own a dinner coat is at a great professional disadvantage in America, I am exaggerating, but not much.

But let us not argue. Assume that I am wrong about that. He ought to spend all his time composing, and think nothing about money. Now nobody works without some incentive. It may be money, it may be fame, it may be the simple satisfaction of feeling that one is a useful member of the community. To be played, and played regularly, is, I should say, probably the most powerful incentive to work that a composer can have. But my correspondent says that he *is* played, and technically, he is right. New American works are beginning to figure fairly prominently on our symphony programs. But there is a catch to that.

Suppose we trace the hypothetical course of a new symphony by a young American composer. Let us assume that it has been a great success at its first American performance. The word goes around among the conductors: "Here's a new American work that is worth playing." The following season you will find it on the programs of most of our major symphony orchestras. The season after that, it will be played by a number of the minor orchestras. And then it will be through. On the shelf. Some other new American piece will be programmed by some prominent conductor. It, in turn, will sweep the country for a season or two. Then it, too, will join its predecessor in the storehouse. The American does get played, but he gets played only once.

That is not because his music invariably deserves oblivion. And it is not, as I so often hear, because our symphony conductors being most of them foreign-born, discriminate against American music. Many of them have little interest in American music, I grant you; but most of them, I imagine, would listen to their audiences. If I am not mistaken, Arturo Toscanini, in all the years that he headed the New York Philharmonic-Symphony Orchestra, conducted exactly two American works. A few years ago he took this great American orchestra on a tour of Europe, during which the orchestra played not one note of American music. Is that his fault? No. Did any great number of Americans complain about it? Did the board of directors of the orchestra protest? Certainly not. When any American symphony orchestra goes through a season without playing any American music, does the board of directors of that orchestra go into action? No. Do the subscribers complain? No. When men like Rodzinski, or Barbirolli, or Stock do program a considerable number of American works, what reception do they get? Complaints, usually, because they neglected the Brahms Third. Do they get any requests for repeats? No.

Is it because the music isn't good enough? No. A good

fifth of the European music you hear during the season of any American symphony orchestra is there—why? Theodore Thomas again—"Popular music is familiar music." You like some music because it's great. A good deal of it you like because you've heard it before. You're used to it. You say to conductors, in effect, "Give me my Mozart and Beethoven and Brahms and Wagner, and you can have all this modern trash"—just as a hundred and fifty years ago you were writing to someone else, "Give me my Palestrina and Bach and Händel, and don't bother me with your Mozarts and Beethovens."

This is no plea for ultra-modern music. I'm not arguing the possible merits of anything that sounds strange to the average ear. I am pleading now for the new American work about which you say, as you come out of the concert hall, "You know, I liked that. I'd like to hear it again some time." And so you would, but do you ever *ask* to hear it again? No. When it is never heard again, do you ever wonder what became of it? No. You stick to the old favorites, and tolerate a few novelties, on condition that you are not asked to hear them more than once. Meanwhile the American composer is very wickedly failing to turn out the vast quantity of music that he should; perhaps because he knows that if he writes one symphony it will be played—once—by every orchestra; and if he writes ten, they, too, will be played—once. But no one of the ten, regardless of its merits, has a chance in a million of getting into the permanent repertoire of any orchestra. Why should he break his heart writing ten, when one will do, for oblivion?

No, the American composer decidedly does *not* stand on the same step with his European contemporary. The attitude of his own countrymen is hardly one calculated to make him feel like an important or even moderately useful person. He knows that among his compatriots not one in a hundred honestly cares a tinker's dam about American music. We get up committees, and we give lunches, and we make speeches, and we give prizes—in fact, we do everything except the one thing that would give him a little hope and self-confidence and self-respect—arrange matters so that a new piece of American music could be heard more than once by the same audience.

II

Transplanted

THE Chicago North Shore Festival of Music, held in the late spring, generally at Evanston, Illinois, has been an annual feature of Midwestern music for a good many years. In 1923 the directors of the festival announced a competition for orchestral works of symphonic dimensions, and offered a substantial money prize for the best work of this kind by an American citizen. I was music critic of the New York *World* at that time, and they asked me to be one of the judges.

We spent a good part of the winter and early spring wading through manuscripts—as I remember, there were nearly seventy entries—and finally agreed on five that we thought were the best. It had been arranged that the five best compositions submitted were to be played by the Chicago Symphony Orchestra, under Frederick Stock, at the closing concert of the festival, and that the judges would then render their decision and award the prize. The names of the five composers were unknown to us, and would not be made public until after the winning composition had been announced.

In order to have plenty of time to make up our minds, the judges met in Chicago a few days before the last concert, heard the five works rehearsed, and then heard a special private concert reading. Then, on the morning of the last day we solemnly assembled to make our choice.

Two or three of the five were well worth playing by anybody, and afterwards *were* played, by several American orchestras. But one work in particular struck us as being head and shoulders above the rest. It was a symphonic poem, called *Memories of My Childhood,* with the subtitle, *Life in a Russian Village.*

As I have said, we didn't know who the composer was —the works were all submitted under assumed names— but we didn't have to know his name to know that he was obviously a master of symphonic form and of orchestration. It seemed inevitable that his work would win on the first ballot, and that our meeting wouldn't take over fifteen minutes. That is not exactly what happened.

You may remember that in the early twenties we enjoyed a witch-hunt in this country that hadn't been equalled in excitement and gusto since the Salem affair, a couple of centuries ago. Only this time it wasn't witches we were hunting, but Communists. Thousands of eminent citizens, including an attorney-general of the United States, never retired for the night without looking under the bed for a Bolshevik. The excitement had died down somewhat by '23, but even then—as even now—the quickest way of winning a political argument was to call your opponent a Communist. And as he looked again at the title-page of the work that we all thought was so good, one of our judges suddenly smelled tainted gold.

"Life in a Russian Village," indeed! was the general purport of his remarks. Did we actually mean that we were going to sit there and award this prize to some Russian immigrant, presumably unwashed, probably with whiskers, and indubitably in the pay of Lenin and Trotzky, some insidious alien who was adopting this dastardly means of taking the bread out of the mouths of honest American composers? A thousand . . . oh, fifteen hundred times . . . no!

That, of course, was exactly what the rest of us did mean that we were going to sit there and do. There was, consequently, a fairly animated discussion. First we asked our superpatriotic colleague whether he didn't agree that this was the best piece of the five. Yes, he did; but that wasn't the point. Then we pointed out that, after all, *any* American citizen was eligible for the prize, that all contestants had to submit documentary evidence of their citizenship, and that if this man turned out to be an alien, we could take the prize away from him and probably put him in jail. We also pointed out that we were there to discuss music, and not politics.

But our friend was hard to convince. It was obviously his conviction that if we awarded the prize to the composer of *Life in a Russian Village,* a large Russian army was going to arrive and put Evanston to the torch before midnight. I can't give you all the arguments pro and con. The memory of the details of that day are a little dim. I do remember that it was a very long day, and that we finally won. About six o'clock, only two hours and a half before the concert, our all-American judge reluctantly yielded to superior numbers and stronger lungs, and consented to cast his vote for *Memories of My Childhood.* To do him justice, I must say that when the envelope containing the composer's real name was unsealed, and he discovered that the prize had gone to Charles Martin Loeffler, a man who had sat at the first desk of the Boston Symphony Orchestra for twenty-one years, who had not a drop of Russian blood in his veins, and who had been an

American citizen for more than half his life . . . when he discovered that, I must say that his face took a mean revenge, and turned the color that is usually associated with Communism.

The case of Loeffler has always been rather a mystery to me. Here is a man who seems to me to belong in the very first rank, not only of American composers, but of contemporary composers anywhere. Yet many people who pride themselves on their interest in American music know little or nothing about his work, and can talk at length about American composers without mentioning his name. Yet if he is not an American composer he's a composer without a country.

He was born French—or, rather, Alsatian, as you might suspect from his name—in 1861. His early childhood, as the Evanston prize-winner commemorates, was spent in Russia; later, he spent some time in Hungary. As a young man, he went to Germany, where he studied the violin with the great Joachim. At the age of twenty he came to this country, where he spent the rest of his life. In 1882 he joined the first violin section of the Boston Symphony Orchestra, and occupied the first desk, with Franz Kneisel, until 1903, when he resigned, to give all his time to composition. He retired to a lovely old colonial manor house in Medfield, Massachusetts, where he remained until his death in 1935. There couldn't have been a more devoted and loyal American than Loeffler. He was an American citizen for the greater part of his seventy-four years, and wrote every bar of his music in this country.

All of his music is written against a rich intellectual background. Not that it sounds cerebral and thought-out; but literary and pictorial ideas have always been its inspiration. His compositions are always superb examples of workmanship, and some of them are really masterpieces. The *Memories of My Childhood* is Loeffler on his pictorial side. Some of his other orchestral works include *The Death of Tintagiles,* inspired by a play by Maeterlinck; *A Pagan Poem,* based on one of Virgil's Eclogues; *La Bonne Chanson,* after Paul Verlaine; *La Villanelle du Diable,* another Russian scene, *The Night Watch of the Ukraine;* and a gorgeous eight-part mixed chorus, written to commemorate a friend who was killed in the war, entitled, *For One Who Fell in Battle.*

All this music has been played, from time to time, and has been praised. But not played or praised nearly as much, to my mind, as it deserves. Americans who know his music are inclined to classify him, almost subconsciously, as a French composer; and the French call him an American.

Someone has evolved a theory that famous men are men of talent who happen to have been lucky enough to be born at just the right time; that Napoleon, for example, born twenty years earlier, would have been too old to take advantage of the last days of the French Revolution, and would have lived and died an obscure Corsican military officer. And that is possibly Loeffler's trouble. He was born a little too early. His music, most of it written between 1903 and 1925, is composed in the cool, impressionistic idiom that we used to call "modern French." When it was played, the critics recognized its value, and praised it. But the general public here didn't warm to it. It spoke a language that we weren't used to; it sounded foreign. Nothing that we were accustomed to associate with American. And so, while we admitted that, technically he was an American composer, we didn't quite believe it.

But the past fifteen years have exposed us to so many varieties of musical speech . . . every man for himself, so to speak . . . that we'll accept anything from anybody. We no longer ask for labels. And Loeffler's manner of musical expression, which once seemed so Gallic to us, is part of the vocabulary of all composers, French, Irish, German, or American. If more conductors would give Charles Martin Loeffler a new day in court, give him the hearing that we would give to a brand-new talent, he would, I think, come into his own; and we might find that we have—long have had—an American composer who belongs, not alone to us, but to the world.

12

Beethoven in the Other Corner

HAVE you ever stopped to realize that music is the one art in which the classics are the staple commodity? In which the works of the classic masters are enjoyed every day, not merely by the cultured and specially educated, but by everybody? The modern theatre doesn't keep modern playwrights out in order to make way for Shakespeare and Molière and Goethe, no matter how much it may produce those masters; the reader of poetry and novels spends much more time with contemporaries than with Milton and Schiller and Keats and Fielding and Dickens. But when a modern composer tries to make his way into the programs of the modern symphony orchestras, who are the people that get in his way? His contemporaries? Not at all. He must prove his ability to stand comparison with Bach, Händel, Beethoven, Wagner, Schubert, Mussorgsky . . . a host of long-dead composers who are still just as alive as when they walked the earth. The fundamental appeal of music changes very slowly . . . probably because it is so innocent of any intellectual complications. It can be enjoyed, and understood, by one who reads no notes, plays no instrument, may even be unable to read or write his own spoken language. An intellectual comprehension of music may enhance one's enjoyment of it; but it doesn't create that enjoyment.

Technical innovations . . . changes in structure, harmony, and whatnot, may make a great deal of contemporary music sound very different from that of our fathers; but they won't necessarily keep it alive. The emotions that music evokes, and to which it appeals, are deep-seated and inarticulate. And they change as slowly as the race changes. I'm inclined to believe that new music has a much harder time than the other arts to prove its right to live. But once it has proved that right, it lives a long time.

13

Godfather to Polymnia

On the morning of July 13, 1918, two American Y.M.C.A. workers faced each other in the Hôtel de France et Choiseul, in the Rue St. Honoré, in Paris. The elder of the two, a man somewhere in the fifties, above the average in height, broad-shouldered, with abundant gray hair, very bright eyes deep set under bushy eyebrows, and a beautiful Greek profile, was, despite an ill-fitting tunic and distressing breeches, obviously a personage, and presumably not a professional evangelist.

As a matter of fact, he was wearing the insignia of the red triangle solely as a necessary incident to his real business in Paris, which was music. He had been asked to recruit an orchestra from among non-mobilized French instrumentalists, and to take it on tour among the American army encampments in France, thus neatly combining entertainment for homesick doughboys with financial aid for some eighty French musicians. Inasmuch as no one could get to France that summer save in uniform, he had chosen that of the "Y."

His credentials were exceptional. Three distinguished Americans—one of them Theodore Roosevelt—had reassured the Y.M.C.A. as to his unimpeachable morality and Americanism, he bore a letter of invitation from the French Ministry of Fine Arts, and his passport had been visaed both by the French High Commission at

Washington and M. Pichon himself, France's Minister of Foreign Affairs. That evening he was to conduct his first concert, in the Théâtre des Champs-Élysées, and on the following day was to play, by special invitation of the French Government, in the Salle du Conservatoire, a hall that no foreign conductor had ever before invaded.

Nevertheless he was in trouble, and looked worried and angry. His tour of the American camps was supposed to begin on the following Monday, and thus far he had been unable to procure the *carte rouge* without which he could not travel in France. The French Ministère des Affaires Etrangères was willing and anxious. The Intelligence Division of the A.E.F. remarked that so far as they were concerned, he was free to go where he pleased. The American Legation was sympathetic, but helpless. For inasmuch as he was enrolled with the Y.M.C.A., only the Y.M.C.A. was empowered to issue his *carte rouge,* and the Y.M.C.A. had not got around to issuing it. Hence this final interview, in which the "Y" was to communicate its ultimate decision.

The other Y.M.C.A. worker cleared his throat. "Mr. Damrosch," he began, "I'm terribly sorry. But thc fact is, Brother, the rules of the 'Y' are pretty strict, and we can't afford to break them. We don't issue travelling cards to Americans of German birth, and as you were born in Germany we can't let you have one. And another thing"—hastily, as the elder man showed signs of having passed the boiling point—"since you *are* of German birth, and can't get your *carte rouge,* the committee asked me to say that they don't think you ought to wear the 'Y' uniform at the concert tonight."

Unfortunately the exact words of Brother's reply have

not come down to us. The gist of them was that he had no other clothes at the moment, that he would conduct the concert either in the "Y" uniform or in his underwear, that his resignation had been written and would be offered Monday, and that furthermore the Y.M.C.A. could etcetera, etcetera, and etcetera.

The concert, need we add, took place, and the following morning another visitor came to the Hôtel de France et Choiseul. This time it was General Charles Dawes, bearing an invitation from the commander-in-chief of the A.E.F. And on the following Wednesday Walter Damrosch, having got his divorce from the Y.M.C.A. and procured his *carte rouge* from some less squeamish source—the French Government, for instance—set out for Chaumont, the general headquarters of the American armies in France, where, at the request of General Pershing, he organized a school of bandsmen and bandmasters, a school that remained in session until the A.E.F. left France.

Up to the time that the Y.M.C.A., with a start, recalled the fact, everyone had forgotten that Walter Damrosch was German-born, so closely had his career been identified with the progress of American musical culture. He arrived here in 1871, when his father, Leopold Damrosch, discouraged with the musical outlook in Breslau, Germany, decided to try his luck in America and accepted an invitation to conduct the Arion Society, New York's largest German choral organization.

Nine-year-old Walter and his brother Frank (formerly head of the Institute of Musical Art) were promptly shipped off to Public School No. 40, in East Twenty-third Street, where, because of their ignorance of English, they began in the lowest class. This was a bit of a comedown for two youngsters who had reached the dignity of Latin studies at the Gymnasium in Breslau, but they rapidly moved up to more appropriate grades. Walter was also studying the piano, with an eye to a concert career. That aspiration, however, was ended by his teacher, Boeckelman, who experimented on his young pupil with a patent finger-arching machine, with disastrous results. The third finger of Walter's right hand was permanently lamed, and although he might—and did—become an expert pianist, there was no possibility of his ever ranking as a virtuoso.

The musical fortunes of Damrosch, the father, prospered apace. He founded the New York Oratorio Society in 1873 (Walter, at the ripe age of eleven, sang first alto in its ranks), and the Symphony Society in 1877. In 1883 the directors of "the new yellow brewery on Broadway" (Colonel Mapleson's blasphemous description of the Metropolitan Opera House) asked him to conduct German opera there during the season of 1884–85. He accepted, despite the heavy labors of the Oratorio and Symphony Societies. In February, 1885, as the season was nearing its close, he caught cold, came down with pneumonia, and died within a week.

That week definitely settled Walter Damrosch's career for him. He had helped his father drill the Oratorio Society, conducted a small choir of his own in Newark, and was a sort of unofficial assistant at the Metropolitan, but was neither well-known nor experienced. Suddenly he found it up to him to save the Wagner season, for no one else at the Metropolitan knew much about Wagner. During his father's last week he conducted performances of

Die Walküre and *Tannhäuser,* and at the close of the New York season took the Metropolitan Company on its road tour.

From then on he moved steadily forward. He continued the Symphony Society concerts, and took over the Oratorio Society in 1886 (he remained its conductor until 1898). The Metropolitan appointed him second conductor and assistant director of the opera house. He retained the double post until 1891, when the return of Abbey, Schoeffel, and Grau banished Wagner from the Met. Three years later, deciding that New York needed German opera again, he sold his New York house and used the proceeds to start his own opera company. He engaged a company that included Gadski, Emil Fischer, and Max Alvary, hired the Metropolitan for eight weeks, and opened in the spring of 1895 with *Tristan und Isolde.*

The profits of the first season were fifty-three thousand dollars. Thus heartened, he made the Damrosch Opera Company a permanent institution, undertook a second season, and managed not only to wipe out all his previous profits but to lose an extra forty-three thousand dollars as well. Bloody but unbowed, he took a partner, Charles Ellis, Nellie Melba's manager, and continued. In 1899 he sold out to Ellis and accepted Maurice Grau's invitation to come back and conduct Wagner at the Metropolitan.

All this time he had been struggling to keep the New York Symphony alive. It was a permanent organization principally in name, as the receipts from road tours, festivals, and what small subsidies he could scrape together were sufficient only for occasional New York concerts, the members spending most of their time playing outside engagements. In 1903 the Philharmonic invited him to become its conductor. He agreed, provided the society would abandon its co-operative basis (a form of self-government under which the principal first violin had voted himself into office annually for forty years) and place its fortunes in the hands of a non-performing board. The negotiations fell through, but Harry Harkness Flagler, one of the Philharmonic committee, offered to help raise the funds to endow the New York Symphony Orchestra and place it on a permanent footing. Damrosch joyfully accepted, and the rest is current history. In 1914 Mr. Flagler announced that he was sick of trying to get money out of reluctant guarantors, and henceforth would finance the orchestra single-handed.

During the years of his various conductorships Damrosch found time to pursue a fairly extensive parallel career as composer and lecturer. He has written three grand operas, *The Scarlet Letter, Cyrano,* and *The Man Without a Country;* a *Manila Te Deum;* a comic opera, *The Dove of Peace,* and incidental music for Margaret Anglin's productions of *Iphigenia, Medea,* and *Electra.* His published songs include the setting of "Danny Deever" without which no baritone can ever bring a recital to a satisfactory close.

In 1926 he made up his mind to retire. The New York Symphony was to merge with the Philharmonic, he was to conduct a few guest performances a season, and the rest of the time he was going to loaf. So he retired, and in 1927 promptly signed up as musical counsel to the National Broadcasting Company, his duties including a series of broadcast concerts and opera lectures. His Music Appreciation Hour, a series of orchestral lecture-concerts for school children, goes out on both networks of N.B.C. and is heard weekly by about eight million youngsters.

He is, simply, the type of man who dies in harness. A real retirement would be a literal impossibility for him. His interest in his work, and in life in general, is too real, and his curiosity and energy too unflagging. He has had a finger in most of the musical pies that have been opened in America during the past forty years. He has edited a series of school music books, he has been a judge in scores of prize-composition contests, he has served on countless committees. Unlike most celebrities who lend their names to worthy causes, he invariably does most of the work of every committee and board to which he is elected.

His interest in new music has always been of the liveliest. His long list of first performances in America includes Brahms's Third and Fourth Symphonies, Saint-Saëns' *Samson et Dalila*, Paderewski's opera, *Manru,* and Honegger's *Pacific 231*. Under his baton the Oratorio Society performed *Parsifal* for the first time here, in 1886. The "stage festival play" was *verboten* outside Bayreuth. The orchestral score was to be had, but could not be used for a performance under penalty of a fine of two hundred and fifty dollars. Damrosch bought the score, had the parts copied, paid the fine, and gave the performance. In 1891 he induced Tchaikovsky to come to America to appear with the New York Symphony at the dedication of Carnegie Hall. A year later, after Tchaikovsky's death, he gave the first American performance of the *"Pathétique"* Symphony. It was he who engaged Anton Seidl to conduct opera at the Metropolitan—an act of self-abnegation if ever there was one, inasmuch as the great German would allow no one else to conduct Wagner and kept Damrosch toiling at *Il Trovatore* and the like for four years.

He was the first conductor to make a practice of playing orchestral works by Americans. Carpenter, Hadley, Chadwick, Hill, Stillman Kelley, Gilbert, MacDowell, Hanson, Gruenberg, Jacobi, Griffes—the list of American composers, living and dead, who have figured on his programs is a formidable one. Most of us, in fact, he introduced. In 1925 he inaugurated the European practice of commissioning native composers to write works for his orchestra. When the *Rhapsody in Blue* gave evidence that jazz was susceptible of serious treatment, Damrosch, one of its earliest admirers, promptly commissioned George Gershwin's Concerto in F. He gave Gershwin's *An American in Paris,* its first hearing in 1928.

His beat as a conductor is authoritative and precise, but lacking in the terpsichorean qualities that are in vogue at present. He is much better than he looks. He has a quaint habit, during the closing bars of some piece that he particularly likes, of half turning to the audience, in the manner of one who says, "Isn't that swell?"

Orchestra players like to perform under him, for they have implicit confidence in him. They have enormous respect for his knowledge of instrumental technique and his ability to detect minor inaccuracies. "He's an old rat!" one of his men once admiringly remarked. His relations with the members of the New York Symphony were unusually friendly, and they gave him unswerving loyalty. Georges Barrère, the great flautist, was with him for twenty years, and his librarian, Hans Goettich, for nearly thirty years. When the Symphony Society merged with the Philharmonic, only about one third of Damrosch's men could be used. Abetted by Mr. Flagler, he promptly turned over the orchestra's pension fund to the others. A sum amounting to more than eighty thousand dollars was thus divided *pro rata* among the men who had been dropped.

The Damrosch house stood in Sixty-first Street, New York, and for years the Damrosch parties were famous. The Damrosch New Year's luncheon was one of New York's institutions. There, every year, assembled an enormous and rowdy gathering, composed of orchestra players, theatrical people, music critics, and all the world's famous virtuosi that were in America and not on the road. One rang the bell, the front door opened mysteriously, a hand came forward bearing a glass of cheerio, and an invisible voice said, "Drink this." There was, incidentally, a lunch, of Gargantuan proportions, served informally by various assorted daughters (he has four) and other feminine relatives, all dressed as waitresses.

There was usually a more or less impromptu vaudeville performance in the back parlor, and a speech by the host. Damrosch talks easily and well on his feet, has never yet failed to say something appropriate and amusing on any occasion whatsoever, and adores doing it. He speaks English, French, and German with equal fluency, and much of his success in France has undoubtedly been due to his ability to address Frenchmen in their own tongue.

His love of France and admiration of French culture is second only to his love of America. He sneaks off to Paris at every opportunity and on any possible pretext. He always stays at the Hôtel de France et Choiseul, and always occupies the same suite. He has a pretty taste in wines, and his choice of a dinner commands the respect even of a French *cordon bleu.* The school for bandsmen that he founded at Chaumont finally evolved into a conservatory for American summer students at Fontainebleau. This service in helping to link the two countries closer won him a Légion d'Honneur, a decoration that he probably prizes above any other honor he has ever received.

In 1928 the Damrosch family decided to sell the house on Sixty-first Street. The daughters were all grown up, the house was too big, servants were too hard to get, and all the rest of it. He would get rid of the house and buy a cozy little co-operative apartment, just big enough to hold himself and Mrs. Damrosch. He bought the apartment, right enough. I have never counted the rooms, but the Damrosch parties continue on the same scale as before, and no guest has yet been crowded out. In 1935 he telephoned me one day.

"My radio work isn't as heavy as it was," he said, "so I think I'll write an opera." And, at seventy-three he did write *The Man Without a Country,* which had its *première* at the Metropolitan in the spring of '37. That same spring the National Broadcasting Company gave a luncheon in his honor, to celebrate, jointly, his tenth year in radio and his seventy-fifth birthday. We talked a bit of the forthcoming opera, and of the future. When I left him he said, "It was nice of you to come to my seventy-fifth birthday party. To show my gratitude, I tell you what I'll do. I'll come to *your* seventy-fifth birthday party."

He'll be there.

14

The Room and Board Problem

IN THE biographical sketch of Jan Sibelius that appears in the *Dictionary of Modern Music and Musicians* there is a phrase that struck me forcibly. It is a simple statement of fact: "A life state grant from 1897 enabled him to devote himself to composition." In other words, here is one composer at least, now over seventy years old, who for more than forty years has been able to compose music without worrying about how to make a living. Thinking that over, I made a list of a number of other great composers, and how *they* made a living; and that list revealed the striking fact that the greater part of the world's symphonic music has been written by men who were, technically at least, amateurs—that is, by men who didn't make a living out of writing music.

Generally speaking, music and poetry are two arts whose practitioners cannot support themselves by their profession. A successful novelist is almost invariably, if not rich, at least comfortably well off. You will have a hard time finding a famous architect who can't pay his rent; a sculptor can make a good living out of sculpture, a painter can live, and live well, by doing nothing but paint pictures. But it is quite possible for a poet or a composer to be at the peak of his creative powers, to be famous even, and, almost literally, starve to death.

Suppose we take a list of famous composers and see

how they supported themselves. First Mozart. He gave piano recitals, taught music, and sold his music to publishers. The first two vocations, which were not his true one, gave him much less than a living income. What he made out of the practice of his art left his widow without enough money to pay his funeral expenses. Schubert gave lessons, and sold immortal songs for three dollars apiece, leaving an estate, at the time of his death, appraised at something under forty dollars. Beethoven gave lessons, conducted, and depended, for the most part, on the sporadic generosity of wealthy patrons. He didn't starve, but his average income was about that of a bank clerk.

Chopin was a pianist. His music brought him very little. Brahms lived, not by the sale of his music, but by conducting orchestras and choruses and appearing as a concert pianist. Alexander Borodine was a physician and a chemist. Rimsky-Korsakoff was a professor in a conservatory and a naval officer. Mussorgsky was a civil service employee. César Franck was a church organist and a teacher. Dvořák was a teacher. Vincent d'Indy lived by teaching. Edward MacDowell made a living as a pianist and as a college professor, and died of overwork.

Bach was a church organist and choirmaster, but was luckier than most, in that part of his job was writing music. Haydn was fairly lucky, too, in that he lived as a sort of superior servant in the household of Count Esterhazy, who hired him to write music. Tchaikovsky lived for a time as a teacher of music, but did his best work on a pension that he received, for many years, from a friend. Rachmaninoff is a pianist. Most of his compositions are Russian copyrights, and as there is no international copyright agreement with Russia he derives not a cent from either their sale or performance. Liszt was a pianist. Saint-Saëns was a pianist. Debussy and Mendelssohn had private incomes, and were comparatively happy men.

There is another category, however. Rossini died rich; so did Verdi; Wagner made a great deal of money out of royalties during the later years of his life. During his earlier years he lived on borrowed money. Puccini died rich. So did Massenet. So, on a lesser scale, did Gluck and Händel.

What does this list show? First, it shows that there is money to be made out of opera. A successful opera composer, particularly during the last century, could become, at worst, comfortably well off, and at the best, wealthy, on his royalties from performances. The composers who have made fortunes out of music have all been composers of opera. In the field of symphonic and chamber music there is a very different story to tell. If a symphonic composer happens to have the luck—and the supplementary talent—to be an instrumental virtuoso, as well, he can make a living, and a good one. But playing an instrument is not composing music. Even one of these comparatively few lucky ones must devote many hours out of every day to the exhausting work of practicing and performances. (Incidentally—though it really doesn't bear on the subject—have you ever noticed that the great virtuoso composers have almost invariably been pianists or organists rather than players on stringed instruments? And I know of no composer who was also a great singer.)

If a composer doesn't happen to be an instrumentalist, what else can he do? For the most part, as the list shows, he teaches music, which is about as dreary a way for a composer to spend his life as any that I know. Teaching is not only a disgracefully underpaid profession; it is a calling in itself. If a man happens to have a gift for it, he can find it an enthralling and exciting profession. But it requires an eagerness to impart knowledge, an endless patience in the presence of stupidity, a willingness to traverse familiar ground day after day, year after year—characteristics that are not generally those of a composer. A few composers, d'Indy for instance, seem to have taken genuine pleasure in their teaching; for most composers, as we know from their own testimony, teaching has been drudgery. The Russians have been luckier, on the whole, in that their living was derived from professions that were miles away from music, so that, at least, they could go back to composing as a respite, a vacation from other work. The luckiest were Mendelssohn and Debussy. So was Grieg, who had a government pension, and so is Sibelius. The modern composer who comes nearest to making a living out of symphonic music is Richard Strauss; he receives very large performing fees. On the other hand, Strauss married into a wealthy family, and derives a considerable part of his income through his activities as a conductor. I can recall only two composers of symphonic music who made a fairly comfortable living by devoting the major part of their time to writing music: Bach and Haydn. For the rest, composition has been a matter of stealing a few hours out of every day, or out of every week, from a life devoted to some difficult and non-creative calling, in order to do the work that they were put here to do, and by which we know them.

Their brethren in the other arts fare less badly, I think. Of course a wholly idealistic painter or sculptor, particularly if he is doing something quite new, has a hard time while he is struggling for recognition. That is to be expected. In fact, one of the attributes of genius, to my mind, is the possession of sufficient strength of character to persist in spite of neglect. That is why they say that it's good for an artist to starve in a garret; it brings out his genius. If that were true, there are several thousand geniuses on relief in this country today! The point is, that if you can still insist on being an artist, even while you're starving, you probably have at least the urge of an artist in you. But when an artist has arrived, has finally been accepted by the public, if he is a painter or a sculptor, or a writer, his economic situation is almost invariably pretty comfortable. But as I said before, it is entirely possible for a composer to be world-famous during his lifetime, and still have to sublet the garret that the painter left when he got his first big commission. I know nothing, for example, concerning the financial affairs of Pablo Picasso; but I find it difficult to believe that Picasso has to worry much about money. I do know of a composer, whose name is as familiar in music as that of Picasso is in painting: Igor Stravinsky. If Stravinsky is not starving, it isn't because his compositions bring him a living. He has to make his living barnstorming around Europe and America as a guest conductor and pianist, when he ought to be at home writing music.

When the painters and sculptors lost their popes and bishops in the eighteenth century, the kings and dukes and counts came to their rescue with portrait commissions; and when royalty began to fade, in the nineteenth, the collectors took them over. But when the poor composers lost *their* royal patrons, the only collectors they ever met, or ever have met, were bill collectors.

15

Accessory Before the Fact

IF EVERY young architect could find a builder ready to turn his blueprints into bricks and mortar as fast as he drew them; if every budding playwright had a producer ready to put his plays on as soon as they were written; if every fledgling composer had a waiting impresario at his elbow—! It can happen. It *has* happened, at least once, in the field of music, and judging from the results one might wish that it would happen oftener. Consider the case of Stravinsky and Diaghileff.

When Igor Stravinsky was nine years old, his parents decided that he showed enough evidences of musical talent to make it worth while to give him piano lessons. Accordingly, they engaged a teacher, and he made fairly good progress, although the family and the teacher both complained that he wasted too much time in improvising instead of practising. There was no thought of making a musician out of him, his parents' sole idea being to give him a good academic education, so that he could get some sort of government position that would assure him a living. He matriculated, in law, at the University of St. Petersburg, and as a matter of fact went through and completed the course. While he was at the university, however, he became more and more drawn to music, studied theory, both with a teacher and by himself, and began to compose in earnest. One of his best friends was the son of the great Russian composer, Rimsky-Korsakoff; and one summer, during vacation time, he summoned up courage to go to see his classmate's father and ask his advice about becoming a composer. Rimsky neither encouraged nor *dis*couraged him. He advised him to keep on studying, but privately; not to enter the Conservatory, but to keep on at the University. A short time later, in 1903, he took Stravinsky on as his own personal pupil.

His educational methods, in regard to his twenty-one-year-old protégé, were hardly orthodox, for he taught him composition and orchestration simultaneously. Stravinsky in his autobiography says, "He would give me some pages of the piano score of the new opera he had just finished, which I was to orchestrate. When I had orchestrated a section, he would show me his own instrumentation of the same passage. I had to compare them, and then he would ask *me* to explain why *he* had done it differently. Whenever I was unable to do so, it was he who explained." Rimsky would also give him Beethoven sonatas and Schubert string quartets to orchestrate, and make him analyze the form and structure of the pieces as he went along. These lessons and discussions continued even after Stravinsky had graduated from the university, with a fine legal education of which he never made the slightest use. During this period he wrote a piece that was the first of his to have a public performance. It was a little suite for voice and orchestra, a setting of three poems by Pushkin, entitled *Faun and Shepherdess*. Rimsky-Korsakoff arranged to have them played and sung privately at a concert of the Imperial Court Orchestra, in the spring of 1907. They did well enough to be given a public performance at one of the famous Belaieff concerts the following season. This same year he sketched the first act of an opera, *The Nightingale;* more of that, later. His famous teacher died in 1908, just as Stravinsky finished his first important work, an orchestral fantasy called *Fireworks.*

Rimsky-Korsakoff never heard it. He did not live to know how completely his faith in his brilliant young pupil was justified. But while *Fireworks* marked the passing of one man who greatly influenced Stravinsky's career, it was the means of bringing another man into his life who influenced it even more profoundly. For it was through this piece that he met Sergei Diaghileff, and began an association that lasted until Diaghileff's death, twenty years later.

This extraordinary man, who was largely responsible for establishing the dramatic pantomime as an independent form of theatrical entertainment, commissioned, and was therefore the instigator, of most of the orchestral works that have made Stravinsky famous. He first came into prominence as the editor of a review called *Mir Isskustva* . . . "The World of Art" . . . which he directed from 1899 to 1905. He had a brief and stormy career in connection with the Russian Imperial Theatres, where his advanced views on ballet production won him widespread unpopularity and made his stay a short one. In 1905 he left Russia for Paris, where he organized an exhibition of Russian art that was a sensational success. In 1907 he turned his organizing genius into a new channel, and dazzled the Parisians with an equally successful series of historical concerts of Russian music. He followed this with a spectacular production of Mussorgsky's *Boris Godunoff* at the Paris Opéra, with the great Feodor Shalyapin in the title role. During the run of *Boris* he met the French impresario Gabriel Astruc, and the two conceived the idea of collecting a company of dancers from the Russian opera houses, bringing them to Paris, and presenting a series of original ballets as an entire evening's entertainment.

The first program of the Russian Ballet included *Le Pavillion d'Armide,* with music by Tcherepnin; a sort of tableau ballet, *Cleopatra,* featuring Ida Rubenstein, who couldn't dance but had a marvellous figure, with music taken from Arensky, Rimsky-Korsakoff, and Glazunoff; a short ballet called *Festival;* and a ballet based on music by Chopin, which they named *Les Sylphides.* The two didn't trust entirely to the ballets to hold their first audience, so played safe by adding an act of Borodine's *Prince Igor,* one act of Glinka's *Russlan and Ludmila,* and a tabloid version of *Ivan the Terrible,* featuring Shalyapin.

It so happened that Stravinsky's *Fireworks* had been played at one of the Siloti concerts in St. Petersburg during the winter of 1908. Diaghileff heard it, and was so struck by the brilliance and originality of the orchestration that he hunted up the young composer and commissioned him, not to write anything, but to orchestrate some of the Chopin music for *Les Sylphides.* It is hardly necessary to record, at this late date, the fact that the entire Russian Ballet venture, which opened at the Châtelet Theatre in Paris, in the spring of 1909, was a sensational success. Stravinsky, although his connection with the affair was a modest one, shared it. He was not there, however, to hear his orchestrations. He was in Russia, working on the score of his fantasty-opera, *The Nightingale.* He had begun it some time before, and was trying to finish it after numerous interruptions. But work on the opera was destined to have one more interruption that would delay its completion for several years. For just as he had finished the orchestration of the first act, a telegram arrived from Diaghileff. Would he write a ballet, based on the Russian legend of the Fire-Bird, for the spring season of 1910? Stravinsky, who was only twenty-seven, and still very much in doubt as to his ability to finish a work by a specified date, was terrified by the invitation, but also fascinated by the idea, and delighted at the chance to be associated with an organization and a producer for which he had great admiration. So he accepted.

He worked at the score all through the winter of 1909 and 1910, in close collaboration both with Diaghileff and his ballet master, Mikhail Fokine, who was to translate the story into terms of dancing. The ballet had its first performance at the Paris Opéra, on the twenty-fifth of June, 1910, and was received with delight. *The Firebird* was important, not only as a milestone in Stravinsky's career, but in Diaghileff's as well; for it was the first real Diaghileff ballet, the first of the many scores that were subsequently written to order, by Stravinsky and other composers, for the Diaghileff productions.

Excited by his success, Stravinsky immediately began planning another ballet, much more extended and ambitious in form than *The Firebird,* to be called *Le Sacre du Printemps* . . . "The Rites of Spring." He described it to Diaghileff, who at once commissioned it. As it happened, however, this was not the next work that he wrote for the Russian Ballet. Knowing that the score of *Le Sacre* would be a long and fatiguing job, he decided to tackle something comparatively easy first, and set to work on a short piano concerto, or rather, a sort of dialogue between the piano and orchestra. He visualized the piano as "a puppet, suddenly endowed with life, trying the patience of the orchestras with cascades of arpeggios." The piece done, he cast about for a name for the puppet-piano, and finally hit upon Petrushka, the unhappy Pierrot of Russian folklore. He moved on to Clarens, in Switzerland, where Diaghileff came to visit him, to find out how the work was progressing on *Le Sacre*. To the impresario's considerable astonishment, Stravinsky played him the new piano piece instead (it eventually became the second scene of the ballet).

"He was so much pleased with it," writes Stravinsky, "that he wouldn't leave it alone, and began persuading me to develop the theme of the puppet's sufferings and make them into a whole ballet. While he remained in Switzerland we worked out together the general lines of the subject and the plot, in accordance with the ideas I had suggested. We settled the scene of action: the fair, with its crowds, its booths, the little traditional theatre, the character of the magician, with all his tricks; and the coming to life of the dolls . . . Petrushka, his rival, and the dancer . . . and their love tragedy. I began at once to compose the first scene of the ballet."

Here we have a glimpse of Diaghileff, not only as the producer of one of Stravinsky's most important works, but as actually taking a part in its creation. Stravinsky, Diaghileff, the painter Benois, who was to do the scenery, and Fokine, who was to stage the action, worked together in close collaboration, and *Petrushka,* when it was finally produced in Paris, during the Russian Ballet season of

1911, became, almost overnight, one of the most famous works of its kind in the world. After the production Stravinsky returned to Russia, where he and Roerich worked out the action of *Le Sacre du Printemps* during the winter of 1911 and 1912.

The Rites of Spring had its first performance in the Théâtre des Champs-Élysées on the evening of the 28th of May, 1913. The choreography was the work of the famous Nijinsky, who, though he did not dance in the ballet himself, devised and directed the actions of the other dancers. The orchestra was conducted by Pierre Monteux. That performance was one of the famous disasters of musical history. The dress rehearsal, which was attended by a number of actors, painters, musicians, and writers, had gone off without any excitement, so that the Diaghileff company was totally unprepared for the behavior of the audience, which, puzzled by the action and outraged by the music, staged what can only be described as a riot. They carried on so that it is doubtful if anyone in the house actually heard the last pages of the score. One reason for the failure was probably the confused manner in which Nijinsky had staged it. He was a genius, but a genius in the sense that Schopenhauer defines one: "ninety-nine per cent will and one per cent intellect." He could do marvellous things, but he didn't know why he did them, nor could he teach others to do them. The action of *The Rites of Spring* was accordingly muddled and overcomplicated. In later years, the ballet was completely restaged by Leonid Massine, and has since been successful wherever it has been performed.

The spectacular failure of *Le Sacre* in no wise shook Diaghileff's faith in Stravinsky. On the contrary, that same year he produced his new opera, *Le Rossignol,* at the Paris Opéra. Seven years later he revived it, in a ballet version, in London. Diaghileff produced nearly all of Stravinsky's major works, sometimes commissioning them, sometimes not, but always performing them as fast as they were written. The year 1920 saw the song-ballet *Pulcinella;* 1922 saw another ballet, *Renard,* and an opera, *Mavra,* both produced at the Opéra in Paris. In '23 Diaghileff produced *Les Noces,* and in 1928, shortly before his death, he sang his swan song, as it were, with a production of his friend's latest ballet-pantomime, *Apollon Musagètes.*

It would be foolish, of course, to say that Stravinsky would not have written music if it had not been for Diaghileff. On the other hand, if it had not been for Diaghileff and the Russian Ballet, it is entirely probable that he would not have written the particular music that he did write, and would not have written his music in the form in which we know it. Stravinsky has given the world *L'Oiseau de Feu, Petrushka, Le Sacre,* and *Les Noces;* and the world is grateful. It owes a little gratitude likewise to Diaghileff, who asked for them.

16

The New Romantics

THERE was a showing of *avant-garde* films the other night, accompanied by *avant-garde* music. As a matter of fact, the films were secondary, for the idea of the occasion was to demonstrate what the modern composer could do in the way of writing music expressive of this, our mechanized civilization. What impressed me most about the performance was something that happened about halfway through the program. One of the films was under way, accompanied by its appropriate music, its title being, as I remember, *Mechanical Principles*. Pistons were plunging, valves were opening and shutting, gears were meshing, and cams were tipping things, and we were all watching and listening.

Suddenly the screen went blank; in place of the squirming gadgets was only a flickering rectangle of white light. The orchestra went its Casabiancan way for a minute or two, and then stopped, baffled. In the uneasy silence that followed, the conductor turned and addressed an unseen accomplice aloft.

"Can you rewind?" he wanted to know.

Apparently the invisible one could not rewind, at the moment. *Mechanical Principles* was temporarily expunged from the minutes, and did not reappear until later in the evening.

The significant part of the occurrence, to me at least,

was that such a thing should happen to a picturalization of the very thing that is supposed to dominate contemporary life. We have been assured—until one of us is slightly sick of hearing about it—that this is the age of the machine. Poets go on about steel girders standing stark against the sky, painters dash off still-life groups of cogwheels and eccentric rods and label them *Civilization*, sculptors do heroic groups of resident aliens socking ingots with sledge hammers, and composers write symphonies based on the noises made by an automobile assembly plant. All the artists are busy Facing Life, while the art critics egg them on to being true to the steely something-or-other of the times, and the philosophers point out that man, having created the machine, is rapidly becoming its serf and slave. Meanwhile, one sprocket of a motion-picture projector fails to catch the proper hole in a film, and the whole silly business comes to a dead stop, helpless.

Never before in the history of art has there been so much self-consciousness about the artist's job as there is today. He is constantly being exhorted to express the spirit of his own age. Nor need he bother to search his own soul in the effort to find out just what that spirit is, for his advisers are not only willing to define it for him, but decline to accept any definition but their own. This is the age of steel, they tell him, the hierarchy of the machine, and you go ahead and express it. Be ruthless and uncompromising; and if you're not, you are just a swooning romanticist, and *ipso facto* old hat.

So the poor devil does his best. The writer comes off fairly well, for his is the medium of ideas, and so, right or wrong, he can express them. But the non-intellectual arts, painting and music in particular, have a terrible time. The best their practitioners can think of is to do the opposite of what they have always done. Painting, which is naturally and obviously representational, has become the medium of abstract thought and emotion; while music, bless its heart, has gone in for imitating contours and masses and planes.

I wonder if there is any such thing as non-romantic art —music especially. The romanticist sees life rather as it might be, or ought to be, than as it is. But the artist who sees it as something other than what it is, or worse than what it is, is no realist, either. We think it rather soft and foolish, now, to invest trees and mountains and horses and dogs with human qualities, to people the forests with dryads and fauns, to make the gods like men—or even to mention them. To me it seems no less silly to swoon over a Ford or a locomotive or an automatic screw machine, to talk about the machine and its slave in terms of Simon Legree and Uncle Tom.

Man is still the master, albeit a damned poor one. Live in a country house for a winter if you want to know the truth about machinery. The day comes (generally a cold and snowy one) when, somewhere up the road, a pole blows down, and a steel and copper wire snaps. Where is your machine then? No heat, no cooking, no water, no light. And does the machine heal itself? Not at all. A gang of men with bad manners and spikes on their shoes sally forth into the cold, blaspheming the while, and right the pole and splice the wire. And all is—until the next time—well.

The machine is neither serf nor master. It is a contrivance whereby either we combine the unskilled labor of many men to produce quickly what a single skilled man once wrought slowly—the factory; or else a means for putting our care and welfare into the hands of servants whom we never see—what is known, roughly, as public service. I used to hire a carpenter to make me a door-frame. Now miners, truckmen, stokers, engineers, laborers, and trainmen, as well as carpenters, all collaborate, through machines, to make that frame and put it in my doorway. Without those men I would have no door-frame. The men who run the power-house, who watch the gauges and tend the generators and string the wires to light my house, are still my servants, just as much as if they picked berries, molded candles, and struck steel on flint.

Merely because it does the work of a man or an animal we must not think of a machine as if it *were* either of those. Forget to feed your horse, and he will still, somehow, draw your wagon. Forget to put gas in your tank, and your car is dead. It cannot move even itself, to say nothing of you. When we wail over being in the grip of the machine we are merely taking a romantic way of evading our own responsibilities. If the factory produces too much, and condemns its workers to industrial slavery, it is only because the factory's owner is unintelligent and greedy. If man falls into the whirling gears and is mangled to death, it is only because man is inattentive and stupid.

Fundamentally, the machine age is one in which we have substituted mechanical servants, that have no life or will or intelligence whatsoever, for servants who formerly possessed a modicum of all those qualities. If any will-power is to be exerted, we must exert it; if any initiative is to be taken, we must take it; if there is any thinking to be done, we must do it—and do it all. If mankind is ever really overwhelmed by the machine, it will not be the machine's fault; it will be only because man is clever enough to invent what he is not intelligent enough to use.

17

Sole Survivor

H. W. FOWLER, author of *A Dictionary of Modern English Usage* (a grand book to have handy in case you are ever inclined to think that you know anything about your mother tongue) is very severe about the use of the phrase "the irony of fate." So far as I can make out (and he wouldn't think much of that phrase, either), there are only about three ways of using it correctly, and two of those are wrong. Even Fowler, I believe, would concede that there was irony lurking somewhere behind the fact that of all the compositions by the inventor and most famous living exponent of atonality and dissonant harmony, the only one to attain the slightest measure of popular favor is a piece that he wrote long years ago, when a major seventh was a dissonance, and atonality was not even a word.

Arnold Schönberg wrote his fourth opus, *Verklärte Nacht* (as a string sextet; later as a piece for string orchestra), in 1899. Even then, its idiom was not novel. Richard Strauss might have written it in the eighties; Richard Wagner might have written—did write, in fact—some of it. It is a deeply felt, thoroughly romantic piece of program music, and there is not a bar in it that would injure the sensibilities of a septuagenarian.

Since those days, of course, Schönberg has become the Lenin of the musical revolution, standing all our accepted notions of dissonance, assonance, form, and melody, upon their astounded heads, and rallying about him a group of disciples who regard a tonic triad very much as a Soviet commissar regards a cathedral. He has written the *Fünf Orchesterstücke*, *Die glückliche Hand*, the *Pierrot Lunaire*, and other public scandals.

Yet it is fair to say that his revolutionary works are, in general, performed only by organizations devoted to giving a hearing upon special, more or less clinical, occasions; that not even his most fanatical champion would claim for them any particularly heaping measure of popular affection. *Verklärte Nacht*, alone, still holds the stage.

Hearing it at a symphony concert, I could not help wondering whether, if it had not happened to be the work of its particular composer, it would have so long survived. It is a worthy work, pleasant, and even, in spots, impressive to hear; but it is not the work of a genius, or even of a first-rank talent. The man who wrote it, had he continued as he began, would have been ranked, I should say, about with Max Reger—a little higher, perhaps, but not much. Certainly never in the same class with Strauss.

Perhaps it survives, not alone on its own merits, but because it allows the average man to say that he has heard a piece by Schönberg—and liked it.

18

Roumanian Proteus

NOT long ago, at a public luncheon, I was sitting at a table that included the musical director of a motion-picture company, a radio commentator on music, a music critic, a member of the board of directors of a great orchestra, and a famous flautist. By a quaint coincidence we were discussing music and musicians. In the course of the discussion, the motion-picture director said, "Of all the composers now living, who, in your opinion, will be remembered, a hundred years from now, as the greatest of our time?" We all had our own opinions, with which nobody else, of course, agreed. Finally the flautist said, "If you'll broaden that definition, and make it the greatest all-round *musician* of our time, I can tell you who the man will be. It will be Georges Enesco."

And that, I find, is the opinion of a great many of Enesco's colleagues. He is what you could call a musician's musician. He is looked upon as eminent in at least three, and possibly four fields of music. Composers regard him with respect and admiration as a composer. Professional violinists flock to his recitals whenever he plays in public. Conductors speak of him as a master of their craft; and pianists tell me that if he would take the time and trouble, he could take his place in the front rank of contemporary pianists.

He comes from a country that, except through him, has

contributed little to the annals of music—Roumania. He was born on a farm near the town of Corderemi, in that country, in August, 1881. He revealed his talent for music very early, for when he was only seven years old his father considered him far enough advanced to send him to Vienna, to enter the conservatory there. The director, Joseph Hellmesberger, was inclined to be a bit skeptical, for when this Roumanian infant appeared before him he remarked that the conservatory was not a nursery. But when he had talked to the child, and heard him play, he not only admitted Master Enesco to the school, but took him to live at his own house.

Enesco himself says that his association with Hellmesberger was the most valuable that he could possibly have had. The director was the third of a line of famous Austrian musicians of that name. His grandfather had known Beethoven, and had played in the orchestra under him. His father, in turn, knew all the great composers of his day. The third of the Hellmesbergers had accordingly inherited, so to speak, a first-hand knowledge of the interpretation of the works of Beethoven, Schumann, Schubert and Brahms, as those composers had played and directed them. All his knowledge was available to young Enesco, who, in addition to laying the foundation of his career as a conductor, was studying harmony and counterpoint, violin, cello, piano, organ, and composition. What he did with his evenings, he doesn't say—or, rather, he does. In the evenings he was allowed to sit in the Hellmesberger living-room while his teacher's friends gave impromptu private recitals of chamber music. It was at one of these evenings that Brahms dropped in to hear a tryout of his new Clarinet Quintet.

By the time he was eleven, young Enesco had taken first prize, among all the students, in harmony and violin playing. About this time, too, he had a job as violinist in one of the Vienna symphony orchestras. In his spare time he used to attend choral concerts. He didn't sing—I can't imagine why not—but he was allowed to sit among the singers and study the scores while they were being sung.

This went on for three years. Then, at the ripe age of fourteen, he left Vienna for Paris, where he studied theory and composition at the Conservatoire under Jules Massenet and Gabriel Fauré. Here again, in 1897, when he was sixteen, he took prizes in counterpoint and fugue, and when he was sixteen, won the first prize for violin playing. In 1898, when he was seventeen, he had made his first public appearance as a creative artist, when Edouard Colonne conducted his Opus 1, a *Roumanian Poem*, at a concert in the Châtelet Theatre. From that time on he rapidly established himself as a composer, virtuoso, and conductor. His compositions began to be widely played, and the ruler of his native country, Queen Carmen Sylva, recognized his eminence as a concert artist by appointing him her court violinist.

He lived in Paris until the outbreak of the war, when he returned to Roumania. During the post-war years he became prodigiously active in promoting the cause of music in his native country. He has conducted numberless concerts, both at home and abroad, has taken a leading part in organizing concerts of modern music in Roumania, and has done much to promote the compositions of his younger fellow countrymen. His first visit to this country was made during the season of 1922–23, when he appeared both as a violinist, and, in January, 1923, as guest conductor of the Philadelphia Orchestra in Carnegie Hall in New York.

Despite his active career on the concert stage he has found time to compose a great deal of music. His more important works include two violin sonatas, a piano sonata, several works for chamber orchestra, two orchestral suites, three symphonies, and an opera. Curiously, in spite of the tremendous respect and admiration that all musicians feel for his achievements, his name is not as familiar to the general public as one might expect. This is probably due to the fact that he is one of the most modest and self-effacing musicians alive, a man who is simply incapable of any action that might be interpreted as self-advertising. For example, when he visited New York during the season of 1936–37 to conduct the Philharmonic-Symphony Orchestra, he was billed as "guest conductor-composer." Thus described, almost anyone might be expected to program a considerable amount of his own music. Not Enesco. During the eight concerts assigned to him he conducted just three of his own works. There is no more versatile musician in the world—and none better liked.

19

The Boosters

ARNOLD BENNETT once wrote, charmingly and at length, of the Passionate Few who, from generation to generation, keep alive the masterpieces of literature. The mob, he said, would never get excited about Shakespeare and Homer and Milton if its interest were not kept alive by the enthusiasms of the few. It is their approval, and theirs alone, that is immortality.

I wonder if the same has been true of the masterpieces of music, and if so, how many the few must be in order to keep a composer's memory green. More, I imagine, than for a literary artist. A book, to live, need only stand on a shelf, to be taken down, say, once a decade. Music, to live, must be performed; and when it is music written on an ambitious scale, performance means considerable time, considerable concerted effort, and considerable expense.

I wonder, specifically, whether the admirers of Gustav Mahler and Anton Bruckner are sufficiently numerous to keep those composers before us as living figures, part of our musical lives, rather than names in the reference book. Mahler, who was being vigorously championed a few years ago, is, for the moment, seldom heard. It has been Bruckner's turn, of late.

How numerous Bruckner's admirers are, I do not know. Even if few, they are certainly passionate. There is a Bruckner Society, with members all over the world, devoted to the task of making his music known and heard. It publishes—or did until recently—a magazine, *Chord and Discord,* devoted to championing the cause of its favorite composer, with a favorable glance out of the corner of its eye at the works of Mahler.

Regarding the propriety of any sort of propaganda, provided it be open, there ought to be no question. Any group of people who are convinced of the rightness of their cause have a perfect right to advance that cause, if possible, by every argument and evidence that they see fit to present. The propagandist runs risks, however, the greatest of which is the result of his frequent failure to memorize and comprehend a statement first made by the well-known Sir Isaac Newton, to the effect that "action and reaction are equal and opposite." That is one of the first laws of physics, and it holds good in the realm of psychology as well. A champion of any cause is, necessarily, an enthusiast, and the more enthusiastic he is, the more difficult is it for him to avoid being annoyed with people who do not agree with him.

He ought to avoid it—or at least conceal his annoyance—as much as possible. For, a propagandist is, in the last analysis, a salesman; and only a poor salesman would spend much time in abusing his prospects for not fancying his wares.

One gathers, from a perusal of *Chord and Discord,* that the Bruckner Society holds the critics largely responsible for the slow advance made by Bruckner and Mahler in this country. I venture to disagree with this opinion, flattering though it is. At the risk of making a damaging admission, I must protest that critics have nothing like the power of life and death over composers and playwrights that they are supposed to have. In the long run, it is the public that renders the verdict. If the critics happen to have agreed with the public, they frequently get the credit for the decision; if they don't, their opinions are forgotten.

Even granted that it is the critics who have kept Bruckner and Mahler out of their kingdom, surely it is a mistake for the Bruckner Society to be so unkind about it. Powerful fellows like us should be flattered, not abused. No good can come from writing, as does a contributor to *Chord and Discord,* "When, on rare occasions, one of his symphonies is performed in England or America, the papers in these countries rehash all the old stupid phrases which were hurled at him by the Viennese papers during his lifetime." We are not only less powerful than *Chord and Discord* considers us; we are likewise less studious.

If present-day critics hurl phrases, even stupid ones, at Bruckner, I am positive that they made the phrases up out of their own heads. The number of American critics who pore over the files of the Viennese papers, looking for derogatory phrases concerning Anton Bruckner, is so small as to be negligible. Perhaps the critics just don't happen to like Bruckner.

Besides, if today's objections to Bruckner are so like those of yesterday that the similarity is noteworthy, that very fact may be significant. Certainly the critics nowadays are not rehashing the phrases hurled at Wagner during *his* lifetime; and if they are not, it was not the Wagner societies that converted them. It was Wagner's music.

Composers are neglected for three reasons: because they have gone temporarily out of style; because their music is inaccessible; or because they are not good enough. The last seems, unhappily, to be the case with Bruckner. He is a reversed Mahler. In the latter's music one senses a great musical intellect crippled by a defective talent. Bruckner has the talent, but not the mind to control it. There are moments, in a work such as his F minor Mass especially, where he is touched with greatness. A theme in the orchestra, a phrase of the chorus, will suddenly emerge, almost startling in its poignancy and eloquence. At last! This is the real thing. Where will it go? Whither will it mount? What will it unfold? You wait for him to speak.

But he has spoken. The moment was all he had. The theme, that started in such brave beauty, drops out of sight, smothered beneath a mass of platitudes; or, worse, it continues, wearisomely repeating itself, reluctant to stop and unable to go on, until its meaning is gone, worn away by too much handling. Just once in the Mass, in the lovely cello interlude between the Sanctus and the Benedictus, does Bruckner really seize one of his themes and handle it like a master; and in that passage you realize what his music might have been if he had been an artist as well as a talent.

It is a pity that he and Mahler could not have been merged into one. He could have given Mahler the pregnant musical ideas that Mahler so much needed, and Mahler could have developed the ideas as they deserved to be developed. Of the two, Bruckner is the sadder figure. Mahler's tragedy was personal; with all his eloquence, he could not think of what to say. Bruckner had much to say, but mumbled it hastily and indistinctly, so that we lost something that we should have been the richer for having heard.

Composer Versus Time

When I was in high school I remember being much impressed to learn that Thomas Gray worked on his *Elegy Written in a Country Churchyard*—how many years was it?—Seven?—Thirteen? I seem to have forgotten. At any rate, it was a long time, sufficient to leave me with a firm subconscious conviction that creating a notable work of art is a slow business. Most of us assume, I think, that the amount of time an artist has spent on a given piece of work has direct relation to its value. Unfortunately for the infinite-capacity-for-taking-pains theory, this is by no means invariably true. Whistler could turn out one of his nocturnes in a day, achieving a result that a lesser painter could not have equalled in a year. Arthur Honegger, the Franco-Swiss composer, owes his reputation as an important contemporary composer to a work that took less than four months to write—his oratorio, *King David.* Six months before it was first performed, Honegger had not the faintest notion that he was going to write it. The story of how he came to do so is not unamusing.

In Mézières, a town not far from Lausanne, in Switzerland, there was a sort of experimental stock company known as the Jorat Art Theatre. It was started in an abandoned car barn by two brothers named Morax, and later, when it became prosperous, moved into an old wooden concert hall. It was very much like one of our own community playhouses, in that its actors, and its musical and mechanical departments, were largely amateurs.

One of the founders of the theatre, René Morax, was a dramatic poet; and some time in 1920 he wrote a biblical drama on the life of King David, which he was planning to produce at his own playhouse and for which he intended to employ considerable incidental music. As he wanted the play to go on in the early summer of 1921, whatever music it needed would have to be written in a hurry. He tried an eminent French composer first; then one a little less distinguished, then another a bit less distinguished than that. None of them would undertake the work on account of the extremely short time allowance.

At last, having exhausted most of his list of candidates, Morax struck bottom. He approached Arthur Honegger. The young Swiss at the time had achieved a certain amount of—well, not so much fame as notoriety—through his activities as one of the *Groupe des Six*. This was a sort of club of young musicians who had banded together with the idea of giving concerts and getting publicity for their own work and that of their fellow members. The other members of the group were Georges Auric, Louis Durey, Darius Milhaud, Francis Poulenc, and one woman, the composer-pianist, Germaine Taillefèrre. Among them they created quite a commotion in Paris musical circles; but although they did attract a measure of rather horrified attention from the conservative musicians, their names did not loom very large on the general musical horizon.

Honegger was, therefore, rather a forlorn hope for Morax. The young composer accepted the commission at once, and started to work late in February, 1921. On April 28 following, nine weeks later, he finished the score. The play and the music went into rehearsal at once, and on June 11, 1921, three months and seventeen days from the time the score was begun, *King David* had its first performance in the rickety Théâtre du Jorat in Mézières, Switzerland. It was a great success from the beginning, and the music attracted so much attention that Honegger conceived the idea of grouping the musical numbers into the form of an oratorio—or, as he prefers to call it, "A Symphonic Psalm," and turning the dialogue of the original play into a spoken narrative to be delivered between the numbers.

He did this, incidentally revising the original orchestration. For the Mézières production he had been allowed only fifteen players, including a piano and a harmonium. The revised version calls for a symphony orchestra. In its oratorio form, *King David* was performed first in Paris, at the church of St. Germain-en-Laye, during the summer of 1923. Its popularity, however, soon took it out of the confines of church performances; it has been done in concert halls and theatres throughout Europe and America. Its first performance here was one given by the Friends of Music in the Town Hall in New York, on October 26, 1925.

Despite Honegger's new term for his work, "Symphonic Psalm," *King David* is essentially a dramatic oratorio, somewhat on the style of Mendelssohn's *Elijah*. It is not, however, a sacred oratorio, strictly speaking, for although the story is a Biblical one, the text does not all come from the Bible. The presence of the Narrator is not quite so much of an innovation as it appears to be. Narrators were used in oratorios and cantatas as far back as the seventeenth century. I do think, however, that the Narrator adds greatly to the dramatic interest of this work, for what Honegger has done is to throw away the old-fashioned recitative passages, whose chief function was to carry the story along, and which, even in the greatest oratorios, have no tremendous musical value, and put them into the mouth of a single speaker, who is thus able to communicate the narrative much more clearly and rapidly than a singer could.

King David opens with a short orchestral introduction, after which the Narrator begins the story. He is followed by a contralto solo, "The Song of the Shepherd David," the text of which is a free rendering of the Twenty-third Psalm. The musical numbers, incidentally, are generally distinguished for their admirable brevity. "The Song of the Shepherd" is only twenty-eight bars long, and most of the other numbers are not much longer. After the song the Narrator is heard again, followed by another Psalm, this time sung by a unison chorus. A brief fanfare introduces a four-bar phrase that depicts the entrance of Goliath. The Narrator then recounts the battle between David and Goliath, the chorus sings a short paean of victory, and the orchestra plays a triumphal march. Two more psalms follow, interspersed with remarks by the Narrator, a male chorus sings the Song of the Prophets . . . "Man that is born of woman . . . ," concluding with yet another of the Psalms, sung by the tenor soloist. In almost all instances the Narrator speaks between the numbers. A descriptive passage for the orchestra shows us the camp of King Saul, and the chorus sings another Psalm, after which the Witch of Endor, speaking against the orchestra, invokes the spirit of Samuel. This is followed by another orchestral interlude, "The March of the Philistines," after which the first section ends with a Lament by the women's chorus.

The second section, which follows after a momentary pause, contains only two numbers: a three-act chorus, "The Song of the Daughters of Israel," and after it, the most extended number in the score, in which the chorus, soloists and orchestra celebrate the "Dance of Triumph Before the Ark of the Covenant." In the third section the Narrator, the orchestra, the chorus, and the soloists tell of David's love for Bathsheba, his repentance, his triumph over his enemies, and the coronation of King Solomon. The work closes with a choral lament for the death of King David.

In Paris, in 1926, not long after the first American performance of *King David,* a friend of mine, an American newspaper man, told me of an interview he had just had with Honegger. After talking about this and that, the American said: "Now in planning this work, did you have any novel style or form in mind? Just how did you conceive the general plan of the score?"

"No," said Honegger, "I didn't. I had only a little over two months in which to write the thing, and I had no time for theories. I did start out with the idea of writing the music in the general style of Bach. Well, after working about ten days at that, I realized that if I wrote the whole work in Bach's elaborate contrapuntal style I'd never get through in nine weeks. Counterpoint takes too long to work out. So then I decided to continue in the style of Stravinsky. Well, after about ten days at that, I realized that I'd never be through in time if I went in for Stravinsky's complicated harmonic progressions. Too many notes to write."

"How did you write the rest?" said the American.

"Oh," said Honegger, "I just fell back on Massenet."

Two Arts Don't Beat as One

ONE way in which music differs sharply from painting, it seems to me, lies in the amount of literalness the two arts are allowed to exercise. Painting is allowed to copy life exactly. Music is not. Representation, in fact, strikes me as being an inherent quality in painting. Not that literal reproduction is the quality that necessarily makes a picture good. A painter attempting to express a locomotive in terms of his art, as Honegger in *Pacific 231* attempts to express one in terms of his, need not—indeed must not—faithfully delineate every bolt and plate. But in so far as he does draw a locomotive he must draw well to be entirely convincing. A good many modernist painters obviously do not agree with this opinion, judging from their determined attempt to divorce painting entirely from representation.

I must confess that nonrepresentational painting worries me. When I see a picture labeled *Skyscrapers,* in which a group of unfortunate flesh-colored office buildings, apparently constructed of taffy, have melted and run against a batik sky, I am so distressed by the reflection that real skyscrapers if erected in such complete defiance of engineering principles wouldn't stand up five minutes that I derive no comfort at all from the artist's assurance that what I am seeing is simply his soul impression of skyscrapers. In fact, I am not interested in the workings of his soul any more than I am in his digestion. I want his painting of skyscrapers to be so devised that it will affect my own soul as the skyscrapers affected his; and unless it is sufficiently suggestive of actual skyscrapers to allow me to forget his drawing and get down to his message, I get no message. I would rather look at Radio City and make up my own message. Complete literalness, no. The difference between an architect's elevation and a painter's conception is largely that the painter is shrewd enough to omit everything except what he wants me to see. But deliberate distortion of outline does not seem to be quite the same thing as the elimination of details.

The case seems to be the opposite with music. There, as soon as the artist represents too faithfully, he becomes irritating. If Honegger's *Pacific 231* were merely an excellent imitation of the noises of a locomotive it would be a great deal less interesting than a real one. What gives his piece real musical value is the fact that he translates his locomotive sounds into terms of music. The noise of the exhaust, as he translates it, is not really like its alleged original; it is double basses playing actual notes in a fixed rhythm accompanied by a roll on the tam-tam. The psychological effect is the same as that produced by a locomotive getting up steam, but the means are entirely different. When his music reaches its climax it contains nothing that remotely resembles the actual roar of a locomotive at high speed, but it is thrilling in exactly the same way.

The episode of the sheep in Strauss's *Don Quixote* is exact representation in terms of painting; in other words, Strauss contrives to make the low reeds, muted brass and strings give an astoundingly life-like imitation of the bleating of sheep. It is startling and amusing at first, but after a few hearings one begins to resent it, because it is not music. An inspired reproduction of an ocular impression, such as one of Frans Hals's portraits, releases the imagination; but a reproduction of an aural impression such as Strauss's sheep music, no matter how inspired, is merely ingenious, and limits the imagination by its very exactness. The best musicians do not think quite in terms of paint, and I have an idea that the best painters do not think quite in terms of notes.

22

Master

It is one of the unhappy paradoxes of music criticism that the very persons and ensembles to whose performances the professional listener looks forward with the greatest pleasure are those about whom it is most difficult to write. There is always something to say about a young artist or a young organization; one can compare this year's achievements with last year's, record improvement and growth, beam approvingly over signs of a deeper artistry, wag one's venerable locks reproachfully at symptoms of bad habits and mannerisms.

A really bad performance, a totally incompetent performer, is, of course, such a glorious stimulant to the critical vocabulary that one's only difficulty is to refrain from bringing up the heavy artillery where a feather duster would have done as well.

But the matured artist, the performer of wholly adult stature, the one of whom we ask only that he remain upon the summit to which he has climbed—what to say of him that has not been said a hundred times before? Fritz Kreisler, for instance. I came away from his latest recital with no particular desire to say or write anything about it whatsoever. Why should I? I had had an evening of music—great music, some of it, and all of it worth hearing—presented by a virtuoso whose artistry is so nearly flawless that it is like a pane of clear glass through which one looks upon beauty. It was an evening of rare, quiet pleasure; something to remember, but nothing to write to the papers about.

Kreisler does not, somehow, invite criticism. Not that he is beyond it—no man is. An industrious analyst, whose interest in violin-playing somewhat transcended his interest in music, could, I fancy, discuss any Kreisler recital at voluminous length. I cannot. I don't know enough about violin-playing in the first place, and I don't care enough in the second. To me, violin-playing is much like cabinet-making: a highly skilled profession, demanding exceptional gifts of its practitioners and interesting to observe, but whose results, nevertheless, are more important than its processes. During the Victorian era, some of the finest cabinet-making the world has ever known produced some of the most hideous furniture upon which the eye of man has ever gazed. And I have heard superlative violin-playing whose net result was analogously abhorrent.

Somehow I never associate Kreisler with fiddle-playing. He seems to me to be one of a handful of interpretive artists whose art transcends its medium. The people who were crowded into Carnegie Hall the other evening—and they filled the stage as well as the auditorium—did not seem to be there primarily to hear violin-playing. They were there to hear music. Kreisler would be the same, his approach to his auditors and the music would be the same, his effect upon his hearers would be the same, if he were a singer, a pianist, or a cellist. In any case, the instrument upon which he played would be incidental to what he played, and how he played.

"Mr. Kreisler played in his usual manner." Which

is the poor phrase that must try to convey the selflessness and simplicity of his manner, the warmth and vitality of his playing, the technical command so complete that it is taken for granted, his mastery of style and phrasing, and above all, his magnificent grasp of form, a musical vision of such breadth that he sees every bar, not only by itself—in the flat, as it were—but in perspective, in its relation to all that has gone before and is to come after.

That is the mark of the master, in all arts, creative and interpretative—that sense of perspective and climax, the ability to conceive a work of art as an object in space, to grasp the thing as an entirety in the process of developing the details. It is the point—and the single point, I think—at which the interpreter becomes a creator. The great actor, and the great musician, sees beyond the lines, beyond the notes, grasps—literally—the big idea, and holds to it, relates to it everything that he says or sings or plays.

Kreisler is at his finest, emerges at his full stature, in unaccompanied passages, in the Bach Saraband and Gigue that he played the other night, or the cadenza of the Mozart G major Concerto. Unaccompanied violin music can be, and usually is, unbearably dull. For in such music everything is up to the player's sense of line and structure. The harmony is necessarily meagre, there is no orchestra to lend deceptive color to his tone or cover up his slips in intonation, no helpful piano to accentuate the rhythm that he may not feel. He must wrestle with his musical angel alone and in the open.

For Kreisler the victory is complete. Without accompaniment, the eloquence of his tone and the subtlety of its coloring, the flexibility and clarity of his rhythms, are more than ever apparent. He spins his single thread of tone, and suddenly you are aware that he is weaving, as well; that what you have heard, and shall hear, is all of a piece, has form and direction. It is more than a purposeless outpouring of beautiful sounds; it is a living, moving organism, with a definite contour and a definite span of life. When it has died away, something has been said that a lesser man, playing the same music, could not have uttered.

None of this applies to the recital I heard any more than to any other. It was a Kreisler recital, and there is little more to be said about it. If it were the first time I had ever heard Fritz Kreisler, I might have written at length in superlatives. There is much to say, after one's first meeting with a great person. After the tenth, or twentieth, one is less communicative. One comes away from a Kreisler recital as one who returns from a visit to a beloved and trusted friend, saying simply, "He is still there."

23

Murder

SPEAKING of great men—and whoever discusses music is bound to do so—it is disturbing to notice that no new musical names of any considerable importance seem to be appearing on the horizon, that among us there seem to be no comparatively young composers to whom we can look to be the Beethovens and Wagners and Debussys of tomorrow. I believe that, on the whole, it is safe to say that this is true. Naturally no one can say with complete authority why this is so, but I have a theory about it, at least. Suppose we discuss it for a moment.

Most men of genius, in music, show unmistakable signs of their powers in their late thirties and early forties. The promise of their younger years begins to be fulfilled. At forty, Brahms, Wagner, Bach, Händel, Beethoven, and a host of others were pretty generally admitted to be great men. Schubert and Mozart never reached that age, but they flowered early. Conversely, if a composer has shown no evidences of being a genius by the time he's forty, he is not likely to turn into one after that age.

I have gone through my biographical dictionaries, and programs, and who's whos, and whatnot, and have collected a list of forty-four living European composers who may be called distinguished. Note that I say *living*

European composers. I'm omitting the Americans for a reason that will be obvious later. Also, note that I say "distinguished." They are not all geniuses, but every one of them has written at least one work that has raised him above the level of mediocrity. The list may lack one or two names, but I think it fairly represents what Europe possesses today in the way of outstanding musical talent.

I shan't burden you with the entire list; but here are the names of some of the best known, together with their ages in the year 1937. Suppose we start with Russia. Shostakóvich is thirty-one years old; Mossoloff is thirty-seven; Prokofieff is forty-six; Stravinsky is fifty-five; Miaskovsky is fifty-six, and Rachmaninoff is sixty-four. There are four other Russians on my list, their ages being sixty-three, seventy-one, seventy-three, and seventy-eight.

Now Germany: Erich Korngold, the youngest, is forty; Schönberg is sixty-three; Hans Pfitzner is sixty-eight; and Richard Strauss is seventy-three. Two others are forty-two and sixty-six respectively.

France: Among the distinguished composers in France are Darius Milhaud and Arthur Honegger, each of whom is forty-five years old. Ravel is sixty-two, Florent Schmitt is sixty-seven, and Gustave Charpentier is seventy-seven. Three others are thirty-eight, fifty-six, and eighty.

Now Great Britain: The youngest distinguished British composer is Eugene Goossens, who is forty-four. Arnold Bax is fifty-four, Percy Grainger, who was British-born, is fifty-five, and Vaughan Williams is sixty-five. Two others are fifty-four and forty-eight respectively.

In Italy we have Alfredo Casella, who is fifty-four; Malipiero, who is fifty-five; Pizzetti, fifty-seven; Montemezzi, sixty-two, and Mascagni, who is seventy-four. Two others are fifty-five and fifty-seven years old.

From Hungary come Kodaly, who is fifty-five years old, and Dohnanyi, who is sixty. Roumania gives us Enesco, who is fifty-six. From Czechoslovakia comes Weinberger, who is forty-one; from Spain comes De Falla, who is sixty-one; and from Finland, Sibelius, who is seventy-two.

Just what does this list tell us? It tells us, for one thing, that among Europe's forty-four most distinguished living composers, just seven are under forty-five years of age. Of these seven, only three are under forty. Of the entire number, only ten are under *fifty* years of age. The burden of creative music in Europe today is being largely carried by men between the ages of fifty and eighty years.

What does this mean? You may say it is natural that the most famous musicians should be the men of more advanced years. Quite true. But discounting that fact, doesn't it seem peculiar that the following seven men should be the *only* distinguished composers in Europe who are under forty-five years of age? Their names are Shostakóvich, Mossoloff, Korngold, Hindemith, Poulenc, Goossens, and Weinberger. Highly talented as these men are, I doubt whether contemporary opinion anywhere would rank them with Brahms or Strauss. Why aren't there *fifty* distinguished composers under forty-five years of age in Europe?

Suppose we figure back. A musically talented boy who was eighteen years old in the year 1914 would normally have been in a conservatory of music. Today, at the age of forty-one, he would just be emerging into his most fruitful period of creative activity. But those boys weren't in the conservatory in 1914. They were in the army. They were at the front, facing death. And most of them died. And the stronger, the healthier, the more alert and intelligent they were, the more certain they were of being taken into the army, and the surer they were of being killed. Not many eighteen-year-olds lived through those four years.

Laurence Stallings published a terrifying book of war photographs a year or so ago, called *The First World War*. But to me, the most sickening war pictures ever printed used to appear in the pages of the *Illustrated London News* and *The Sketch* and *The Graphic*, between 1914 and 1918. They were the portraits of young English officers who had been killed in action . . . page after page, week after week, year after year, of those slaughtered boys of eighteen and twenty. They were officers, of course. The dead private soldiers outnumbered them ten to one. England lost 900,000 men in the war; France, Germany, and Italy lost over 1,000,000 apiece; Russia lost nearly 2,000,000. Killed. Not casualties.

Now do you think you know what became of a whole generation of potential composers, painters, poets, novelists, playwrights, architects, sculptors? Europe murdered them . . . a whole generation of them. Travel through the battlefields of Europe. Visit the cemeteries and cenotaphs of England, France, Italy, Roumania, Germany, Poland, Austria, Russia. Somewhere among those rows and heaps of skeletons you will find what is left of those who should have been the geniuses of today. If great men are to walk the earth again, we shall have to look for them, largely, I think, among a generation that is not yet ready, a generation that was too young to kill and be killed, twenty-three years ago. And if the world keeps its feet upon the road that it seems to be walking, it may well be that even that generation will be murdered, too; that we shall have to give up hoping for great art and great artists until the race of man has grown intelligent enough to avoid this bloody, profitless, imbecile business that he calls war.

PART THREE

Tomorrow

I

What's Wrong with Opera?

AMONG the more elderly of our more respectable jokes is one whose wording may vary, but whose accompanying picture never does. The latter always shows an opera box, in the front of which sit two or three ladies examining their neighbors severely through opera glasses. In the rear sit two or or three gentlemen in a state of collapse, one at least being sound asleep. The text, as I say, may vary in form, but in substance it conveys the general idea that women go to the opera to see other women and be seen by them, that men go because they are dragged there, and that the parties of the first and second parts haven't the foggiest notion of what it is all about.

To any dispassionate observer of the operatic situation in this country, there seems to be no particular reason for disputing the soundness of that joke. During the past ten years the general public has made it disconcertingly clear that it considers opera a highly dispensable luxury. One by one the few permanent opera companies that we could boast were disbanded. The Metropolitan Opera Company, in New York, remains, and the Chicago Civic Opera has been revived; but they are our only *permanent* producing opera companies. If they, and a few of the "short-season" companies, were to go, it would be quite conceivable that there would not be a performance of grand opera to be heard in America.

Naturally, I, for one, would regard such a thing as a national calamity. I have been going to opera since I was fifteen years old, I have heard nearly all the great singers of the past thirty years, and virtually every work in the active repertoire—that means between seventy-five and a hundred—and I should like to go on hearing them. Besides, I have written three operas of my own, and hope to write more, and could hardly be expected to view with pleasure, exactly, the prospect of having nowhere to get them produced. On the other hand, I shall have to admit that grand opera means very little in the life of the average American; much less than the symphony orchestra and infinitely less than the theatre and the movies.

Our attitude, or lack of it, in this respect is curious when it is contrasted with Europe's attitude. The average Frenchman, Italian, German, or Austrian not only goes to the opera regularly but is even willing to have part of his taxes go toward its support. And Europeans, I might add, are no more anxious than we are to be taxed for the support of things that they don't want. We have taken over, and supported, and made our own, every other form of art that the Old World has sent us. Above all, I should say, are we a good audience for music and the theatre, in whatever form. Yet the one form that is a combination of these two—the opera—is the very one in which we take the least interest. A few of us support it, for various reasons—usually the wrong ones—at great expense, and the man in the street, who is the majority of us, simply ignores it.

Why isn't he interested? There are two reasons that people usually give, and neither makes sense. Some say that opera is over our heads—which is to say that a public that listens to *Hamlet* and Brahms's Second Symphony is unable to grasp the profundities of *Lucia di Lammermoor.* Well, then, they say, opera is unworthy of our serious attention—meaning, presumably, that a public that can understand *Three Men on a Horse* could hardly be expected to condescend to *Carmen* and *Don Giovanni* and *Götterdämmerung.*

You may argue that the *Three Men on a Horse* public and the *Carmen* public are not made up of the same people. In this country they are not, although I believe that they ought to be and might be. Certainly they are in Europe. Has it never struck you as worthy of note that Tony, your barber, who knows and likes all the latest jazz, also knows several opera scores almost by heart? The backers of opera in this country have always been obsessed by the knowledge that opera in Europe is backed by wealth and aristocracy, and have ignored the fact that it is also attended by the proletariat. They have not, apparently, realized that the gallery of the Paris Opéra was full, even on nights when the imperial box was empty, and have, accordingly, built opera houses in which all the emphasis is on the boxes and the boxholders, with the common, run-of-the-mine public more or less of an afterthought.

We have imported opera much as we import caviar and Scotch grouse—as something rare, exotic, and expensive. The fact that it has been a wholly alien product has only added to its fascination, and the fact that it has not been to the taste of the average man has given us a feeling of exclusiveness and superior culture. All of which is fair enough, so long as our wealthy and superior backers of opera are willing to foot the bills. But they are no longer willing, or able, to foot them. The comparatively small group of Americans who used to meet opera's annual deficits now find it far too expensive an amusement to maintain. If opera is to survive, it must go to the great public for support. It must find a large popular audience; and, generally speaking, there is no popular audience. Why not?

In order to find out why not, suppose we invite an average, intelligent American business man to attend a performance of grand opera. He likes to go to the theatre, and his taste in plays is neither provincial nor puritanical. He is rather fond of music too; listens to symphony concerts over the radio, and has occasionally been hauled by his wife to performances by the local symphony orchestra. He has never before seen an opera, however, and we shall assume that he knows nothing of its origins and history, and has only a vague idea of what he is going to hear and what he is supposed to get out of it. His state of mind as he settles into his seat can be described as a mixture of pleasurable curiosity and apprehension.

The curtain rises on a performance of *Rigoletto*. The opening chorus is all that he had hoped for—gay, lively music, with certainly nothing complicated or abstruse about it. He can't make out the words, but that would be too much to expect of any opening chorus. Then two men enter. One of them is the leading tenor, as our disciple discovers from the outburst of applause that greets his appearance. The other is a tenor, too, but not so good. The two hold a brief conversation in song, not one word of which the American understands. He is a little disappointed when he realizes that they are singing Italian, for we had forgotten to tell him that the performance was to be given in a foreign language. However, a soprano enters, rather young and good-looking, and the tenor sings her a pretty song. Matters might be worse. The music is certainly tuneful and well sung, and perhaps our American can get a general idea of the story by watching the actors.

But the plot is a trifle puzzling. A hunchback enters —a baritone, and, judging by the applause, another big shot—to whom the other members of the cast seem to have taken a dislike. An old man is dragged in, singing bass, and makes a long and indignant speech to the leading tenor, who seems annoyed. The hunchback refuses to take the old man seriously, whereupon the old man turns and gives him a piece of his mind, ending with what looks like a good old-fashioned curse. This frightens the wits out of the hunchback, who cowers in terror as the old man is led away by the gendarmes.

During the intermission, our American has plenty to think about. The leading tenor, he decides, is somebody important—a king, probably—and not far wrong, at that; he was a king, until the censor made Verdi change him into a duke. The hunchback must be his court jester, and the old man is presumably a political prisoner, though why he should be so sore at the hunchback remains a mystery. Ah, well. Things will probably clear up in the next scene.

But they don't clear up. The scene shows a garden on one side and a street on the other, with a wall running down the center of the stage. The hunchback enters and sings a solo. Then a basso appears and sings another solo, the only distinguishable word of which is something that sounds like "sparra—foo—cheel, sparra—foo—cheel" over and over. Then the basso leaves, and the hunchback, after another solo, unlocks a gate in the wall —he might have saved time by stepping over it—and enters the garden, whereupon a beautiful girl appears —at least she is dressed in white and wears a blond wig—and throws herself into his arms. They have quite a chat. An older woman appears and joins in, after which the hunchback and the girl sing a duet.

By this time, the unfortunate American is hopelessly befuddled. Abandoning all hope of disentangling the plot, he decides to concentrate upon the beautiful voices and the orchestra. But a whole evening of unrelieved, meaningless singing and playing is too much. It is a rare power of concentration that can stand the strain of a vocal concert lasting nearly three hours. About half-way through the third act, our American, having received a vicious jab in the side from a scowling neighbor, comes to with a start, to realize that he has been fast asleep, and probably snoring.

Americans are a hardy race, and so, little daunted, our hero tries again another night. This time, the opera being *Die Walküre,* he takes precautions. His knowledge of German, picked up during the war, is confined largely to *"Kamerad," "wie viel,"* and *"danke schön,"* which, he dimly suspects, will not get him very far with Wagner. So he buys an English translation of the libretto, which he studies earnestly, reading and rereading it until he feels that he has a firm grip on the plot.

So he goes to *Die Walküre*. The introduction to the first act is exciting, and the first scene, with the exhausted fugitive staggering into the hut to take refuge from the storm, he finds doubly impressive because he knows what it is about. But as the action progresses, he finds himself more and more out of touch with what is going on upon the stage. These people stand about, without moving, for hours. Just talking. And he keeps getting ahead of them. He is sitting up, waiting for Siegmund to pull the sword out of the tree, just as that hero is warming up to an account of his life's history for Hunding's benefit. The orchestra is magnificent, and the voices are fine; but there are no set musical numbers, and as he remembers only the general idea of each scene, and has no idea what the actors are saying, he finds it hard to keep his attention from wandering.

During the intermission he overhears an enthusiastic lady telling another, "I love to just sit and close my eyes and listen to the voices and the orchestra." So he tries that, with the result that, not being a student of music, but only an average theatre-goer, he ignominiously falls asleep, just as he did at *Rigoletto*. Some time later he awakes with a start, to find Brünnhilde standing exactly where she was when his nap began. This is the end. He is a brave man, but he knows when he is licked. Declaring that opera is too highbrow for him, he goes back to his theatre and talkies, leaving Art to shift for herself.

There is just one important reason why the American opera audience is so small. It is the fact that opera, as produced in this country, is sung in virtually every language except that of the inhabitants of this country.

There is one other country in which this is done—England. And England and America are the two highly civilized countries in the world where opera has never taken root. A hundred and fifty years ago, the question of language was not so acute. Opera then was the only spectacular, and almost the only musical entertainment to which the public had access. There were no elaborately staged musical shows; no spectacular motion pictures; no public song recitals or symphony concerts. To the average man, opera was a little bit of all these. But the picture has changed. So far as concerns spectacle, ballet, orchestral music, even singing, opera finds itself today outstripped by its newer competitors. It must hold its place as a musical form of dramatic entertainment—the *dramma per musica* of its Renaissance inventors—if it is to survive at all.

Europe has, of course, long recognized this fact. Mention the famous air, "*La fleur que tu m'avais jetée,*" to a German, and he will not know what you are talking about. But if you call it "*Hier, an dem Herzen treu geborgen,*" he knows at once that you are referring to the "Flower Song" from *Carmen*. He has never heard Bizet's masterpiece sung in any language but his own. Standing outside the Paris Opéra Comique one day, I saw posters announcing a forthcoming performance of what I assumed to be a new opera—*Paillasse*. Not until, reading further, I came to the cast of characters and saw the familiar Nedda, Canio, Tonio, Silvio, did I realize that it was only our old friend, *Pagliacci,* which, as this was a French opera house, was being sung in French. My friend Edward Johnson, general director of the Metropolitan Opera Association, knows the roles of Tristan,

Parsifal, and Lohengrin in Italian, because he has sung them in Italy. He does not know them in the original German, because he has never sung in Germany, and he does not know them in English, because he was never asked to sing them in English.

To realize why opera has never really taken root here, why its audience is one-twentieth of what it should be, and why so few American composers have written grand operas, try to imagine the state of the American theatre today if it had faced the conditions under which its sister art has had to struggle. Suppose that, fifty years ago, a group of public-spirited New Yorkers had built a magnificent theatre and installed therein a company of first-rank actors, prepared to give the finest plays written. For fifty years, then, this company has been presenting the works of Molière, Racine, Rostand, Hauptmann, Sudermann, Schiller, Goldoni, Ibsen, Shakespeare, and other playwrights. None of these plays, however, has been done in English. The French plays have been played in French, the German ones in German, Ibsen in Norwegian, Dostoyevsky and Tchekoff in French or Italian—never English—translations. The company, which at first was entirely European, is now about one-third American. Most of these American actors have received their training in Europe, and know their roles only in foreign tongues; for even Shakespeare, in this imaginary theatre, is played in Italian.

Under such conditions, just how large a theatrical audience would the United States have developed? What would the average citizen make of a performance of *Faust* in German, or *The Cherry Orchard* in Italian? How many theatres would have sprung up in response to popular demand, how many American playwrights would we have developed, how many American actors would be playing today? How large a following do you suppose Walter Hampden would have built up for his *Cyrano* if he had played it in French? How big a hit would *Liliom* and *The Swan* have been if they had been offered in the original Hungarian? What would Katharine Cornell's position be today if she had received all her training abroad and played only in German and Italian?

This comparison is not, of course, wholly fair. There is no music to fill in the gaps of a spoken play. In opera, on the other hand, there is undeniably much pleasure to be had from listening to the music, even if the action is unintelligible. But the fact remains that however great that pleasure may be for the listener who is unusually sensitive to music, it is not enough to attract and hold the listener who is not definitely musical. If you don't believe me, look at the state of opera in this country today.

Most of the greatest composers of opera—Gluck, Weber, Wagner, Verdi, Strauss, and Puccini, for instance—have been as much concerned with the dramatic qualities of their librettos as with the aesthetic qualities of their music. Music is only half the opera. If it is all, as some people insist, why scenery and costumes? Why the pretense of a story? Why expect any acting of the singers? Why not save time and expense, hire a concert hall, play and sing the music without words, and let it go at that?

Opera is theatre. And the essence of the theatre is that the spectator sees a story unfolded in his presence, is in on the ground floor, so to speak, when things happen. And it is one of the paradoxes of the drama that the words are essential, and yet not important. They are not important in that, as you watch a play, you are conscious not so much of the individual words of a scene as of the ideas of which those words are an expression. They are essential in that, if the lines are incomprehensible, you have no chance to get at the ideas.

But in opera, they tell me, this problem can be solved by studying the libretto beforehand, so as to familiarize oneself with the story. In the first place, that's a bore. When I go to a play, I don't have to bone up on it beforehand, as if I were getting ready for a mid-term examination. Why must I do research work in order to understand an opera? In the second place, no amount of homework can take the place of understanding every line as it is delivered. Unless I go to the trouble—which nobody would—of actually memorizing the entire libretto, both in the original language and in English, I bring to the performance only a general idea of the purport of each scene. When the curtain goes up on the first act of *La Bohème* I remember that the studio is cold, and that Rudolph and his companions finally decide to burn his play in order to keep warm. So I sit, firmly clutching that idea, while four singers get through ten minutes of chatter that is only incidentally interesting from a musical point of view, but which I would probably find amusing if I knew what they were talking about.

Tony, your barber, understands the words of the operas that he attends in your country's greatest opera house. When he goes to *Pagliacci* and hears *"Vesti la giubba,"* he not only listens to a tenor singing a famous aria but he follows a dramatic situation, hears an actor playing a touching scene. No wonder he is several times as enthusiastic about opera as you are. If the Metropolitan, most of whose repertoire is sung in either Italian or German, managed to pay its way for more than a score of years, that phenomenon may not be unconnected with the fact that New York's Italian-speaking population outnumbers that of Milan, while her German-speaking residents would populate Leipzig.

The Metropolitan is still probably the greatest single opera house in the world, giving every year performances of about fifty different Italian, French, and German operas that average better than similar performances in Italy, France, and Germany. A few years ago I traveled four thousand miles to hear, among other things, some festival performances of opera in Salzburg and Munich; and Salzburg's *Der Rosenkavalier* was just about as good as the Metropolitan's, while Munich's *Die Meistersinger* was not only just about up to the Metropolitan's average but presented singers whom I had already heard at the Metropolitan. New York's famous opera house is an international museum of opera, just as New York's other Metropolitan is an international museum of painting and sculpture. At the Metropolitan—the opera house, that is—you can hear all of Europe's great operas, produced in a manner that frequently surpasses the European standard, with most of Europe's great singers.

Nevertheless, unless opera can be sold to America, unless it can find a new, large, popular audience, it may shortly pass out of existence. That audience must be trained, since it does not now exist; and the only way to train it is to make it take opera and like it. And the only way to do that is to produce opera, somewhere, strictly for an American audience, and wholly from the American point of view.

Somebody—perhaps it was Plato (quotations are not my strong point)—said that "to know what to ask is to know half the answer." Which encourages me to the belief that I know fifty per cent of the solution of this opera problem. At least I know what I should like to see, without regard to whether it is possible or could ever be made so. I should like to see some American opera companies, run by Americans—schools of opera appreciation, so to speak, to which the Metropolitan would be a post-graduate course. What would they be like, and how would they differ from what now exists?

First of all, such a company would be housed in a modern theatre. By "modern," I mean designed for a contemporary audience of citizens of a republic, rather than for an imaginary audience of kings, nobles, and rabble. Our existing opera houses, even the newest of them, pay more or less respectful tribute to the famous houses of Europe; and the more famous a European house is, the less likely is it to have anything that we need. Covent Garden, in London, dates from the fifties; the Paris Opéra was begun in 1861; and La Scala, in Milan, goes back to the seventies—1778, to be exact.

Suppose we admit that these houses have served their purpose, and forget them, putting our hypothetical opera company in a theatre equipped with a revolving stage, projection booths before and behind the curtain, plenty of storage space, plenty of rehearsal rooms, the last word in lighting systems, and so on. The auditorium will be shallow, to bring everyone as close as possible to the stage, will seat not more than three thousand people—the Festival Opera House at Bayreuth seats only twenty-four hundred—and the best places in the house will not be given over to the boxes—or rather they will be; for I would put the boxes downstairs in the rear of the house, where the occupants can see and hear perfectly without being seen.

The general manager of such a company would be a theatrical producer of culture and taste. He would be interested in opera, and know something about it, and interested in music, although his most important qualification would be his showmanship. Two years before his house opened he would carefully go through the hundred-odd operas that compose the existing repertoire, picking out, not those that he thought he ought to produce, or those that impresarios always produce, or those that the music critics would like to see produced, but those that he believed would have some dramatic and musical interest for an average better-class American theatre audience.

This would give him a working repertoire of about thirty-five operas. One or two of your especial favorites would undoubtedly be omitted, but be patient; remember, this is a popular opera house. Having selected his repertoire, he would proceed to have it translated into English. And here I must digress to explain what I mean by "English."

Mention opera in English to the average opera-goer, and he thinks you mean the curious doggerel into which librettos are generally translated for English-speaking readers and auditors. It has its merits, but it is hardly a language in which I should ever care to hear an opera sung. It is the result, partly of the practice among foreign publishers of paying as high as one hundred dollars for an "English" translation, and partly of their habit, when commissioning a translator, of hiring someone who knows the language of the original, but does not know any English. He may know it in the sense that he speaks it, but he cannot write it clearly, beautifully, or always intelligibly. Judging from the way he fits the words to the notes, he knows nothing whatsoever about music.

What I mean by a translation of a libretto is an English version written by someone who is a master of the English language, who is sensitive to music and knows a little about it, and who is able to reconcile the rhythms and accents of music to those of English poetry—an English version, in short, that has the same literary and poetic distinction as the original, and fits the music just as well. Most people would say that such a thing is impossible, and most people would be wrong. It has never been tried. To my knowledge, no first-rank American writer of English has ever been asked to prepare a singing translation of a foreign-language libretto—chiefly, I suppose, because he would be expensive. He would probably have to be paid as much as the prima donna gets for three or four performances of the opera. Offhand, I can think of half a dozen Americans who could do the job to perfection—Brian Hooker, Maxwell Anderson, Stephen Benét, Archibald MacLeish, John Erskine, and Edna St. Vincent Millay.

While his English librettos were being prepared, our producer could be recruiting his company and his chorus. It would obviously be impossible to develop a group of American singers into such a company of international stars as the Metropolitan can offer, inside of a year; but one could make a creditable start. It is not a question of voice. We have produced many magnificent voices in this country, and could produce many more if there were any demand for them. But voice is no longer enough for an opera singer. He must be an actor, and a good one, and, for an American audience, he ought to be able to look something like the character he is impersonating. Perhaps the best way to train our opera company of beginners would be to select candidates with good voices, interesting personalities, and a knowledge of singing style —they could be found—and then make them do what Lawrence Tibbett did—put in a hard course of training in theatrical stock companies. Six months would be enough to weed out those who were hopeless as actors, and another six months would develop the survivors into good raw material for the stage director.

I envy the stage director. He could work, for once, free from the dead hand of operatic tradition. To understand how tradition works, and why it is necessary, bear in mind that every opera company in the world is a repertoire company, presenting anything between fifteen and fifty operas in a given season. Naturally, with such a large number of works to perform, no company has any great amount of rehearsal time to give to anything but new productions. In consequence, and also because singers travel from one company to another, the stage business, the properties, and the plan of the scenery for any opera tend to become standardized.

When an opera is first produced, the positions of the singers on the stage, even their important gestures, are carefully worked out and rehearsed. If it survives, and is produced in another opera house, these positions and gestures are more or less faithfully copied. So with its third production, and its fourth, and so on. In time, after ten years or so, it may be receiving simultaneous performances in a score of opera houses, scattered throughout the Western world, all substantially alike.

The practice has obvious advantages. When the manager of an opera company decides to produce some hitherto unperformed opera, half his singers have probably sung it elsewhere, and are thoroughly familiar with the staging. His scene designer, having the original plans before him, is saved the trouble of having to work out fresh solutions of construction problems. Singers become easily interchangeable—like automobile parts. The Metropolitan, let us say, engages a tenor by cable from Buenos Aires. Two weeks later he arrives in New York. It would be quite possible for him to dock at five in the afternoon, go direct to the opera house, dress, and step upon the stage at eight o'clock for the evening's performance of *La Bohème,* without ever having seen another member of the company, knowing exactly what they are going to do and where they will be upon the stage at any given moment.

But, inevitably, a traditional performance tends to become stereotyped and mechanical. Some perfectly accidental and meaningless gesture, some mannerism of the singer who first performs a role, may be solemnly perpetuated through two or three generations, with never a question as to its suitability or significance.

They tell a story of a young tenor who was studying the title role of Verdi's *Otello*. At a certain moment in one scene, the coach informed him, while the chorus was singing and he was not, he must turn, go upstage, mingle with the crowd, and then come back in time to sing his concluding measures. Dramatically speaking, there was no sense to this procedure, and the tenor objected. But the coach was adamant. "That is the tradition of the part," was his only explanation.

"But why?" the tenor persisted.

The coach didn't know and didn't care.

"Who created this role?"

"Tamagno."

The name of the world-famous tenor was enough to crush any beginner's objections, but still the young singer was not satisfied. A year later, when he was in Italy, he hunted up Tamagno and asked for an interview.

"Maestro," he began deferentially, "I have come to ask you about a certain piece of business in *Otello*"—and proceeded to outline the troublesome scene.

The old man looked puzzled. "Did I do that?"

He thought hard for a moment, then took down a copy of the vocal score and studied it. Suddenly his face brightened.

"I have it!" he cried triumphantly. "It is very simple. You will notice that in the final passage Otello has to sing a high B flat. So, while the chorus is singing, I go upstage to spit!"

If this were all that tradition did to opera, we might make the best of it. But it does worse, in that it tends to keep methods of acting and stage handling completely static. Generally speaking, the opera lags, mechanically and histrionically, half a century or more behind the spoken theatre. Rossini's *The Barber of Seville* was first produced in 1816. I would lay odds of 8 to 5 that if a member of the original first-night audience could be resuscitated and taken to a performance of *The Barber* in almost any opera house in the world today, he would notice nothing new or strange about it. *Rigoletto* is performed today with much the same kind of acting and *mise en scène,* and about the same scenery, that it received at its world *première* in 1851. When Wagner's *Ring* cycle was first performed complete, at Bayreuth in 1876, it represented the last word in modern scene designing, acting, lighting, and stage direction. The lighting has been a little modernized since then, but any attempt to bring the acting, or even the scenery, a little more abreast of contemporary stage ideas, is greeted with roars of disapproval of such violation of the sacred traditions established by the master. Yet do you suppose that Wagner, who was nothing if not a progressive, would stage the *Ring* today exactly as he did over sixty years ago?

I still remember the historic night at the Metropolitan when Maria Jeritza dared to sing *"Vissi d'arte"* lying on her stomach. We critics wrote reams about this epoch-making event in operatic history. Yet, in the modern dress version of *Hamlet,* I once saw Basil Sydney deliver all of Hamlet's soliloquy lying flat on his stomach, and the critics didn't even bother to mention it. In the contemporary theatre it is taken for granted that actors and directors will try to find new ways to do old things. In the opera, what was good enough for our great-grandfathers is good enough for us.

Our imaginary opera company being, as I say, a local affair, and being composed of singers who need not fit into European productions that have remained unchanged since the sixties, would be free to put on its repertory according to the best standards of American scene designing, stage direction, and acting, and without regard to any tradition that could not pass an intelligence test. Bosom-heaving would, I imagine, be reduced to a minimum, and arm-waving would be largely confined to the traffic cops outside the opera house.

It would be an interesting opening night. The performance would be pretty crude in spots, I imagine. The singers would hardly be in the same class with the great singing actors of operatic history. At least, though, the audience would be able to understand two-thirds of what they were saying; which is two-thirds more than the average American audience now understands. Think of being able to follow the action of an opera as if it were a play, with the added emotional excitement of the music! The orchestra would be first-class, and the conductor as well. The latter would be, if a good one were available, an American; otherwise, not—the occasion being a theatrical and not a patriotic one. The lights and the sets and the stage direction would be, as they generally are in the American theatre, unconventional and interesting. Despite the company's lack of experience, there would be something about the whole performance—something new and electric and dramatic—that would hold its hearers spellbound.

They would come again, I think. Not to perform a duty, or absorb culture, or be seen by somebody socially eligible, but to spend an evening in the theatre—the theatre that is music. I think they would come often enough, and in sufficient numbers, to make the company able to pay its way; and, in other cities, other companies. People would get to know the operas, not merely as concerts but as dramas; and some they would reject, and some they would take to their hearts. When they came to New York they would drop in at the Metropolitan as a matter of course, exactly as they would drop in at any other great theatre. America would have, in short, an operatic audience; one that was on an equal footing, in its interest and understanding, with French, German, Italian, and other audiences, including the Scandinavian.

2

Der Doppelgänger

One of the crying needs of this generation is a school for teaching opera singers how to play upon dummy orchestral instruments. Never yet, for instance, have I seen a tenor who achieved the faintest illusion with his harp-playing in the Venusberg and song-tournament scenes in *Tannhäuser.* At the last performance I saw, the hero did manage to strike the first chord of his hymn to Venus in perfect unison with the real harp in the orchestra; but thereafter, apparently demoralized by success, he achieved unanimity only by coincidence. Moreover, his technique was deplorable. No matter what the real harp was playing—solid chords, after-beats, or arpeggios—he stuck to a relentless, clocklike stroking motion that might have served to soothe an Airedale but would never have extracted much co-operation from a harp. The young woman who played the role of the shepherd boy in the second scene was just as much out of practice in her playing of the English horn. Her solo had been going on in the orchestra some little time before, with a start of surprise, she began to perform, and she blew several effective measures after her orchestral double had ceased to function. She, too, employed a peculiar technique which consisted in fingering all the low notes near the mouthpiece and all the high ones up by the bell. It does seem as though it would not be beyond the capabilities of the human intellect for an opera singer to learn the outlines at least of the accompaniment to his solo. The intellectual strain might be severe, but the resultant gain in illusion might almost be worth it.

3

Polyandry on Parnassus

ALONG with our increased interest, as a people, in symphonic music, has come an increasing tendency to extend the seasons of our symphony orchestras. The city that, ten years ago, could support a season of thirty symphony concerts, now supports fifty, sixty, or seventy. This is all to the good for music, but it puts an ever-growing strain on the strength and nervous systems of our symphony conductors, so that most of them now take midseason vacations in order to keep from becoming nervous wrecks.

In order to provide the scheduled number of concerts, our orchestras began the practice of importing guest conductors. This seemed a good idea at the outset, for it not only gave the regular conductor a breathing spell, but gave the audience a chance to meet a new musical personality. Unfortunately, the guest-conductor idea has proved so popular that the regular conductor is frequently so only on the prospectus of the orchestra; it is by no means unusual for an American orchestra to have three, four, or five guest-conductors in a single season.

It ought to be obvious why this system is bad for our orchestras, but to a great many people, apparently, it is not. "After all," they say, "an orchestra's an orchestra. Why shouldn't it play under a dozen different conductors if the subscribers want them?" The reason why not is simple enough. Teamwork is the secret of a great orchestra precisely as it is the secret of a great football team. If the world's greatest aggregation of football stars, instead of being drilled by a single coach, had to go through its season under six successive head coaches, each with a different system of plays, nobody would expect it to reveal any very brilliant football, except by accident. Similarly, the board of directors of any symphony orchestra are not living in the world of reality if they expect their orchestra to approach greatness under a procession of guest conductors.

Just what are the qualities that make an orchestra deserving of the adjective "great"? Technical proficiency is, of course, the fundamental one, in the sense that without expert musicians in its ranks no ensemble can play really greatly. But let us assume that. On the technical side most of our orchestras can hold up their heads in any company. What are the other essentials? At least five, I should say: (1) beauty of orchestral (as opposed to individual) tone; (2) transparency; (3) precision of attack and release; (4) balance; (5) flexibility. There may be others, but these will serve for the present inquiry.

If every conductor of an orchestra had an unlimited number of rehearsals at his disposal he might, by dint of ceaseless practice over a short period of time, be able to make his men play a given program perfectly even though he was a comparative stranger to them. But no conductor gets unlimited rehearsals with a modern orchestra. Under the union rules the players must be paid a certain minimum fee for every morning or afternoon rehearsal and their regular concert fee for evening rehearsals, with an extra charge for every minute over two hours and a half. A single rehearsal, therefore, of a huge organization such as the New York Philharmonic-Symphony cuts a substantial slice out of a thousand-dollar bank note. Economic factors, accordingly, tend to cut the number and duration of rehearsals to a minimum. Four rehearsals for one program are an exceptional allowance. Three, or even two, is the usual figure. Under such conditions a part-time conductor must concentrate all his energies upon the interpretation of the works he is performing, and is forced to take the actual qualities of the playing almost for granted. Yet these qualities, to be developed properly, demand the closest possible understanding between conductor and orchestra.

Let us consider the first of these enumerated: beauty of tone. Now this is a matter of skill plus confidence. A horn player who has a difficult and important solo passage will probably play it beautifully if he has faith in his conductor and knows that the conductor has faith in him. But suppose he is playing that same passage under a conductor whom he does not know well. Did the conductor indicate that entrance at rehearsal or was he to find it for himself? Did he wait on this note or hurry over it? When the conductor made a brushing motion with his left hand just what did he mean? These and a thousand other questions run through the unfortunate soloist's mind. He nervously awaits the cue, hesitates a fraction of a second too long, and comes in late. This makes him more nervous than ever. He gets out of breath, begins to phrase badly, plays flat, and finishes by "blowing a bubble" on a high note.

This is an extreme example, perhaps, but it can happen and has happened. And what is true of one player is true of the whole orchestra. If they know their conductor and trust him; if long association with him has taught them the meaning of his every lift of eyebrow and finger; if they are familiar with his reading; if, in short, they not only are freed of any fear that he will spring something unexpected on them, but know almost without prompting exactly what he wants of them at any given moment—then, naturally, their response to his directions becomes almost automatic, and their consciousness is free to concentrate upon tonal and technical refinement.

Transparency is a quality that should, perhaps, be included in tonal beauty. It is the quality that particularly characterizes a good string quartet—the purity of the sound produced by four solo instruments, the almost visible movement of the four voices. This perfection of intonation and timbre—the brasses and woodwind sounding almost as one instrument, the five string choirs playing like five soloists—is the ultimate refinement of orchestral playing, and is the result only of years of common experience. The late W. J. Henderson, speaking once of the Boston Orchestra under Wilhelm Gericke, said: "Why, he had that orchestra to such a point that you could see through it!" No part-time conductor can hope to produce such results. For remember: if three violins out of the eighteen firsts fail to remember to begin an accelerando at precisely the right point; if one of the four horns is a fraction of a second late with an attack, you will not hear the offenders clearly enough to know what is the matter, but the tone of the orchestra will no longer be transparent. There will be just the faintest blurring, just enough of a veil over the sound to keep it from being absolutely pure.

Precision and balance are likewise qualities that it takes time to obtain. If a conductor have an exceptionally clear beat he may be able to get the attacks and releases sharp and clean in a comparatively short time; but though he may obtain perfect instrumental balance upon occasion, he can never be sure of it until he and the men understand one another completely. He may train them ever so patiently, may show them over and over again exactly what degree of loudness or softness he wants in any particular passage; but he will never be able to count upon perfect results in performance until his directions have penetrated the subconsciousness of his players. And that process may take years. If, when the "Banner" theme of the *Meistersinger* overture enters, the third and fourth horns play the forte the slightest degree louder than they should; or if, in the opening of the last movement of Brahms's Fourth Symphony, the trumpets enter just a bit too strongly, the woodwind instruments, which in these particular passages outline the melody, will be drowned out, and the effect will be spoiled. You cannot blame the individual player for forgetting just how loudly he is expected to play every note. He is playing "blind." He has only his own part before him and hears little of the music beyond what is being played by the instruments nearest him. If you do not tell him what to do he will never be able to tell by listening what he ought to do. And if, as is frequently the case, he is faced by several conductors in one season, each with a slightly different notion of how a given set of notes should be played, you can hardly blame him for forgetting occasionally and playing the notes in Mr. A's way during a performance conducted by Mr. C.

Flexibility and alertness, the ability to rise to emergencies—these are qualities that no orchestra possesses to any degree unless it has had one conductor whom it understands perfectly. I remember once hearing the Chicago Orchestra play Liszt's *Les Préludes* under Frederick Stock. The piece came at the end of a program which, thanks to the soloist's far too numerous encores, was becoming unduly long. It was quarter to eleven and the audience was getting restless. "We'll have to make a cut," said Mr. Stock. "Let's see; where can we do it? . . . Ah! here's a spot. Eighty bars." So out he went, and just before raising the baton he leaned over the desk and said in a stage whisper, "Gentlemen, cut from letter G to five bars after L"—or whatever it was. *Les Préludes* began, the cut was negotiated without a moment's hesitation and all ended triumphantly without the audience's having the slightest suspicion that the piece was several minutes shorter than it should have been. Several years ago at an upstate music festival I saw the same conductor successfully make his orchestra skip five bars in order to catch up with a singer who had come in too soon. Neither of these feats sounds difficult for any intelligent group of instrumentalists, and neither is, perhaps. The trick is to get ninety men to do what you want at the same moment. Stock could accomplish the feat because his men, through long association, knew that a certain gesture meant, "Watch me closely," and when he said, "Cut from G to L," he meant just that. If a stranger had said that, one-third of the players would have done it, perhaps. Another third would have thought he said,

"E to L," and another would have thought he said, "Repeat." As for skipping five bars, if an orchestra saw a strange conductor suddenly beat five four-four bars as fast as his hand could move—as Stock did—it would merely assume that he had suddenly gone insane.

"He knows what he wants." That is the highest compliment an orchestra player can pay a conductor, and it is a significant remark. For in it is implied, also, "We know what he wants." Not two conductors have the same gestures, or attach the same meaning to those they have in common, or mean precisely the same thing by the words "forte," "allegro," "largo," and the like. When a conductor has a chance to work with his men season after season, he arrives at a completeness of understanding with them that saves time and energy and leaves both free to polish details instead of delaying over first principles. I have seen Leopold Stokowski rehearse the Philadelphia Orchestra in the Beethoven Fifth Symphony in less than twenty minutes, after a season's silence, and subsequently give a gorgeous performance of the work. He could do this because the men knew his readings and he knew their playing. He could afford to trust them to play the easy passages perfectly, saving his and their energy by rehearsing only the difficult spots. A part-time conductor cannot afford to trust his orchestra for anything. He must take it wearily over ground that has been covered a thousand times, losing precious minutes and sometimes hours merely in trying to explain what he means by what he says. Then just as the orchestra has begun to work comfortably with him Mr. B arrives with a new set of interpretations and a brand-new vocabulary and everything must be unlearned—at three hundred dollars an hour.

4

The Living Instrument

Most of us rather take an orchestra for granted. When it plays well, we praise the genius of the conductor. "Mr. A," the critics remark, "gave a performance of *Le Sacre du Printemps* that was a marvel of technical brilliance and temperamental fire." When it plays badly, we either commiserate with the conductor for having to deal with such intractable material, or curse him for his sloppy technique, as if he were a pianist out of practice.

Now it is undoubtedly true that a fine conductor can make an orchestra play better than a poor one can. On the other hand, as any conductor—or football coach—can tell you, the human material of which an organization is composed has a good deal to do with whether it functions well or ill.

When Mr. A gives that brilliant performance of *Le Sacre* we are prone to forget that some of that brilliance was due to the fact that sitting before him were ninety or a hundred men who possessed the technical skill necessary to play the hideously difficult notes of Stravinsky's score. An orchestra is not an organ, and it doesn't play itself, and the conductor doesn't play it. If he wants to take a certain passage two metronome numbers faster than any other conductor ever ventured to take it, he must find an instrumentalist who can play it that fast;

if he desires to evoke certain beauties of tone and nuance, he is likely to discover that the production of a lovely sound involves not only somebody to ask for it, but somebody who can give it.

The strings get a certain meed of credit. Most of us know a violin from a cello, and if we don't actually play, ourselves, we probably have a friend who scrapes a bit, or we have heard Kreisler and Zimbalist and Salmond, and know what's what.

But, barring saxophones (and would God one could), who plays wind instruments, or knows anyone who does? Yet the average first-class wind player is not only a technician whose relative skill is that of a good concert pianist, but an all-around musician whose acquaintance with the history and aesthetics of his profession would put most singers to what is frequently known as the blush.

He has to be an all-around musician, and a strictly trained one. A singer, or an instrumental soloist can, at a pinch, find his place in an ensemble by ear; either he is playing or singing the tune, or can take his cue from someone else who is playing it. But as I said before the orchestra player cannot guess. Before him, on his desk, is a sheet of paper containing one part: his own. The notes he must play may be buried somewhere in the middle of a harmonic mass so complicated that his ear is of no avail at all. If he has seventeen bars rest, followed by a sixteenth-note entrance after a rest of a dotted eighth, he has got to be able to count seventeen bars and come in on that note at the proper time. And coming in on the note, and playing it, means that he must be a sight-reader of superlative skill. For the concert that takes two hours to play he may get six hours rehearsal; more than likely, he gets three. In any case, the time is spent on practicing interpretation, not notes. His ability to play virtually anything at sight is taken for granted.

If he is a brass player, half of his time is spent in playing notes that aren't there. For he is playing all sorts of imaginary instruments that existed when the older scores were written, and whose parts still remain unchanged—trumpets in E and F, trumpets in D flat, horns in low C and high C and E and B flat alto. These parts must all be transposed at sight, so as to sound right on the modern instrument he happens to be playing.

Lastly, if he is to have any fun in life, he must be a paradox—a musician without vanity. For he must be ready to put in years of practice, to become a master of his instrument, and have his most brilliant performances taken for granted by ninety per cent of the people who hear him. Once in a great while he does get a break, of course. The evening comes when he plays the horn solo in the Tchaikovsky Fifth as no one ever played it before. And in the morrow's paper he reads: "Mr. A's playing of the slow movement was a miracle of lyric beauty and plangent melancholy." Mr. A is the conductor.

5

How Large Is an Orchestra?

NOTHING seems to worry our symphony conductors so much as the problem of how to perform the works of the composers of other centuries. One would think that the simple thing would be to go ahead and play them as well as possible. But no. What bothers our baton wielders is the size of the modern orchestra. Their theory seems to be that a symphony orchestra, like a hat, should be of a size appropriate to its wearer—in this case the composer. I agree enthusiastically, in principle; but I do wish they could make up their minds whether our orchestras are too small or too big.

So far as I can determine, the symphony orchestra of the present day is too small for the nineteenth century and too big for the eighteenth and seventeenth. The proper way to play Beethoven, for instance, is to add half a dozen extra woodwind players to an orchestra that already numbers 112 men. This, the conductor explains, is to make up for the fact that we have more string players in our orchestras than Beethoven had in his. One could, of course, reduce the number of strings; but that isn't to be thought of in the case of Beethoven.

In the case of Mozart, Händel, and Bach it *is* thought of. The proper way to interpret these masters is to reverse the Beethoven process: cut down the strings until your orchestra contains no more than just the number of players for whom they wrote. This, according to our best conductors, gives you the music exactly as Mozart, etc., conceived it and heard it. If they are really sincere in this belief, they ought to go a step further and see to it that the woodwinds are as out of tune, the brasses as raucous, and the strings as dreary in tone and as sloppy in technique as were those of the seventeenth and eighteenth centuries. Also, making the supreme sacrifice in the cause of art, the regular conductor ought to step down from the podium and let the orchestra get along with what indications it could get from the concertmaster. Then, and then only, would we really hear Bach and Händel and Mozart exactly as they heard themselves.

There is another phase to this cutting-down business which, I think, deserves a little discussion: the effect upon the morale of the subscriber. Having bought series tickets at no small expense, on the expectation of hearing music played by a full symphony orchestra, he finds, upon going to the concert hall, that the conductor has arbitrarily reduced his forces to two-thirds or one-half of their full strength. Do not be surprised, therefore, if he should become aggrieved, and demand a discount.

He might argue thus: If the Philharmonic-Symphony Society comprises 112 players, and the average symphonic program contains four numbers, the listener is therefore entitled to count upon hearing the playing equivalent of 448 man-power. (In this estimate, time spent in counting rests is considered as playing, since the player, if he is thus engaged, obviously cannot be elsewhere. If he is a timpani player, he might hire a substitute to count the rests for him; but since he would have to pay the substitute, the economic loss involved would equal the time he saved.)

On the other hand, if the conductor elects to play a Händel concerto grosso, followed by a Haydn symphony, and reduces the orchestra, for half the evening, to fifty-six men, the listener suffers a serious loss. Instead of hearing 448 man-power, he has heard only 336, a reduction of twenty-five per cent. On Händel and Haydn evenings, consequently, he is technically entitled to a discount of fifty cents on a two-dollar ticket.

I call this to the attention of the boards of directors of our symphony orchestras wholly in a spirit of helpfulness. They may, all unwittingly, be sowing the seeds of revolt. There is too much unrest among the masses as it is.

Besides, this cutting down the size of the orchestra must be bad for the morale of the players, too. Suppose you are a performer on the bass clarinet, or the contrabass tuba, or the contrabassoon. You spend the afternoon practicing, you have a hasty dinner, and you rush down to Carnegie Hall at eight o'clock. When you get there, you find that the program includes a concerto grosso for spinet and three violas, a quartet for oboes, and a divertimento by Monteverde for violas, three theorbos, and a tromba marina. Consequently, you will not be needed until nine-forty.

What do you do? You can't go home; and you can't practice, because it annoys the audience. Eventually you play pinochle, perhaps with some subscribers who were late, and, not being box holders, were locked out. The chances are that in that hour and a quarter you will lose your life's savings (late subscribers are marvellous pinochle players; they get so much practice, waiting for the doors to be reopened). And all because you were kept in idleness, instead of being allowed to pursue your vocation.

Even if you don't play pinochle (which is improbable, if you belong to the musicians' union), and spend the evening reading Marcel Proust, the moral effect is bound to be bad. You get a bit discouraged, you neglect your practice, and you develop habits of unpunctuality.

Your technique begins to be sloppy, and the conductor notices it. Then, some fatal evening, when there is a concert on, you think to yourself: "Oh, it'll just be Caccini and Corelli and Palestrina. The hell with it." And that very evening, probably, will be the one on which the conductor had planned to produce something by a Soviet composer calling for four tubas, two bass clarinets, and three contrabassoons. And you won't be there; and you are fired. And there you are, on the bread line, or else playing in a beer garden, all because some conductor can't bear to look 112 men in the face for two hours.

Nor is this reducing the orchestra so overwhelmingly good for the programs. I remember an evening when an eminent conductor sent most of his men to the showers in order to do justice to a youthful serenade by Brahms that dispensed with all the violins and all the brasses except two horns.

It is a pleasant piece, undoubtedly, and played in someone's living-room would be good entertainment. Besides being pleasant, it is also the longest piece ever written for the concert stage—or at least it sounded so. I thought enviously of those exiled pinochle-players. Thirty violins, two more horns, three trombones, and a bevy of kettledrums might have made it sound a good deal more important.

6

Stunting

SO MANY pianists have a nasty trick of swooping down upon an inoffensive group of sixteenth or thirty-second notes and tearing through them at a breakneck speed that has nothing to do with the main tempo of the piece, merely because they can. The practice is a survival of the bad old days of piano-playing, when pianists competed very much in the spirit of track athletes. The player who could get through Chopin's "Minute" Waltz in 55 3/5 seconds was *ipso facto* better than the unfortunate rival whose best record was 58 flat. The pianola, and its descendant, the player-piano, stopped all that. In sheer speed, it was to the human hand what the automobile is to the bicycle, so that the keyboard virtuosi perforce began to base their claims to pre-eminence on more aesthetic grounds than that of velocity.

However, most of them still cherish a sneaking desire to show how fast they can play, and still take an occasional chance of breaking the speed laws. Not, of course, that they call it that. They call it Accelerating the Tempo in order to infuse their playing with the Spirit of Improvisation. Which would be a grand thing if anybody wanted it. Who wants to be confronted with the spirit of improvisation in a performance of Philip Emmanuel Bach's Sixth "Prussian" Sonata? We all know the pianist didn't make it up; and his chopping the tempo into small pieces does not convince us that he did. It merely damages Bach.

7

Don't Blame Radio

DEVOTE any appreciable amount of your leisure time to attending vocal and instrumental recitals and concerts, and you are likely to be impressed, and a bit saddened, by the enormous gap that separates piano programs from others, aesthetically speaking. In general the pianists seem to be the only performers who decide beforehand what sort of audience they want to attract, and build their programs accordingly. If you like Bach and Brahms and Chopin, you can safely go to a recital that offers these composers with a reasonable assurance that the rest of the program will not insult your intelligence. Pianists who begin with Bach and Beethoven do not as a rule finish off with a group of Leybach and Heller and Chaminade.

Most of the violinists and singers, however, seem never to have made up their minds whether they are performing before music lovers or vaudeville audiences. Perhaps they are trying to appeal to everybody; that, at any rate, is the only charitable explanation of the trash that creeps into the programs of even reputable violinists. Your average fiddler starts off bravely with a Händel or César Franck sonata, only to go back to the restaurant by about the third group. He has, of course, the ready excuse that the violin repertoire is painfully small compared with that of the piano. Small as it is, however, it is large enough for artists like Kreisler and Spalding and Menuhin to make up programs that never fall below a decent standard of musical taste. Many of their brethren, unfortunately, seem to have no taste at all. One gathers, listening to what they play, either that they are deliberately condescending to their audiences or that they play the classics because it is the thing to do, and play gaudy rubbish because they like it.

The singers are the worst. In the first place, an idiotic tradition has standardized their programs almost beyond the limits of endurance. In ninety cases out of a hundred you are safe in predicting that a New York song-recital program will contain the following items, to wit: one group of songs in Italian, either native classics or Händel; one group of German lieder, selected from about fifty of the hundreds available; one group of French songs with Fauré, Franck, and early Debussy predominating; one group of songs in English, the majority of which will be American ballads of a low order. Just why this cast-iron polylingual arrangement must be followed nobody seems to know. If a singer's diction is bad in Italian, I get no particular thrill out of discovering that it is equally bad in German, French, and English; and if he knows nothing of lieder style, I am not consoled by learning that he cannot sing French songs either. And if the singer must sing several languages, why must he segregate them so relentlessly? I still remember a program of songs that a young soprano gave five or six years ago. Her songs had been grouped according to their contrasted moods, regardless of the language of the text; and the result, although she was by no means a great singer, was one of the most interesting song recitals I ever heard.

As to musical standards, the singers are below the violinists, if such be possible. No consistency in style, no appropriateness in grouping, no sense of cumulative effect. The only aesthetic principles that they seem to follow with any fidelity at all are that any German song is good, any French song is full of "atmosphere," and that any concluding group must contain one or two of the most appallingly banal American songs that performer can exhume. (If the song is particularly terrible, it has probably been dedicated to the singer.) There are honorable exceptions, of course, singers who are obviously musicians of taste and discernment, who build their programs as carefully as they sing them and who can keep an intelligent listener interested. But they are the minority. The majority are an uninspired and uninspiring lot.

8

The Lowly Immortals

WHAT goes to the making of a "hit"? Not a contemporary song hit, the sort that sweeps the country like the black plague for a month or two and then vanishes. That sort of thing defies analysis. What makes one particular tune out of a revue or musical comedy more popular than all the rest is something that will ever, probably, remain more or less of a mystery. As a matter of fact, if any one of us could solve it, he would probably be busy making a fortune, without wasting time talking about it.

But the so-called popular classics, the songs whose pretensions, at least, are slightly more elegant than musical comedy, that belong in the category of what may loosely be called salon music—what of them? Why should some of them hang on for years and years, while others, no better and no worse, die a-borning? Why should their appeal to simple minds—and to minds not always so simple—continue almost indefinitely?

There is no final answer, of course. Nevertheless, it is amusing to try to analyze the reasons for the longevity of certain tunes. It is quite possible, I believe, to discover some, if not all the reasons for their perennial popularity.

Take "The Rosary," for instance. The words probably contribute a good deal to its success. It is one of the original "torch" songs, in which the party of the first part tells the party of the second part what a miserable time he or she has had since they parted, and assures her or him of his or her undiminished—and, indeed, undiminishable—affection. Any song of this "me to you" type has a head start toward popularity, for it affords otherwise diffident young people the opportunity for uttering sentiments of the most intimate and personal character, under the pretext of trying over an old favorite together. I wonder, by the way, whether anybody in this generation still sings Amy Woodford-Finden's *Indian Love Lyrics.* I hear restaurant orchestras play them once in a while, and am instantly transported back to an undergraduate epoch when piano lamps were still extant, and young men used to gaze earnestly and significantly into young women's eyes, the while songfully adjuring them, "When I am da-high-ing, lean over me, softly, tenderly."

But there are a couple of musical reasons, also, for "The Rosary's" popularity. One is the modulation in the first and second bars (on the words "spent with thee, dear heart"), where—to lapse into technicalities—a tonic chord of D flat (first inversion) passes by chromatic steps through the dominant seventh of D natural (second inversion) to the dominant ninth of D flat. It is a common enough harmonic excursion, and has long since become a "barber-shop" chord of such familiarity that amateur male quartets venture it—successfully—by ear. But Nevin was the first to use it in a popular ballad, and it has become a sort of trade-mark for "The Rosary."

The other sure-fire musical device of "The Rosary" is the downward sweep of a minor seventh on the word "sweetheart" toward the end. This particular interval has always been tremendously moving. No matter where it is used—whether in *Tristan, Louise,* "Nur wer die Sehnsucht kennt," or "The Rosary"—it is invariably arresting.

The words have little, if anything, to do with the popularity of "From the Land of the Sky-Blue Water." The tune itself is the thing. It has freshness and simplicity, and the combination of its smooth lyricism with the Scotch "snap" (which is also Indian) is a novel one. Cadman's accompaniment is well and unobtrusively harmonized, and repeats the rhythmic pattern of the melody with admirable effect. This is one popular classic that a musician can admire.

Of the older favorites, Tosti's "Good-by" is another torch song, older even than "The Rosary." The tune lives because it successfully incorporates a section of the falling chromatic scale. This is a melodic device as infallibly successful as the downward minor seventh. In using it, "Good-by" shares the honors with the "Evening Star" air from *Tannhäuser,* and Delilah's incorrigible "My Heart at Thy Sweet Voice."

There is a later one that seems on the point of rivalling "The Rosary" as America's choice—a musical setting of Joyce Kilmer's "Trees." Here, of course, the words play an important part. Ever since it was written, a good many years ago, "Trees" has been the sort of poem that people cut out and carry about in their pocketbooks. It is safe to assert that if you don't know that "only God can make a tree," you probably don't know how to read.

The music sounds pretty bad to this untutored ear, but it has one thing in its favor. While it is not exactly a transcription of Rimsky's "Song of India," it is so like it, in rhythm and melodic pattern, that the two could be played simultaneously without discomfort. "Trees," therefore, does not have to beat its own path to the brain. It travels a furrow already ploughed for it by its famous predecessor.

Not that all the popular classics are necessarily bad. Most of them are; but there are a few exceptions. Just which, I forget at the moment. However, good or bad, do not deny them one important virtue that they possess: vitality. Remember the humble immortelle. Its beauty is not striking; it looks rather dry, and brittle, and artificial. But it keeps. It lasts through the winter, long after the orchid and the roses have withered and died.

9

On the Wagon

On an evening not long ago when Beethoven's Fifth Symphony constituted the second half of a Philharmonic-Symphony program, one member of the audience did not hear it; and the reason he did not hear it was that he walked out on it; and the reason he walked out on it was that he has a Three-Year Plan of his own.

Every once in a while this friend of mine declares a three-year moratorium on some famous and overplayed orchestral classic. For thirty-six months he resolutely declines to hear it under any circumstances. It may be the sole interesting number on an otherwise inconsequential program; it may be the prize offering of some master conductor whose reading of it is world-famous; it may be the only four-hand piano arrangement that two piano-playing friends have in common; it may be the big event of his favorite chewing-gum hour on the radio; it may be the only uncracked record in the cabinet.

Nevertheless, this gentleman will have none of it. He turns off radios and gramophones, leaves parties, walks out of concert halls, quits parks, retreats from music festivals, and withdraws from beer gardens, rather than listen to it.

This he does, not because he dislikes the piece, but because he finds himself in danger of getting used to it, and employs this heroic method of regaining his freshness of approach. The first work he tried the plan on was Schubert's Unfinished Symphony. Three years ago he laid it, figuratively, on the table. Not until this year did he hear it again. And when he did hear it, he says, after the long silence, he found its original charm and freshness redoubled, had the fun of discovering all over again that it is a masterpiece.

Two years ago, in the course of a musical pilgrimage through Europe, he heard the Beethoven Fifth played by eight separate orchestras, as interpreted by eight separate conductors. Whereupon he laid the Beethoven Fifth away in lavender, and will not hear it again until next season.

It is an excellent idea. Theoretically, one characteristic of a musical masterpiece is the fact that one can hear it repeated indefinitely without wearying of it. This is not literally true, and in every art except that of music we make no pretense that it is.

One's pet author may rest undisturbed on the bookshelf for months, or even years. When I say that I consider Hardy a great man, nobody assumes that I spend three days a week with my nose buried in *Tess of the D'Urbervilles* or *Jude the Obscure*. I don't consecrate an hour a day to staring at *The Night Watch,* even though I do consider Rembrandt an immortal painter. If *Hamlet* were running now, my veneration of Shakespeare would not necessitate my going every other evening to see it.

The fact is—and it is a commonplace fact enough—that any pleasurable sensation tends to diminish upon too frequent repetition. One's first *Filet Mignon Béarnaise* is a ravishment. The second, unless it occurs after a suitable interval of repose, is likely to be considerably less effective; a third, in rapid succession, is hardly to be contemplated with equanimity. Any aesthetic experience, like any gastronomic one, requires a pause for thought and rumination if it is to do the utmost possible good.

Works of art that are merely a glorified form of amusement do not, notoriously, stand repetition at all. An inconsequential novel, or a meretricious picture, or a pretty good piece of music, may be vastly pleasing at the moment; but read it, or see it, or hear it once too often, and you are sick of it, through with it for life.

This is not true of real art. We don't grow sick of a great book, or picture, or symphony. On the other hand, we can—which is almost equally disastrous, grow accustomed to it. Read your favorite poem too incessantly, and the words lose their meaning. Meet your favorite picture, or your favorite composition, too frequently, and you find yourself growing blind and deaf to it. You take for granted the beauties that once thrilled you. The truth that is beauty, shows dangerous symptoms of becoming a platitude.

This temporary laying aside of art treasures goes on, with most of us, quite unconsciously. We take an artistic vacation whenever we please, and hardly think about it. We put the book back on the shelf, stay away from that room in the museum, go to another theatre, with no one —least of all ourselves—the wiser.

But in the case of music, it is not so easy. We are not privileged to make up our own programs. We hear music at such times as it is offered, and in such variety as is vouchsafed us. Almost any program may contain some work that we have heard almost to the point of satiety. If we are to preserve the sensitivity of our musical palates we must do so, with premeditation.

I, for one, shall try the scheme. When next you catch me tiptoeing out of a concert, and inquire, anxiously, "What! Aren't you staying to hear the *'Pathétique'?"*—you may expect to hear me whisper, intrepidly:

"No, thanks. I'm on the wagon."

10

Homer Does Nod

I HEARD an all-Beethoven cycle not long ago, and it had by-products of considerable interest. First of all, it demonstrated once again the fact that there are few neglected masterpieces. Naturally, if you are planning an all-Beethoven program, one of your principal aims is to play something of his that is seldom if ever heard. In consequence, you do considerable archeological expeditionary work among the kitchen-middens of Beethoven's unfamiliar compositions. The cycle I heard included, among other things, his *Namenstag* and *King Stephen* overtures, and an extraordinary descriptive piece called *Wellington's Victory.*

And the conclusion that one reaches after hearing *King Stephen* the *Namenstag* and *Wellington's Victory* is that if they are not played nowadays it is for the simple reason that they are not worth playing. Beethoven could write just as bad music as the next man, upon occasion—and so could Mozart too, as a round of Mozart festivals would probably reveal. Time has dealt fairly with them both. If the Seventh and E flat Symphonies survive it is not because Beethoven and Mozart wrote them but because they are great music. And it is a great comfort to know that. It is comforting too to hear musical trash and know that a great man wrote it. The fact makes him more human, and therefore more likable. One warms to him, discovering a kindred streak of mediocrity that proves him, however distantly, one's own cousin. Only a genius could have written the Ninth Symphony; but the man who composed *Wellington's Victory* was obviously thinking about the rent.

It is not only comforting to know that great composers do not invariably write great music, but it is highly important that the fact be freely admitted and announced with considerable emphasis. There are fundamentalists in music as well as in religion, and they succeed in making just as many skeptics. This country is full of people who are kept away from music because they are afraid it is going to bore them. They don't put the case in those terms, however. They say, "This classical music is over my head." Finally one of them is dragged to a concert by a hundred per cent music lover and is made to listen to, say, the *Namenstag* overture. It bores him. But he does not know that the reason it bores him is that it is commonplace music. He has been told over and over again that Beethoven was one of the greatest composers that ever lived and that his music is "inspired." So he blames himself. If this be classical music there is nothing in it for him. Another potential concertgoer lost simply because no one thought to say, "Never mind this stuff; let's go up to Carnegie and hear the last movement of the Fifth."

11

A Plea for Grade B

THERE is a symphony of Dvořák's that answers to two names. It is sometimes called "Dvořák's First Symphony," possibly because he wrote five others preceding it; at other times it is known as "Dvořák's Third Symphony," I suppose because it was published before any of his others. So far nobody has thought to call it "Dvořák's Sixth Symphony."

At any rate, he did write this symphony, in 1880, and saw it published in 1882. The Philharmonic, under Theodore Thomas, gave it its first American hearing in 1883, which doubtless explains why one of the concert guides says that it was "composed in 1884." The Philharmonic played it again, under Anton Seidl, in 1893, after which there was a long silence.

The silence remained unbroken until 1931, when Erich Kleiber had the Philharmonic-Symphony play it, after thirty-eight years. You would assume, naturally, that if a work had been left lying unplayed as long as that, that there must be some good reason for its neglect; that, when it finally was played, it would turn out to be a piece of no particular importance, historically or musically; that it was not nearly as good, for instance, as Dvořák's familiar "From the New World" Symphony.

The assumption would be quite correct, too. The Dvořák's First—or rather, Third—that is to say, Sixth

—Symphony is pleasant, lightweight music, and that is all—no ill effects if you take it, no harm done if you let it alone. There is no particular thing about it that Tchaikovsky or Brahms or Beethoven does not do as well, and better.

Just the same, it is a pity that there is no room for a piece like this on the working programs of our symphony orchestras. For while it may not be enthralling, it is anything but dull. It is a gay, tuneful little work, with an attractive folksong atmosphere and a rattling good third movement in dance rhythm. Its misfortune is to be, not bad, but not good enough.

If it were a play, as good of its kind as it is a symphony, and showing as few signs of wear and tear, it would not have to wait thirty-eight years for a performance. Our theatre is so organized that there is room for the little fellows as well as for Shakespeare and Ibsen. When a new play opens in New York, the critics and audience say of it: "It is a good show," or, if it is a bit better than that, "an interesting and well-written play." Once a month they wax enthusiastic and call something "the finest play of the year."

If they compared the new plays with *Hamlet* or *The Wild Duck,* they would hardly find one a year that was worth praising. But they don't. Nobody does, and nobody would dream of doing so. When you come out of the theatre saying enthusiastically, "By George! That's the best show I've seen in a long time," you don't mean: "Viewed in the light of what the greatest dramatists of all time have achieved, that play is worthy to hold high rank." You mean merely what you say: that you have spent an interesting and adult evening. You are not thinking of the classics, and you wouldn't drag them into the discussion if you did. There is suffering enough in the theatre, as it is, without having to think about Shakespeare.

But in the concert hall, as I have said before, the situation is entirely different. Our standard orchestral repertoire, the one that we hear regularly, is largely made up of the greatest music ever written. You can hear masterpieces twice a week in Carnegie Hall whose equivalent in the theatre you would not see as many times in a year. Naturally, the concertgoer has the best of it. He is wonderfully lucky to be able to hear the classics of his chosen art whenever he pleases.

But there is another side to it. For one thing, new music is at a frightful disadvantage. If young Bilgeheim writes a symphony, and is lucky enough to get it played by a major symphony orchestra, his hearers judge his work, not in the light of Junksky's symphony, that was played last week, but according to how it stands up with the Beethoven Seventh. If he does not hold his own with the handful of survivors among the thousands who have been composing music during the past three centuries, his work is promptly dropped, to be heard no more. Imagine the feelings of a young playwright whose audience was there to see if his comedy was as good as *Candida!*

The situation is fair enough, in one way. There is no commercial market for music, as there is for plays. Pure aesthetic value is the only value the average orchestral piece can hope to possess, so it is only right that conductors, hearers, and critics unite in demanding that it possess at least that. Our symphony orchestras are so superlatively good, our conductors such masters of their art, and our repertoire so replete with masterworks, that there would be no point in lowering standards merely to give the near-great a chance.

Nevertheless, there is a flaw somewhere in the system under which we produce and hear music. The so-called "pop" concerts and the radio ought to fill the bill, but they don't. What they offer, as a rule, is music that would seldom get even a first hearing with a great orchestra. You know the list—Massenet's *Scènes pittoresques,* the Rakoczy March, the first and second *Peer Gynt* suites, *Pomp and Circumstance,* overture to *Die Fledermaus,* selections from *Natoma.* The music I mean is more ambitious than most of those. Music like Liszt's *Liebestraum,* another "pop" favorite, is what one might call first-rate *second*-class music. It survives because it is popular, despite the fact that it is more or less innocent of any intellectual and spiritual content.

On the other hand, there is a mass of second-rate *first*-class music, that fits in nowhere. It is better than the radio average, a little too highbrow to be a popular heart-throbber; and it is not quite good enough to stay in such fast company as Bach, Beethoven & Brahms, Inc. The Dvořák symphony is a good example. Once in thirty-eight years by the Philharmonic-Symphony is about right; but at least once every two years by somebody else would be even righter.

What this country needs, aside from a good five-cent cigar, is a good fifty-cent orchestra—or shall we say seventy-five? We need a lot of first-rate second-class orchestras to play second-rate first-class music to audiences that have graduated from *Zampa* and are not quite ready for *Le Sacre du Printemps.* Walter Damrosch did the sort of thing I mean, several years ago, in a series of radio concerts. He played the classics, but he also dug up any quantity of minor works by Saint-Saëns, Dvořák, Raff, Borodine, and a dozen others; works that did not deserve the front rank, certainly, but that deserved better than to fall out entirely.

Unfortunately, those concerts stopped, and no one has exactly resumed them. Meanwhile, there is a lot of orphan music wandering about, of whom no one, apparently, is willing to assume the custody.

Getting It Said

REZNIČEK'S overture to *Donna Diana* is one of a number of what might be called musical headstones over the graves of departed music. That is to say, it is one of a group of compositions that are the sole surviving parts of forgotten larger works. There are a good many of these in the literature of music. For example—a very obvious example—who in this generation heard a performance of the opera *Poet and Peasant,* whose overture is still the delight of military bandmasters; or of another opera, *Jocelyn,* whose incorrigibly popular *berceuse* has almost attained the dignity of a folksong? When *Donna Diana* was produced, less than half a century ago, it was hailed as a masterpiece. Now there's nothing left of it, except the overture.

It's a little saddening to think of all the hard work and anguish and hope that went into the making of these operas, and oratorios, and symphonies, that are now gone with the wind, remembered only by their fragments. But there's another side to the picture. I once heard a friend of mine say that every composer has just one thing to say, and spends all his life trying to say it perfectly. That statement is possibly a little too sweeping to take literally. It's hardly accurate to say that men like Bach, and Beethoven, and Wagner had only one thing to say. But it is true that every one of them had his own particular manner of musical speech . . . the thing that we vaguely call style . . . the thing that makes you say, hearing a piece of music . . . "Ah, that's Bach . . . that's Beethoven . . . there speaks Wagner." Even these giants didn't always succeed in being completely themselves. Every one of them has plenty of forgotten music in his repertoire.

So it is small wonder that a lesser man succeeds only occasionally in uttering the particular thing that is himself. But it is heartening to realize that when a composer does succeed . . . if only for sixteen bars of a song, one movement of a suite, one overture . . . when he does write something that makes you say, "I don't know just who that is, but he *is* somebody" . . . the world doesn't allow it to die. Rezniček wrote a vast quantity of music that we no longer have time to hear. But in one little overture he did say a completely charming, perfect, personal thing; and we are still glad to listen to him as he says it.

13

Celestial Airs

I HAD a rare opportunity, not long ago, to hear some Chinese music—the real thing, played on Chinese instruments by Chinese performers. The program was given under the auspices of the China Institute of America, and offered instrumental pieces, operatic airs, and folksongs.

One difficulty connected with the printed program rather gave me pause. Chinese names, charming as they look, are not very revealing to the ignorant eye; and as the program was not as explicit as it might have been, we had some slight preliminary difficulty in distinguishing the instruments from the players. During the opening number, for example, I was under the impression that Pi-Pa was playing *Ko-Wu-Yin* upon the *Han Chuan-Hua,* until an anguished glance at the printed glossary exposed the fact that it was Miss Han Chuan-Hua, playing the *Pi-Pa.*

After that we got along famously. I can now distinguish between the *Hsiao* (vertical flute) and the *Ti* (horizontal flute); I know a *Tung-Ssu-Chin* (bronze-stringed dulcimer) when I see one; and with practice I could probably tell a *Yueh-Chin* (moon guitar) from a *San Hsuan* (three-stringed banjo). And as for the *Sheng—!*

I would really like to own a *Sheng.* It is described as an "ancient organ," which is pitifully inadequate. It resembles a group of badly matched pieces of macaroni stuck in a snub-nosed teapot, and it is the honorable remote ancestor of the mouth-organ. The player inserts the spout of the teapot in his mouth, cuddles the bowl in his hands—as if he were trying to keep his fingers warm—and inhales.

It all looks very difficult and somewhat uncomfortable, but the results are worth the trouble. The sound that proceeds from the *Sheng* is a remote, slightly nasal warble, very sweet and minute—somewhat as if someone were playing a pipe-organ in a doll's house. It plays all sorts of diatonic tunes (it has a large, long-nosed cousin, called the *Yeu,* that plays chromatics), and could, I imagine, in the hands of a very expert player, manage chords. It played fifths and fourths the other evening. A couple of *Shengs* and a *Yeu* would be a delightful addition to a chamber orchestra.

Before the concert we were warned that the players were all students, and were not by any means to be considered as anything but amateur instrumentalists. Which was well. It is only fair, hearing an exotic instrument played for the first time, to ask how well it is being played. A Chinese audience, for example, hearing a piano for the first time, as played by myself, might easily receive a less favorable idea of the instrument's possibilities than it would get from the playing of Mr. Vladimir Horowitz.

Concerning this concert, my guess would be that Miss Han Chuan-Hua is a fairly accomplished but easily frightened performer upon the *Pi-Pa;* that Mr. Ho Shu-Cheng, at the *Hsiao,* needs a lot more practice; and that Mr. Tsu Kuo-Mo, on the *Sheng,* is good enough to be a professional. Judging from the anxious minutes that the string players spent in tuning their various instruments (the *Erh-Hu, Yueh-Chin,* and *Hu-Chin*) to accurate thirds, fourths, and fifths, I suspect that some of the strange intervals heard later were not so much examples of Oriental subtlety as plain sour notes.

The music itself, after what we have gone through at the hands of the various contemporary left-wing schools, sounds as simple as "Old Black Joe." Most of what was played at the concert I heard consisted of diatonic airs, many of them easily recognizable tunes. They differed from Occidental folk music chiefly in their over-addiction to reiterated short phrases and in their unmeasured rhythm. Incidentally, the unmeasured rhythm seemed to result, not from design, but from uncertainty. In the ensemble pieces (played in unison, with an occasional fifth or fourth by way of harmony), the players were obviously unanimous in their agreement as to pitch, but seemed to have some trouble in keeping together.

Altogether, I found none of the subtlety and incomprehensibility that I had expected to encounter in Chinese music. Concerning Oriental music, far too much, I think, has been made of its antiquity, and not enough of its primitive character. To talk about the marvels that might be wrought by grafting Chinese and Japanese music upon Occidental music is, in my belief, to talk nonsense.

The plain truth is that most Oriental music is in a state of arrested development. Most of its characteristics—its rhythmic irregularity, its intonational vagaries, and its lack of harmony—are the obvious result of the fact that the Oriental has never been able to evolve a satisfactory system of music notation. The Chinese method, that of indicating separate notes by separate characters, is all right for determining pitch, but gives no inkling of duration.

Music that cannot be written down, but must be transmitted by ear, cannot develop, any more than can literature that cannot be written down. Just as a language must be capable of being written before it can develop a complex grammar and rhetoric, so must a music be written before it can develop harmony and counterpoint. If Chinese music is what it is, the reason is not particularly obscure. Chiefly it is because, since the T'ang Dynasty, the study of music has been banned from education and scholarly pursuits.

The T'ang Dynasty ended A.D. 907. In other words, about one hundred years before Guido of Arezzo made his incalculably fruitful discovery that music, to be transmitted properly must be, not written, but drawn, the music of the Chinese world stopped developing. Had it continued to do so, it would, I believe, bear the same easily recognizable relation to our music as Chinese art and literature bear to our own painting, sculpture, and poetry. As things are, however, in one of the arts at least, the East has, I suspect, everything to learn from the West.

14

Art for God's Sake

I DON'T know just why the term "amateur," used in connection with music, should be taken so generally to imply music badly played. The word is used in its pure sense in the world of sports, and no one misunderstands it. An amateur golfer, or an amateur tennis player is a person who engages in those games for the fun of it rather than for a living. The average professional is undoubtedly more skilled than the average amateur, because he has to be. On the other hand, nobody is surprised when an amateur golfer, for example, is skilled enough to beat the best professionals.

But when you call a man an amateur, in music, you had better smile; because you are assumed to be saying that he is not good enough to be a professional. The reason for that is, of course, that whereas millions of Americans play golf and tennis for the fun of it, hardly anybody, comparatively speaking, plays the piano or the violin for the fun of it. Plays really well, I mean. Cross-examine the average conservatory pupil, and you will find that, carefully cherished in the back of his or her mind, is a picture of that pupil on the stage of Carnegie Hall, or the Metropolitan Opera House, bowing to cheering thousands. What we need here are more people who would find it as exciting to give a good performance of a Beethoven sonata as to hold a tennis champion down to a 6-3, 6-4, 7-5 score.

That is why the example of an organization such as the Beethoven Association in New York is so valuable—to say nothing of the fun of hearing the concerts. For here is a group of headliners whose interest in music as an art, as well as a profession, is so genuine that they are willing to take a busman's holiday, to spend time and energy in rehearsing and giving concerts whose only reward is the satisfaction of having done a good job.

And that satisfaction, that joy of the craftsman doing good work for the sheer love of his craft, is manifest in everything they do. The impressive thing about hearing an artist like Felix Salmond play a Beethoven sonata, at one of their concerts, is not at all the fact that he is not getting paid for it, but the obvious pleasure he is taking—and communicating—in the music. Listening to a Brahms quintet, one thinks, not of the expensive time that must have gone into rehearsing it, but of what fun the players must be having, hearing the music come out like that.

15

Guaranteed Hand-Made

An astonishing number of people will ask a serious composer, "And do you actually orchestrate all that music yourself, or do you hire somebody to take all that manual labor off your hands?" People ask this who really ought to know better, people who wouldn't dream of asking a painter if he actually colors his pictures by hand after he has drawn them. There is this excuse for their asking it: the music that is most in evidence around us, that is, jazz and musical comedy, is almost invariably scored by someone other than its creator. I know of no contemporary popular composer who does all of his own orchestration. Most of them, as a matter of fact, could not write an orchestral score if they wanted to; some of them cannot write even a piano arrangement of the tunes that they whistle or pick out with one finger.

There is nothing essentially immoral in a popular composer's hiring a specialist to do his orchestration for him. It has always been done. Arthur Sullivan occasionally used assistants for rush jobs of scoring; so (although rarely) did Victor Herbert and Julian Edwards. Contemporary dance music is so frightfully monotonous in its forms and rhythms that the services of an expert arranger are almost essential to give it variety and interest. In former years the late Frank Sadler did the best of the musical comedy scoring. He was succeeded by the ingenious and resourceful Russell Bennett. The music libraries of our large broadcasting stations employ staffs of talented young musicians whose sole job is to make special orchestral arrangements for radio.

And why not? The writing of popular music is an industry, and its practitioners are in it for one good and honest reason: to make money. Most of them are as innocent of any artistic intentions—or pretensions—as plumbers, and so long as they can turn out a sound, salable job it is nobody's business what labor-saving devices they choose to employ. But if we are to discuss serious music, that is a different matter. For serious music (that is, a piece of music intended to be taken seriously as a work of art rather than a commercial job) is, like all forms of art, presumably conceived in terms of its medium. Just as a good architect thinks, not in terms of blueprints, but of wood and stone and steel and terra cotta, so a good composer thinks, not in terms of abstract music, but in those of instruments and voices.

It is doubtful whether, in the higher stages of art, matter and form can be separated. A Rembrandt etching has obviously been conceived in terms of line and black and white rather than in terms of paint, and it is not probable that Shakespeare wrote Hamlet's Soliloquy before deciding into whose mouth to put it. Most of Chopin is so completely music for the piano that it defies any attempts to translate it into orchestral terms. Wagner, on the other hand, thinks wholly orchestrally, and no piano arrangement has ever done justice to one of his scores.

Consider the flute part of Debussy's *Faun,* the horn call in the finale of the Brahms's First Symphony, the *cor anglais* solo in the third-act prelude of *Tristan und*

Isolde. In every one of these instances you have music that was created in terms of the instrument that plays it, and that would not sound right if played by any other. Consider the counterpoint of Palestrina, meaningless unless it is *sung*, and the counterpoint of Bach's Chromatic Fugue, which must be played. Obviously, therefore, a composer who cannot write his own orchestral score, or choral piece, or piano part, is incapable of really *thinking* music in the only terms in which it exists—those of sound; and if he cannot do that, he has no control over his medium, and is no artist. A tune, or a theme—a musical idea, in short—is, like the plot of a story or play, only the raw material. Whether the finished product is trash or a masterpiece depends largely upon who develops the idea.

Craftsmanship is not the whole story, of course. A man might be a master of orchestration and still have nothing to say. On the other hand, not to know one's chosen business, to be too lazy or incompetent to master the technique of the art over which one pretends to mastery, is hardly a recommendation for respectful consideration. A real playwright does not hire gag men to insert funny lines in his comedies; a real architect does not rely upon the contractors to tell him whether to build of masonry or wood. Art is a one-man job, and a composer who invades the field of Beethoven, Debussy, Brahms, and Strauss so ill-equipped that he must call in another man to help him give expression to his ideas is either a hero or a fool. We may admire his courage or his impudence, but we would do well not to take him too seriously.

Dancing in the Dark

THE temptation to dance to music that was not written for dancing seems to be as strong in terpsichorean circles as is the impulse, among singers, to put words to music that was not meant to have any. In both instances the results of the experiment are of debatable value. There is no real harm, I suppose, in singing "goin' home, goin' home" to the tune of the slow movement of the "From the New World" Symphony, although I like it better on the English horn; and no lasting damage is done to a string quartet by dancing to it if one feels in the mood to do so. Where I part company with such performances is on the question of their entertainment value.

I heard a dance program of chamber music not long ago, a series of interpretative pantomimes devised to go with music by Bach and Ernest Bloch. There was nothing frivolous or irreverent about either the intent or the execution of the program. As a matter of fact, the nearest approach to a light touch during the entire proceedings was provided by Bach himself; for much of his music seemed to contribute an undercurrent of optimism and good cheer that was not always in keeping with the solemnity of the occasion.

His was the opening number, a toccata and fugue in D minor, mimed by a masculine soloist and a feminine ensemble. The idea seemed plausible enough, for Bach, like Beethoven and Wagner, is a composer of completely articulate music. Relax and listen to him, and you will never be in doubt as to what he is trying to say, nor as to his complete success in getting it said. This being so, one might expect to have little trouble in devising stage action for his music. But the trouble is that Bach's ideas are all musical. He is almost innocent of any dramatic or literary prepossessions. His music speaks, with tremendous clarity and eloquence, in a language that is self-sufficient and untranslatable.

The stage action for the toccata, therefore, while no doubt interesting and significant in its own right, did not seem to get along very well with the music. Perhaps it was too interesting. One saw Mr. Blank standing in a flood of light at the foot of a flight of low steps, making significant gestures. Eventually he turned, to face a group of young women clad, apparently, in robes of cellophane. They moved, graciously and gracefully, and arranged themselves in various groupings, all of which, while vastly pleasing to the unprejudiced spectator, were apparently unsatisfactory to Mr. Blank, who retreated downstage with unmistakable signs of disapproval. Meanwhile, one had forgotten Bach, who, as one finally realized with a start, was being very well played on the organ. The curtain fell to respectful applause.

The other piece of formal music thus visualized was Ernest Bloch's String Quartet. There seemed to be a little difference of opinion as to what this music signified. According to advance information from the producers, "the Bloch *Quatour à Cordes* for string quartet [*sic*] is rich in dramatic content, revealing the composer's disgust with the bitterness and strife of the war which engulfed the world at that period, and breathing his hope for the future." On the other hand, according to the scenario printed in the program, Bloch meant other things: "In the first movement the individual, in this instance a woman, is seeking a key to her own direction. In the second, she is confronted by the more formalized demands of the Group Force. In the third, she seems enveloped by and identified with the destiny of the Eternal Woman. In the fourth, the consciousness of the Group Force surges over her more violently than ever"—you get the general idea.

Having deliberately abstained from reading both explanations before the rise of the curtain, I was interested to see what was going to happen, and I must admit that not much, either of Mr. Bloch's disgust with the war or of the scenarist's Group Force, came over. One saw a danseuse, moving very beautifully. Later she met Mr. Blank. The two were thereupon confronted by a group in black, whose—one might say—thinly veiled hostility to the happy pair gave rise to the suspicion that they must be the in-laws. The part about being identified with the destiny of the Eternal Woman did come over the footlights very clearly, more clearly, in fact, than one might have expected from the scenarist's roundabout way of putting it. In the end, however, Miss Dash, having got rid of the committee from the Group Force, lost Mr. Blank as well.

The trouble with devising stage action for abstract music is that it is rather unfair to the composer. The minute you put people on the stage, and give them movements and gestures, you create some sort of dramatic situation. Whereupon you begin judging the music according to its success or failure to convey the mood of a scene with which the composer has nothing to do, and of whose putative existence he was utterly unconscious when he wrote his music. There were times, during the evening, when Mr. Bloch seemed to have missed the point of the scenario completely—which was a bit rough on Mr. Bloch.

One incidental shortcoming of the performance confirmed me in an opinion that I have always held, which is that there is a definite relation between the number of people on the stage, in any performance, and the number of people in the orchestra. I doubt if this relationship has ever been analyzed and explained, and I am not at all sure that it could be, completely; I do know that most performers, especially dancers, ignore it. Just the same, it exists.

The impressions received by the eye and the ear differ in kind, but they do correspond. If the eye receives one sort of sight impression, the ear expects instinctively to receive the corresponding sound impression. There are exceptions, of course. Sometimes the unexpected impression is more interesting, may be all the more convincing because of its unexpectedness. Nevertheless, it is safe to say that, as a rule, when the ear registers loud, the eye expects to see bright; hear soft, and you look for dark. Thus, when the orchestra blares the triumphal march in *Aïda,* the eye accepts it as fitting and proper that the scene should be brilliantly lighted and colorful; just as anything louder than a murmur would hardly do for the inky blackness of the castle vault into which Golaud and Pelléas descend. There is yet another relationship, more subtle, perhaps, but none the less real. And it is the one that dancers are most prone to violate. It is the one that causes the ear to expect small when the eye sees few; large, when the eye sees many.

What is a small sound? The English horn solo at the opening of the third act of *Tristan und Isolde*. Imagine that the curtain, instead of rising upon the lonely figures of Tristan and Kurvenal, in that scene, rose upon a stage crowded with people. No matter how quiet they were, I doubt whether the voice of a solitary English horn would sound appropriate. The whole string section of the orchestra, in such a case, would be infinitely better. The strings might be muted; the whole sixty-four of them, combined, might not make as much actual noise as the single English horn. But their sound, however soft, would be bigger.

A crowd is a big thing, and needs a large sound to express it. A good rule of thumb, for dance performances at any rate, might be that up to seventy-five, the crowd should never outnumber the orchestra. Ten people on the stage, not less than ten in the orchestra; fifty on the stage, fifty in the pit. The consequences of ignoring this relationship were particularly apparent while the Bloch quartet was being interpreted in terpsichorean terms. As long as Miss Dash and Mr. Blank were alone together, the quartet of string players was always adequate to support, in sound, anything that the dancers essayed in motion and gesture. But when the ensemble joined them, when there were fourteen people on the stage as against four in the pit, the quartet was swamped. The body of sound that one heard was at no time commensurate with the collective body that one saw. In moments of violent action the instrumentalists were nowhere. Scrape and pant as they might, the music sounded dwarfed, inadequate—not as music, but as a sound. The Bach toccata, on the other hand, fared very well in this respect, with just as many on the stage; for it was played on the organ, and the organ always has magnitude, no matter how quietly it plays.

The scenario for the Bloch Quartet might have been more convincing if it had been a little less cosmically phrased. As a rule, plots in which Woman is seeking something, or Man is in quest of anything, do not make very good theatre. Collective nouns are likely to be bad actors. The best way to keep an abstraction impressive is to keep it an abstraction, and not to let it go on the stage. Put Woman in bare feet and a tunic, and she is likely to turn out to be simply Miss Dash.

Audiences don't reason from the abstract to the concrete. As a matter of fact, they reason, if at all, only after the performance. Show them an individual and tell them that he is a type, and they won't believe you. Call him an individual, and it is just possible that later, if you have done your work well as a dramatist, they will go out telling each other that he is a type. Thousands of people have decided that Candida is a perfect expression of a certain protective, mothering instinct in women. If Shaw had dramatized the instinct, and forgotten to call it *Candida,* it is highly probable that those thousands would have stayed away from the theatre with disconcerting unanimity.

Catching Them Young

THE guest of honor was famous as a brilliant leader and a clear thinker, a man of exceptional intelligence and broad culture. After dinner, the talk turned to music.

"I wish it meant something to me," he said, "but it doesn't. I enjoy reading, looking at pictures, and going to plays. I always have. But aside from the names of a few composers, I know nothing about music. And, frankly, I care nothing. I know I'm missing a lot, but it can't be helped. I've been to the opera a couple of times, and sat through a couple of symphony concerts; but I got nothing out of them. A popular tune I can understand and enjoy. But serious music—anything you fellows would approve of—sounds too mysterious and complicated to be any fun. I have often wondered why," he continued. "The truth is, I think, that I'm afraid of it—afraid of not understanding it, and afraid of being bored. I came to it too late. Books and pictures I've had as long as I can remember; but there wasn't much music at our house when I was a boy. Perhaps, if there had been—"

He is no exception. The average American parent, bent upon instilling culture in his progeny, sees to it that their formative years are spent in an atmosphere of the best in literature, poetry, and art. But the average American child, even today, grows up either with no musical background at all, or with one that is the equivalent of Nick

Carter and the comics; whereupon his worried parents wonder why his musical taste is so low-brow.

Good music is exactly as mysterious and complicated as any other of the arts; and no more so. The way to appreciate it is to hear it, and the way to understand it is to be familiar with it. If a good many otherwise sophisticated Americans of the last generation—and this one—are musical illiterates, the reason is, not that they have no inherent taste for it but that they came in contact with it too late. They weren't caught young enough.

How are we to catch them young enough? Assuming that you like music—or, whether you like it or not, that you would be glad to have your children like it—how do you go about introducing it to them? What is the musical upbringing that any child might reasonably expect? When does it begin, and of what does it consist?

It ought to begin, I should say, at about the age of six months. Naturally, his course of instruction at this period is nothing elaborate. It consists of playing him some music at a definite hour every day. Any music will do, provided it is tuneful and strongly marked in rhythm. The point is to accustom him to hearing music as part of his daily life, and to give him pleasure by appealing to the most primitive of all musical impulses—the impulse to keep time. Give him a week of it—not more than ten minutes or so every day—and at the end of that time you will probably find him swaying back and forth as he listens. He won't necessarily keep exact time to the music at first, but he will sooner or later.

The best time of day for his music is in the late afternoon, some time between his nap and his bath. Don't make it too late in the day, and for heaven's sake don't play or sing him to sleep! The old-fashioned lullaby is a beautiful thing to talk about; but it is as much a habit-forming drug as the old-fashioned dose of soothing sirup. It tends to make him dependent upon an artificial aid for the performance of what should be a natural and effortless function. Besides, it is going to associate music with sleep, in his subconsciousness, to a degree that is likely to make concert-going, in his adult years, simply an ordeal of trying to keep awake.

Naturally, if you play the piano, you will play for your child yourself. If you can't, try to bully someone else to do it for you. If that attempt fails, or if you have no piano, buy a gramophone—the best you can afford—and play him records: jigs, dances, marches, and the like. Failing the gramophone, turn on the radio, around five o'clock, and try to get one of the periods of teatime music. But be sure to have it gay, vigorous music, that will stimulate rather than depress him.

This daily ten- or fifteen-minute period should go on until he learns to talk. When he begins to develop some conversational powers—at eighteen months or two years, probably—take up the second stage of his musical education. Again, do your own playing or singing, if you can. If you can't, the faithful gramophone is a good substitute. Since your youngster is in the early talking period, words are the most fascinating things in his life; so you proceed to introduce him to music by associating it with words. Buy books or records of all sorts of folksongs and nursery rhymes, and teach them to him. Put the apparent emphasis on the words, but be sure he gets the tunes right. Sing them or play them over and over, and get him to sing them after you.

Let the folksongs be his main diet. These are the ideal

form of music for young children. In the first place, they are good music, for the simple reason that music possessing vitality enough to last through many generations is bound to have some merit. Second, they are easy to grasp and to remember; for they are airs that have been passed from mouth to mouth for centuries. They have been worn smooth by constant handling, so that the awkward and difficult phrases have been simplified. Third, they are the purest form of music—unadorned and unaccompanied melody. Any child who has grown up on folk songs has a musical background that he need never discard and of which he need never be ashamed. He will find these friends of his infancy embedded in the works of Beethoven, Brahms, Wagner, Tchaikovsky, Rimsky-Korsakoff, and a dozen other symphonic writers.

Be careful of one thing. Songs for children, whether of the folk or manufactured variety, are almost invariably pitched too high. Apparently the editors of such collections, having read much fiction in which "the shrill piping of childish voices" figures prominently, have taken it to be an ideal instead of a calamity. The average young child has a comfortable vocal range of little more than an octave, beginning with middle C. His vocal cords are relaxed and undeveloped, and the production of the "supported" tone necessary to sing endurable high notes requires a control of his throat muscles that is beyond his powers. To sing a high note he must yell; and while yelling may be an allowable and even desirable element of his playtime activities, it has no place in his musical education.

Be very sure, therefore, that his songs are comfortably within his vocal reach. As a rule they should not go higher than the D on the fourth line of the treble staff. Don't hesitate to sing them a whole tone or so lower than they are written, if necessary. If you are teaching him via the gramophone, slow it down until the pitch is right for him. This is not an ideal method, but it is better for his songs to be too slow than too high.

As he grows older, begin to bring him in contact with more complicated forms of music. For this purpose the gramophone is ideal. Try him with all sorts of orchestral and chamber music, not only the so-called "popular classics," but symphonic poems and parts of symphonies. The radio, by the way, also furnishes symphonic concerts that —in reasonably small doses—are good for him. Don't be afraid of giving him music that is too advanced for his taste. There is no telling what may strike his fancy. He is just as likely to be fascinated by the Immolation Scene from *Götterdämmerung* as by Schubert's "Serenade." If he likes it, whatever it is, let him hear it.

At just what age he should begin this sort of listening it is hard to say. Serious music may begin to interest him as early as his third year. On the other hand, he may be six or seven before he begins to take any particular notice of it. The best rule is to try it on him early, and see what happens. If he pays attention, keep it up. If he doesn't, don't try to sell the music to him. Don't say, "Now keep quiet, darling, and listen to the lovely symphony, or Mummy spank." Just put the records away, and try again after a couple of months.

If you are within commuting distance of a good symphony orchestra, by all means take him to the children's concerts. But don't take him too young. A child's world is a very small one, and he pays conscious attention only to what is close at hand. To the average child of four, an orchestra a hundred feet away in a concert hall simply does not exist. If you try to make him listen to it, at that age, he is likely to pay much more attention to the little boy two seats away than to the music. If by some miracle he should be interested, his powers of concentration will fail him after ten or fifteen minutes. He will grow tired, and correspondingly cross, and you will probably have to carry him out, howling, about halfway through the second number on the program. Better wait until he is six or seven before trying the children's concerts.

If you can manage it, have him taught the elements of reading and writing notes about the time he starts school. One of the great mental hazards that the neophyte music lover has to overcome is the cabalistic look of the signs in which it is written. The strange and apparently irrational series of dots, lines, and miscellaneous squiggles has the same effect upon him as the sight of a stenographer's notebook or a Chinese laundry ticket. It looks secret and insoluble, and he is convinced that he can never be on really intimate terms with anything so complicated and esoteric. As a matter of fact, the rudiments of musical notation are not one-tenth as difficult to master as the spelling of the English language. Almost any normal child can learn them—and should—at a comparatively early age. Any vocal, piano, or violin instructor can teach him.

I can say one thing for the system I have just described: it works. I tried it out on my own daughter. From her fifth month to her fourth year she heard music regularly for about fifteen minutes every day. Before she could talk it was played and sung to her. She began to learn songs when she was about two years old, and to hear music on the gramophone when she was about four. At ten, she knew upward of thirty or forty folksongs—French, English, German, and Russian—by heart. She has attended several symphony concerts and parts of opera performances, all of which she enjoyed. She knows the names of a number of composers, and can identify many of their simpler works. Her favorite compositions, at the moment, are Debussy's *Fêtes,* the Flower Maiden chorus from *Parsifal,* and, I regret to state, "The Love Bug Will Get You If You Don't Watch Out." She is taking piano and violin lessons at her own request, and knows notation. She has also composed and written down some piano pieces. Music, in other words, is a natural and necessary part of her life, as simple and enjoyable as playing store, swimming, and reading fairy tales. She will listen to music, without pose or self-consciousness, and derive pleasure and comfort from it, all her life.

But she, as you will point out, is the child of a professional musician, and has probably inherited some aptitude for music. Some, yes, but I am pretty certain that her natural bent lies elsewhere. The point is that her intellectual curiosity, which, like that of any child of her age, is insatiable, has been directed into channels that are going to yield her cultural returns later on. She has been getting no more than any of her contemporaries should be given. The treatment of special talent is another story.

What is special talent? Every professional artist of any sort is the target of anxious inquiries from parents who want to know how to handle their more-or-less-gifted offspring. Almost without exception they ask the same questions: how can I be sure that my child is talented? If he has talent, what is the best way to go about developing it? How can I avoid spoiling whatever talent he has?

The only honest answer to the first question is that you can't be sure. When Ludwig Geyer lay dying, he said of his eight-year-old stepson, Richard Wagner, who was playing the piano in the next room, "Is it possible that he has musical talent?" This was not blindness. It was the honest caution of a man who had lived his life among actors and musicians, gifted and mediocre, and had learned that flowers and weeds look much alike when they are sprouting.

However, even if you cannot be sure, you can make a fairly good guess. There are three symptoms of special aptitude in music—or any other art. The first is urge, the impulse toward the art, the desire to practice and master it. The musically talented child will not only enjoy music when he hears it, but will be fascinated by it. He will make opportunities for hearing it, and will try to create it for himself, either by singing or by picking out tunes on the nearest available instrument. The second sign of talent is technical preoccupation. He wants to learn, wants not only to play or sing, but to play or sing well. He doesn't have to be forced to practice, and will tackle technical problems by himself, without waiting for his teacher to set them. He wants to know the why and the how of everything musical. The third sign is intuitive grasp. He seldom makes the same mistake twice. He not only remembers what he has been told, but really comprehends its meaning, and can apply it. He is likely to progress at a speed that is out of proportion to the amount of instruction he gets or the degree of conscious effort he seems to put forth. He may not be exceptionally bright, compared with other children, but in music something outside his brain steers him toward the right conclusions.

Granted that your youngster displays these signs of musical talent, what are you to do about it? One thing you must not do about it is to jump to the conclusion that he is destined to become a great artist. A successful career in music involves other things beyond ambition and technical brilliance. A singer, for example, may have a glorious voice; but if his singing lacks musical intelligence, taste, and emotional power, if he cannot grip and hold the attention of an audience, he will not go far. Technique and tone will not avail an instrumentalist if his playing lacks the something-or-other that makes people eager to hear him. A composer may know as much about counterpoint and symphonic form as Bach and Beethoven; but unless his themes, his musical ideas, have the breath of life in them, his music will not live.

On the other hand, interpretative genius, the greatness of personality that makes a Kreisler or a Paderewski; creative genius, the greatness of ideas that makes a Wagner or a Debussy—these are generally the attributes of maturity. Not one musician in a million is likely to display them in childhood. In other words, don't worry about them. If you—and whatever musicians you happen to meet—honestly believe that your child has talent, foster that talent—keep it weeded and watered, so to speak—and let the future take care of itself. Give your child, in music, the equivalent of the academic education you would give to a child who might, you thought, grow up to be a writer.

First of all, see that he masters the fundamentals of

technique. It is a tradition of tennis playing that if you don't learn certain things about footwork, position, and stroking before you are sixteen, you never will learn them. A good tennis player doesn't consciously figure out the spot on the court to which his opponent is going to return the ball, deliberately go there, and as deliberately select the best stroke to use in getting the ball back. He moves into position and hits the ball, literally before he has had time to think about what he is doing. He uses his mind between rallies to size up his opponent and plan his game; but once the ball is in motion, he has no time to think at all.

The same holds true of any other technique, from driving a car to playing the violin. It is no good to you until you have forgotten it—that is, until it is part of your subconscious mind. Give your musically gifted child a sound, clean, unconscious technique, whether in playing, singing or composing. The fact that he is a child—that the habit-forming part of his brain is more active than the reasoning part—will cause him to absorb it faster and more surely than any grown-up could. Once absorbed, once definitely transmuted from a conscious effort into a nervous and muscular reaction, it will never leave him. When he is older, he will be free to concentrate on what to do, without having to think so much about how to do it.

So, if your young hopeful wants to play an instrument, have him taught to play well and easily. If he shows signs of breaking out into composition, give him harmony, counterpoint and the elements of composition as early as he can grasp them. If he has a voice, be careful. Let him be taught proper breathing, and phrasing, and reading, and interpretation, but don't let his teacher spend too much time on placement—that is, the actual production of tone—or in trying to extend the natural range of the voice. A boy's voice drops an octave some time between his twelfth and sixteenth years. A girl's voice does not drop during the corresponding period, but it is equally affected by the bodily changes that mark the end of childhood and the beginning of physical maturity. Hard usage at too early an age may ruin it. Rigorous vocal training, for either a boy or a girl, should not begin until after fifteen or sixteen.

Whatever variety of musician your child shows signs of becoming, see to it that he gets a broad musical background. Let the budding composer learn to play an instrument; let singer or instrumentalist learn something of composition and musical history. Make him aware, whatever he is, that his particular branch of music is not the whole of the art.

Be sure to give him the best teachers you can possibly afford. Don't argue to yourself that it would be a waste of time to engage an expensive teacher for a child. An incompetent teacher may give him bad technical habits that will hang on for years. Ten lessons with an instructor who thoroughly knows his business are worth a year with a third-rater.

It is hard to spoil a real talent, but it can be done. One good way is to push a child faster than he wants to go, in the hope of making a prodigy of him. Keep him long hours at practicing when he would rather be doing something else, and you have an excellent chance of making him thoroughly sick of music before he is fifteen. If he happens to be so extraordinarily gifted that he can stand the drudgery, and does become a child prodigy, he may astonish the neighbors, or even the public, for a few years. But the chances are that his vitality will be so drained by hard practice and unhealthy nervous stimulation, his mind made so narrow by overspecialization, that at twenty-one he will be a tired young-old man, with nothing left to give to music or the world.

Don't let him get a swelled head, no matter how much he seems to be a genius. Do your bragging, and let the neighbors do their marveling, behind his back. For once get it into his head that he has nothing more to learn, and he will learn nothing more. His career will stop short on its threshold, and it will be your fault. Don't go to the other extreme of never praising him. You will merely discourage him and kill his ambition. Try to maintain the attitude that his gift is a great privilege—which it is—and that it is up to him to make the most of it.

Beware of making his development lopsided. Until he is well into his teens, music should not necessarily be the major part of his life. See that he has a good general education, even at the cost of slowing down his musical progress. Make him read, study, and exercise. See to it that he has a sound body, a solid foundation of good health, and a first-hand acquaintance with life and people. Whatever else a great artist may be, he is always a great person, someone whose bigness of outlook is reflected in his art. Make your child a real person, if you want him to become a real artist. Talent is only one ingredient of genius. The others are training, culture, and character. They are yours to give or withhold. Be wise, and generous, and give them.

The Chick and the Ego

SPEAKING of talented children, I have had three letters from a gentleman who wants me to hear a child genius that he has discovered. She is a little girl of six, who has composed a number of small pieces of music—not "composed" in the sense of writing them down, but in that of picking out the melodies on the piano and retaining them in her memory, so that she can repeat them whenever she is asked to do so. Her parents are not musical, and are too poor to pay for the development of her talent. She has, however, been accepted as a pupil by an excellent music school, and is receiving free instruction. She is, he thinks, a musical wonder, and if I could hear her compositions I would be greatly impressed. I must, positively, not fail to come.

I am not going, for two reasons. The first is the purely selfish one that I dread arguments. And there would be an argument, because what would actually happen would fall so far short of what the little girl's parents and admirers would expect. There seems to be a good deal of confusion in many people's minds concerning the precise duties and powers of critics—particularly music critics. The latter are assumed to resemble Cinderella's fairy godmother far more closely than they actually do.

I might, of course, go to hear the little girl's compositions, but the audition would do neither of us any particular good. All that would happen, probably, would be that I would catch the eleven fifty-two from Stamford, it would be ten minutes late, and I would arrive just at lunch time, very cross.

Lunch would be hastily shelved, and the little girl would play five pieces: *Stars; Doll's Lullaby; Morning Thoughts; March; Dance of the Sparrows.* There would be an expectant silence, and I would then say, with the air of one who says something original and important: "That's fine. Very interesting. She certainly has talent, and should go to a good music school."

Then they would tell me that she is already attending a good music school, which would leave me nothing to say except, "Good. Then let's wait and see what she does ten years from now." Then the argument would begin.

The other reason I am not going is that I don't believe that any child of six can compose music which, considered solely upon its merits as a work of art, is worth my hearing. I may be wrong. This child may be a phenomenon unique in history, and I may be pointed out as the dunce who refused to hear her first works. Nevertheless I shall take that chance. I would rather be lazy than right.

The child who can play the piano or violin or cello with precocious skill has at least a fighting chance of becoming a great virtuoso. Technical command of an instrument is a trying and laborious accomplishment, and if it can be achieved at an early age, so much to the good. The player has just so much more leisure in which to become a person and an artist as well as an executant.

But technique in creative art is solely the artist's business, being entirely meaningless otherwise. A poem may have fourteen lines, all containing five perfect iambi, with all the rimes absolutely correct, and still not be a sonnet. A child of six might, by some stretch of the imagination, conceivably develop two themes in perfect sonata form; the result would not necessarily be the first movement of a symphony. We might grant the technical correctness of what she produced, but still we would ask, "What are her themes like, and what does she do with them?"

There she would fail, I believe. For music, above all other arts, is preoccupied, not with the mind, but with what we may, loosely, call the emotions. That doesn't mean, as so many people assume, that the invariable effect of great music is to dissolve its hearers into tears. It does mean that music, when it is more than an agreeable sensation to the ear, touches something beyond and behind the mind, something larger and deeper—the thing that some people call the imagination and others used to call the soul. And the power to make that appeal is an adult power.

I can imagine a child of six being able to play Rachmaninoff's Second Piano Concerto as well, technically, as its composer. I will admit that it is within the realm of possibility that she could play it with as much expressiveness and dramatic power. I cannot possibly imagine her being able to compose it.

And I ought to be able to imagine that, if it is to be worth my while to go to hear her music. For the age of the artist is no concern of his—so to speak—customer. Either a work of art is good or it isn't. However interesting children's art products are, as promises for the future, they are seldom valuable in the present. In recent years I have read and seen and heard many poems and paintings and compositions by adults that fooled me into thinking they were done by ten-year-old children. I have never yet encountered a work of art by a ten-year-old that made me believe, for an instant, that it was the work of an adult.

There is no such thing as a work of art that is wonderful, considering the artist's age. If it is wonderful, considering, it is not a work of art.

If that little girl's friends and admirers really believe that she is a genius, let them, for art's sake, never allow her to know that they think so. If she is getting good schooling—which she is—she is getting all that anyone can give her. Let them not ask publishers to print her, or critics to hear her, or virtuosi to play her.

Let her alone. They might encourage her a bit, if they feel like doing so. But not too much. They cannot make her an artist if she is not to be one, but they can make her miserable by arousing false hopes. On the other hand, if she is to be one, we shall hear about it from her, not from them.

19

Child Prodigy

THERE are exceptions, of course. Once in a while, in the field of interpretative music, a child appears whose performance is so miraculously adult that one is content merely to marvel, without trying to explain. Such was Yehudi Menuhin, the violinist, at his first New York recital, and such was the boy pianist whose first American appearance occasioned the review that I take the liberty of quoting herewith:

"Those who run after the marvellous without caring even to try to fathom its nature, those who like to exercise their wits in explaining the seemingly inexplicable, and those whose hearts warm at the thought that a genius may come down in this matter-of-fact age . . . all found a rich reward in the concerts of the wonderful boy who made his first public appearance in America on this occasion. For a year past reports concerning his remarkably ripe powers as a pianoforte player had reached our ears, first from Berlin, then from London. He had played at a concert of the venerable Philharmonic Society [London Philharmonic] under the direction of Sir Arthur Sullivan, and royalty had condescended to smile on him, as a century and a quarter before it had put its head out of a carriage and nodded vigorously to the boy Mozart as he took a walk in the park. Then he gave a series of recitals in St. James's Hall, and when the time came to announce the last in the newspapers, lo! it was a needless thing to do, for the tickets were already sold. Such a startling occurrence in the history of concert-giving could not escape the notice of the foreign correspondents.

"In the literature of no other art are tales of precocity so common as in that of music. They furnish opening phrases for the majority of biographies of a certain class. There is some color of reason why this should be so. Some elements of a musical nature must be direct gifts or they will never be owned. . . . Yet all these things have not prevented the critical part of the world from viewing the tales of premature ripeness with suspicion. . . . The uncritical and unthinking, of course, are always ready to be astounded and bewildered. From the utterances of the two extreme classes it would be difficult to come to a decision in such a case as that of this child. It was obvious enough at this first hearing that he is gifted in music far beyond any child presented to public notice in recent times; and if the inquiry were to stop here there would be little occasion for controversy. From the technical point of view solely, his playing of the pianoforte is phenomenal. All the features of his playing are admirable in themselves, and nothing short of remarkable as elements in the playing of a lad of ten years.

"But it is none the less true that all of them might be the fruits of imitation, and are not necessarily indicative of the possession of extraordinary musical talent. For the proofs of such a possession we generally look at other elements in pianoforte playing—to its intellectual and emotional contents. In the nature of the case we cannot talk about emotional depth in a child's playing, even though he be a prodigy; when this boy approaches feeling at all, it seems rather the product of an instinctive appreciation that some effect is necessary for the sake of beauty in music; and it would be the course of wisdom to exclude from his programs all the music of such composers as Schumann and Chopin, with whom the emotional element is dominant. But there is a high degree of intelligently directed taste in his playing, which bears testimony to a genuine musical nature.

"The majority of his intuitions are a delight to the judicious. At his first concert he played two numbers which lifted this side of his ability into prominence—the slow movement of Beethoven's first concerto, and the theme and variations by Rameau. It would be difficult to convince a musician that the exquisite phrasing and lovely shading in the former, and the solidity of style and lucidity of exposition in the latter were acquired by an exercise of a merely imitative faculty, no matter how abnormally developed.

"Josef Hofmann is a wonderful child. The ripeness and maturity of his pianoforte playing, coupled with the perfection of his finger technique, fill the musician with amazement, and tempt him strongly to declare the boy to be a genius. And so, perhaps, he is. If the dreadful adjective be pardoned, he is a pianistic genius, such as Liszt was at his age, and Rubinstein.

"His genius ought to be an interesting subject of study for physiologists as well as psychologists. Here is a child of ten years, with undeveloped mental faculties, with the emotional element of his nature absolutely quiescent, with immature physical outfit, who nevertheless performs feats on the keyboard which from a purely mechanical point of view are bewildering. Like Liszt, he has a piano hand—

not abnormally large, but with muscles, nerves, and sinews adjusted to enable him to grasp chords and propel his fingers powerfully and independently. His touch is truly musical, moreover. The taste of the lad is exquisite, his command of tone-color amazing, his reposefulness of delivery would reflect credit on any older artist, his sense of symmetry is most delightful, and his digital agility as great as that which the majority of pianoforte players attain after practising as many years as this little lad has lived."

So wrote Henry Edward Krehbiel on November 30, 1887, after Josef Hofmann's first New York concert. You notice that he said that the boy was too young to play Chopin. If he could have heard Hofmann play the Chopin concerto as I heard him play it one afternoon in 1937, I think he would have admitted that the child of that concert of 1887 has long since reached the intellectual maturity, the spiritual insight, and the emotional depth that Chopin's music asks of the artist. The boy prodigy of half a century ago is surely a boy no longer. But we all agree, I think, that he is still prodigious.

20

Balanced Ration

My first opera was *Tannhäuser,* at fourteen. I did not see a performance of it, but I was personally conducted through the piano-vocal score by a gentleman named James Fuller Berry, who, besides being a rabid Wagnerite, was a professor of mathematics in the New York public high schools. I never went to public high school, and my mathematics was—or is it were?—always terrible; but I am indebted to a mathematics professor for opening before me a world that I had not known existed.

My first contact with orchestral music on the grand scale was likewise the music of Richard Wagner. I am not absolutely positive just where it was that I first heard it, but I think it was Willow Grove Park, outside Philadelphia. There were two flapper cousins and myself, ranging in age from twelve to fifteen, and we used to go out to Willow Grove to hear the band and orchestra concerts.

There was an afternoon concert, and an evening one. The round-trip fare to the park was twenty cents, and admission was twenty-five. Adolescent allowances being what they were, it was obviously out of the question to pay another fare and admission to hear both concerts. Equally was it out of the question to dine in the park restaurant. Consequently, at dinner time, we would pool our resources and purchase fifteen cents' worth of the cheapest and worst candy the park's refreshment stands had to offer (no faint praise, that). This, when consumed, would make us so ill that the very thought of food was abhorrent. Thus we were easily able to wait for the evening concert without fainting from hunger. I have often wondered why the idea has not become more popular.

Sousa and his band played at Willow Grove; and Victor Herbert and his orchestra. It was the latter, as I remember, playing excerpts from *Lohengrin* and *Tannhäuser,* that first gave me an idea of what symphonic music might be like.

I venture these reminiscences because there is a moral attached to them. *Tannhäuser,* elementary as it may be in the Wagnerian scheme of things, spoiled all its predecessors for me. The first opera I actually saw performed was Donizetti's *L'Elisire d'Amore,* and I nearly wept with rage and disappointment. I could not forgive it for not being on the large scale of the Wagnerian work, for being light and frothy and prettily tuneful, instead of serious and symphonic.

So with all the pre-Washington nineteenth-century operas of the Italian and French and German schools. It is only within the past decade or so that I have come to realize that, granted their premises and conventions, many of them can rightfully claim to be works of art. I heard only the frequent dramatic inadequacy of their melody, not its classic form and balance; only the poverty of their harmonic system and the thinness of their orchestration, not the charm of their vocal line.

So, too, did Wagner's music spoil Beethoven for me. It took me years to realize the bigness of Beethoven's conceptions, his masterly and unerringly right handling of colossal forms. After the sensuous beauty of Wagner's themes, the opulence of his harmonic and instrumental color, the torrential fluidity of his musical speech, Beethoven's material sounded square-toed and homely, his harmony rather drab, and his development sometimes naïve. Not that any of these things are true of Beethoven's music. Nevertheless it was a long time before I perceived that the tropical luxuriance and flaming volcanoes of Wagner are not the only wonders of the musical world; that there is grandeur, too, upon the lonely, wind-swept, granite heights of Beethoven.

In short, I was steeped in modern music (Wagner was actually ranked as a modern in the paleolithic days of my adolescence) much sooner than was good for me. The experience was one that must have happened to many others besides myself, and must be happening now to thousands. It is one to avoid.

The idiom of art is constantly changing; only the things it says remain eternal. But the trouble is, that in the mind of one who is aesthetically inexperienced, idiom becomes confused with subject-matter. He sees only that the way in which Beethoven expresses himself is not the way in which Stravinsky, or Béla Bartók, or Alban Berg expresses himself; that if a present-day composer were to write a symphony that was developed, harmonized, and scored in the manner of Beethoven, he would hardly get a hearing. What he may not see is that the essential Beethoven is utterly independent of Beethoven's medium of expression—a living man in an old-fashioned costume.

The beginner in music, whether he be fourteen years old or forty, should approach it in the only safe way: that is, chronologically. If you begin with Haydn, Mozart, and

Donizetti and Bellini, you will never lose them. You may proceed safely through Verdi and Brahms and Wagner and Strauss and Debussy, straight on to whatever ultramodernist represents the limits of your musical appetite, secure in the knowledge that the new will never spoil the old for you; that a mind nourished in infancy upon plain, simple food can assimilate richer fare later on, without risk of indigestion.

This is, of course, in violent opposition to the opinions held by many moderns, who announce that it is better to abolish the past entirely, and have dealings only with the present. It seems a meagre, poverty-stricken sort of regime to me. If music is a good thing, why not be able to enjoy as many kinds and styles of music as possible? Even a gourmet, it seems to me, must, if he would keep his health, be able to neglect his caviar long enough to take an occasional fling at roast beef.

Music was written to be enjoyed, and we might as well enjoy as much of it as we can. The man who talks of Strauss as being old-fashioned, and Wagner as Victorian, and Beethoven as outmoded, and Bach as a primitive, may be getting himself a great reputation as a connoisseur; but he is certainly missing a lot of fun.

21

The One-Time Visitor

ONE of the oldest and bitterest struggles in the world is that which goes on between the novice and the professional. It goes on year after year; the novice determined to make the professional show him the road to success, the professional equally determined to do nothing of the sort—or so it seems to the novice.

All practitioners of all arts are, I imagine, engaged in this struggle. Even so, the musician is probably more vigorously and continuously assailed than any other. The painter has an answer that is comparatively easy. He can generally silence, if not satisfy, his inquisitor by saying, "Paint pictures and show them to dealers." Even the dramatist can say something definite; for managers produce plays and engage actors, and almost any neophyte who is persistent enough will, sooner or later, be given a chance at something or other.

But the actor who looks for a part in a play is looking for a job. He is seeking definite employment, to do definite work as a member of an organization. As such, his responsibility is limited. No one actor, unless he be the star, can make or spoil a play. The producer knows this, and can afford to take an occasional chance with untried talent.

The musician, however, is the whole show, unless he sings in a choir or plays in an orchestra (two jobs that, by the way, can definitely be sought). Otherwise, he is wholly responsible for the success of what he undertakes to do, and is, consequently, very much of a gamble for anyone who undertakes to back or manage his career. And concert managers have learned, painfully, not to do much gambling.

Which is why, I suppose, any musician's weekly mail is sure to include numerous requests to tell aspiring youngsters how to become concert singers, composers, opera stars, and piano and violin virtuosi. How shall they begin, whom shall they ask to hear them, what do they do next?

If the musician tries desperately to avoid giving them any advice whatsoever, it is not through natural wickedness, or a determination to crush young talent, but simply because he does not know what to say.

How *do* people become professional musicians? To which William Howard Taft's once-famous answer is the only one possible: God knows. Every musical career is unique, and its beginnings, when they are not wholly fortuitous, are largely the result of the character and personality of the musician. Study the beginnings of Lucrezia Bori, Lily Pons, Lawrence Tibbett, José Iturbi, and Rosa Ponselle, for instance, and you will realize that to parallel any one of their careers you would have to be one of them. Marcella Sembrich became a world-famous singer by studying to be a concert pianist; Enrico Caruso became the same by studying to be a blacksmith.

However, there is one answer that one might make to any ambitious seeker for light. It is not a very satisfactory answer, but it possesses the bleak virtue of being to the point. It is this:

Learn your trade.

This sounds like a truism, but apparently it is not. Out of ten young singers who appear, trembling, at one of the Metropolitan's periodical auditions, two, perhaps, have the slightest notion of what would be expected of them in the way of repertoire and stage routine if the miracle were to happen, and they were to be engaged.

Of fifty young composers whose songs are being neglected by singers and whose symphonies are being ignored by conductors, how many know anything of the technique of singing, or the playing of orchestral instruments? Of ten young opera composers who cannot get a hearing from the Chicago or the Metropolitan companies, how many know anything at all about the theatre? How many young pianists and singers know anything about building a program, or even taking a bow?

Not that these details are the secret of success. But really to learn one's trade involves the mastery of standard practice as well as the acquirement of a technique. There is much, in any career, that only experience can teach; which is another way of saying that it is not a bad idea to go after experience before going after a career.

How to get it? That is another thing for which there is no ready formula. I know only this: that there is no such thing as an unskilled genius. If he has not mastered his job he is, more than anyone else, aware of that fact. If there is no one handy to teach it to him, he learns it for himself. He takes his gifts for granted, and goes after his failings.

Genius is an infinite capacity for taking pains—yes. But not in the sense that it is a capacity for meaningless, unintelligent drudgery—activity for its own sake. It might better be defined as an infinite capacity for dissatisfaction, for looking about to see what remains to be learned, and learning it.

Also, a part, at any rate, of genius is an infinite willingness to work, not at one's career, but at one's art. So many young musicians are looking for a chance, not just to sing or play or compose, but to make a little money and gain a little applause as well. It is better not to ask too much, at first.

Better, too, not to insist upon an opportunity that promises something definite. Not only does she knock only once, but she generally does so disguised as something else. It is safer, on the whole, to answer every knock and to be up and ready to go in case it were really she. Otherwise, there is the risk that, when she does come to the door, she may find us having breakfast in bed and reading the Sunday papers.

The People at the Other End

It is nearly time for the fresh crop of prophecies concerning the imminent extinction of orchestra concerts and opera. Every time the radio or the gramophone is improved, someone prophesies that anew. It will not happen. The time is not far off when the electrical reproduction of any voice or single instrument will be indistinguishable from the original, even at close hand. It is at hand, for that matter. Twice, on days when the radio was left running and the announcer's voice came over particularly well, I have thought there was a salesman downstairs, and have rushed down to throw him out. Once it was a piano that deceived me. I would have sworn that someone was playing in the living room, except that our piano is in tune.

But I have never for a moment been deceived into thinking that the Philadelphia Orchestra or the Philharmonic-Symphony was playing downstairs. Not only because the probabilities are against such a thing's happening, but because of the *size* of the sound. An orchestra, even when playing under its breath, is a large sound, just as any radio set or gramophone, however loudly it plays, is a comparatively small one. Consequently, any reproduction of the sound of any large group of singers or instrumentalists, no matter how perfect in quality, will always be a miniature—something heard, so to speak, through the small end of a telescope. There will always be an audience for the real thing.

The only other time I tried my hand at prophecy was in 1922, when I made the New York *World* the repository of a brilliant analysis of the radio situation. I forget the details, but I do remember proving, incontrovertably:

(A) That radio reception would never get any better than it was then, which was terrible;

(B) That performers would soon get tired of speaking and singing for nothing, and would demand adequate payment for their services, which would make broadcasting unprofitable;

(C) That since broadcasting was being carried on solely for the purpose of selling radio sets and accessories, as soon as everybody had a set, broadcasting would be superfluous; and that, therefore,

(D) The whole business would blow up in about three years.

Altogether, it was an excellent prophecy, greatly admired at the time, particularly by its author, who carried it about with him and would read it aloud on any or no provocation. Just how closely it anticipated the present facts of radio is something we won't go into, if you don't mind. It is enough to say that during the winter and spring before this book was assembled I talked, every Sunday, to an invisible audience that had gathered to hear the broadcast programs of the Philharmonic-Symphony Society of New York. That audience was estimated, by radio engineers, to number nine million people. Assuming that every concert given by the Philharmonic-Symphony since its founding, in 1845, was attended by twenty-five hundred people (a lavishly generous estimate, by the way), something over eight million people have heard the orchestra in the flesh, as it were, since that year. In other words, *one* Sunday afternoon broadcast is heard by more people than have heard the orchestra in concert during the entire period of its existence!

Now radio presents an interesting paradox. It is listened to by the largest audiences that ever assembled in the history of the world; and it is at the same time the most intimate form of entertainment in the world; for when one plays or sings or talks over the radio, he's doing so, not to millions, but to the average number of people around the average radio set . . . in other words, he plays or sings or talks to about three people. And these average three are not in the least conscious of being a vast public. They are not influenced by the reactions of the people around them, as they would be in a concert hall, because there aren't any; and they listen to a speaker, if at all, not as a remote, impersonal figure gesticulating upon a platform, but as a conversationalist sitting in the room with them. And they answer back. Not orally, of course, but by mail. During the Philharmonic-Symphony season I received between six and seven thousand letters—a very small so-called fan mail for a variety show or comedy program, a very large one for a symphonic hour. For the public that listens to the Philharmonic-Symphony and the Metropolitan Opera over the radio broadcasts is the most sophisticated radio public in America; and as such it is not addicted to letter-writing. It might amuse you to know something of what it said in such letters as it did write.

One thing that overwhelms me in reading radio mail is the extravagant estimate many people have of the knowledge, wisdom, and powers of a radio commentator, to say nothing of their overestimate of the number of minutes and hours there are in his day. During the season I received about seventy shipments of manuscript music, ranging from single sheets to bundles of orchestral scores. Their composers wanted me to tell them, first, what I thought of their music; second, how to get it published. Five wanted me to have them put at once on the programs of this orchestra. Seventy-nine people sent song poems, either to be criticized, sent to a publisher, or set to music. One author wrote, simply, "Please write some inspiring music to this." (I regret to say that up to the moment I haven't been able to think of any.) Five people had Stradivarius violins which they wanted appraised, eighty-nine singers wanted interviews, seventy-eight singers wanted to know how to get to sing in radio, and fourteen pianists wanted to play for me. Two young women wanted a complete list of books to start a music library, a lady in a neighboring city wanted me to come over and help select a piano for her daughter, another lady wrote from Annapolis to tell me to have two tickets in her name at the box office in Carnegie Hall for next Sunday's concert, and a young woman in Chicago wrote, "My life's ambition is to be a conductor. Do you think I am nuts?"

Big-game hunters like to hold forth about the thrill of waiting for the leap of a hungry tiger in the jungle. If any big-game hunter wants a real thrill, he ought to sit at a microphone some Sunday afternoon, with the consciousness that thousands of hungry wolves are ready to leap at his throat at the slightest mistake in facts or slip of the tongue. My worst blunder, of course, was in carelessly saying that Oscar Hammerstein first produced Strauss's *Salome* in America, and that the Metropolitan never gave a public performance of it. As several score of purists had considerable fun in pointing out, *Salome* was publicly performed at the Metropolitan on January 22, 1907, and Hammerstein didn't produce the opera until 1909. I had a very good excuse for that mistake, although I must admit that it eludes me at the moment. Other slips that received instant correction were listing Glazunoff and Schillings as living composers, and calling Leopold Auer a Russian when he was a Hungarian. The *Don Quixote* controversy was a historic one. I pronounced it "Quick-sawt" and several dozen correspondents pointed out that the only proper pronunciation is "Kee-ho-té." I promptly hurled the Century Dictionary, the Standard, and Webster's New International at their heads. All three support my pronunciation, so I'm still sticking to it. All three dictionaries failed miserably to back me up when I said *ad*ult one Sunday, instead of ad*ult*. Either the dictionaries are wrong, or I was. I also said "orghy" one Sunday, instead of orgy; but nobody caught me at that except my mother. Aside from these breaks, I seem to have come off pretty well, except that I once tossed off the statement that Jean Cocteau was a member of *les Six* in Paris. Etienne Auric promptly wrote to me from East Orange, New Jersey, to point out that Cocteau was not a member, and that his uncle, Georges Auric, whom I had forgotten to mention, was.

Thus confessed and—I hope—shriven, let me say a few things about the audience. One of them is the discovery, or rather the confirmation of a suspicion, that a good many people are unable to listen accurately. I happened to say, one Sunday, that most people would agree that the four most *eminent* living composers are Sibelius, Strauss, Stravinsky, and Ravel. Whereupon a surprising number of correspondents commented more or less heatedly upon my choice of the world's *greatest* living composers. Now I had very carefully not said "greatest." I wanted to keep out of just that controversy. I said "eminent"; and "eminent," according to Webster's New International, means "high in public estimation." I wasn't discussing their merits, only their reputation. One lady was so agitated that she sent me her own list of the world's greatest composers. According to her, they are Mascagni, Stravinsky, Chaminade, Paderewski, and Whistler. I don't know yet whether she meant Whistler and his mother or Whistler and his dog.

There is one type of letter that I find really annoying, and rather disquieting. This is a sample: "Dear Mr. Taylor: I am a student at blank high school, and am making a music project of the lives of famous composers, living and dead. If you could send me any information I would appreciate it very much. Thank you, etc." Now that is so naïve that you smile at it. But you stop smiling when letters like that come in by the dozens every week, from high-school and college students all over the country. They're doing projects, or term papers, or notebooks, and they want you to sit down and write them facts, dates, statistics, personal opinions, biographies, and whatnot. And virtually everything they want to know they could find out, if they weren't too lazy and badly taught, by spending a couple of hours looking through dictionaries and encyclopedias. And their teachers encourage them to do it. Half the time, the letter closes: "My teacher says I can have an extra credit if you will sign this information." Many of my friends, who are writers, tell me they are similarly pestered. The thing is getting to be a national educational racket. When I went to high school I did my own homework.

Such an overwhelming majority of the letters expressed appreciation of the fact that the concerts were available on the air, that it is a little disproportionate to refer to the handful that did not, except that they possessed a certain interest as curiosities. First prize, so far as I am concerned, goes to a gentleman from Winnipeg, who wrote, "Your program for next week is rotten." Inasmuch as that particular program consisted of a *Dance Symphony* by Aaron Copland and Honegger's *King David*, neither of which had ever been played by the Philharmonic-Symphony, and I am sure had never been played in Winnipeg, one could not but admire his clairvoyance. A lady from Philadelphia wrote, "As for the Philharmonic, if I lived in New York, I'd give up my subscription just on the strength of the wretched programs." I decided to answer that one, and after considerable pondering suggested that she ask for her money back.

As commentator I naturally received a few individual brickbats. Some were scoldings, based on the assumption that the choice of conductors and the making up of the programs were entirely in my hands; others were simple and heartfelt expressions of personal aversion. I had devoted one intermission to a discussion of Wagner's character (it appears in this volume under the title of "The Monster"). One lady who was moved to write about it ended her letter, "You are a liar, a traitor, a snake, and a moron." I have a suspicion that she didn't care for that talk. Incidentally, I quoted her letter on the air, and the following week received a second communication from her, expressing her unaltered opinion that I was still a liar, a traitor, a snake, and a moron.

As I said, it is out of proportion even to mention the adverse mail. The overwhelming majority of one's radio correspondents are friendly and generous. One thing that amazed me is the enormously increased interest in music among men, particularly among classes of men that are, in this country at least, traditionally uninterested in music. I had letters containing not only intelligent, but often deeply thought discussions of musical matters, letters that revealed a genuine love and understanding of music, from lawyers, insurance brokers, printers, garage proprietors, travelling salesmen, day laborers—every trade and profession that one could imagine. American women have always supported music. It is the interest that American men are taking in music today that so particularly interests me. I think we have the radio to thank for that.

What they used to say about newspaper work can also be said about talking on the radio: "It must be wonderful to meet so many interesting people."

It *is* wonderful.

ABOUT THE AUTHOR

DEEMS TAYLOR *was born in New York City in 1885. After receiving his A.B. degree from New York University he studied music and held several editorial positions. In 1916 he became assistant Sunday editor of the New York* Tribune, *leaving shortly afterward to represent that paper in France. From 1917 to 1919 he was associate editor of* Collier's Weekly, *and from 1921 to 1925 music critic on the New York* World. *He was editor of* Musical America *from 1927 to 1929, and music critic on the New York* American *from 1931 to 1932. More recently he has acted as commentator for the New York Philharmonic Symphony Orchestra's Sunday afternoon broadcasts.*

In addition to writing about music, Deems Taylor also composes it. In 1910 he wrote The Echo, *a musical comedy, and in 1912 his* Siren Song *won the orchestral prize awarded by the National Federation of Music Clubs. His most famous compositions since then include* Through the Looking Glass, *an orchestral suite that is in the repertoire of virtually every major symphonic organization in America and Europe,* The King's Henchman, *with a book by Edna St. Vincent Millay, and* Peter Ibbetson, *both of which were commissioned and performed by the Metropolitan Opera Association. A third opera,* Ramuntcho, *based on Pierre Loti's novel, is now on the press.*

Index

INDEX

INDEX

INDEX

INDEX

INDEX

INDEX

INDEX